ARISTOTLE IN LATE ANTIQUITY

STUDIES IN PHILOSOPHY
AND THE HISTORY OF PHILOSOPHY

General Editor: Jude P. Dougherty

Studies in Philosophy
and the History of Philosophy   Volume 27

Aristotle in
Late Antiquity

edited by Lawrence P. Schrenk

THE CATHOLIC UNIVERSITY OF AMERICA PRESS
Washington, D.C.

The paper in this publication meets the minimum requirements of
American National Standards for Information Science—
Permanence of Paper for Printed Library materials,
ANSI Z39.48–1984.

∞

LIBRARY OF CONGRESS CATALOGING-IN-PUBLICATION DATA
Aristotle in late antiquity / edited by Lawrence P. Schrenk.
    p.   cm. — (Studies in philosophy and the history of
philosophy ; v. 27)
    Includes bibliographical references and index.
    Contents: Plotinus and the rejection of Aristotelian metaphysics /
Lloyd P. Gerson — Plotinus on the nature of eternity and time /
Steven K. Strange — Galen and the logic of relations / R. J.
Hankinson — Alexander on Aristotle's species and genera as
principles / Arthur Madigan — Proof and discovery in Aristotle
and the later Greek tradition / Lawrence P. Schrenk — The Greek
Christian authors and Aristotle / Leo J. Elders — Hippolytus,
Aristotle, Basilides / Ian Mueller — The Aristotelianism of
Photius's philosophical theology / John P. Anton — Averroes /
Thérèse-Anne Druart.
    1. Aristotle—Influence.   2. Philosophy, Ancient.   3. Philosophy,
Medieval.   4. Philosophy—Byzantine Empire.   I. Schrenk,
Lawrence P.   II. Series.
B21.S78   vol. 27
185—dc20
93-6867
ISBN 0-8132-0781-9 (alk. paper)

Contents

Introduction

Fashions change in scholarship as in other areas of human life: thinkers neglected in one period become objects of intense study in others. The history of ancient thought is by no means immune to these fluctuations. Many scholars are currently turning their attention to late Greek thought. New texts, translations, and studies now regularly appear, and already our understanding of the philosophers of this period has undergone substantial change. Situated at the end of the Greek epoch, late Greek thought is correspondingly complex in its appropriation of earlier philosophies; the Presocratics, Socrates, Plato, Aristotle, and Hellenistic philosophy are all important source material. While this period can most accurately be described with the neologism "Neoplatonic," it would do great disservice to overlook the important influence of other thinkers of classical Greece. After Plato, Aristotle must be regarded as the dominant influence, but the attitude of late Greek thinkers to the Stagirite was hardly homogeneous. Plato was regarded with almost universal devotion, but philosophers from the Middle Platonists onwards diverged in their attitudes toward Aristotle, from admiration to open hostility. Few thinkers, however, remained unaffected by his thought.

This volume brings together nine studies that focus on the influence of Aristotle, from Plotinus through Arabic thought. While these do not constitute a comprehensive survey of his influence,[1] they should

1. An introduction to the influence of Aristotle on later Greek thought can be found in H. B. Gottschalk, "Aristotelian Philosophy in the Roman World from the Time of Cicero to the End of the Second Century AD," in *Aufsteig und Niedergang der Römischen Welt* II.36.2, ed. Wolfgang Haase (Berlin: De Gruyter 1987); reprinted as "The Earliest Aristotelian Commentators," in *Aristotle Transformed: The Ancient Commentators and Their Influence*, ed. Richard Sorabji (Ithaca: Cornell 1990). An introduction is also provided in "The Ancient Commentators on Aristotle" by Richard Sorabji (also in *Aristotle Transformed*). Both of the aforementioned volumes contain a variety of fine studies that will be of interest to the reader. In addition, *Aristotle Transformed* includes a substantial bibliography of the Greek commentators on Aristotle, and *Aufsteig und Niedergang der Römischen Welt* II.36.1 contains several relevant bibliographical studies, including ones on Platonism in Imperial Rome, by L. Deitz; Plotinus, 1951–71, by H. J. Blumenthal; and Plotinus, 1971–86, by K. Corrigan and P. O'Cleirigh.

nonetheless present a series of specific insights to Aristotle's influence
on thinkers throughout this period. In "Plotinus and the Rejection of
Aristotelian Metaphysics," Lloyd P. Gerson shows how Plotinus develops much of his metaphysics in conscious opposition to that offered
by Aristotle, though the two do share certain metaphysical positions,
e.g., that being is neither univocal nor equivocal. Within Plotinus's
arguments, Gerson discerns a two-fold attack on Aristotelian metaphysics: first, Plotinus denies that Aristotelian νοῦς, i.e., self-thinking
thought, can be the ultimate ontological principle; and, second, he
shows the One to have a series of properties not possessed by Aristotle's unmoved mover. Steven K. Strange ("Plotinus on the Nature of
Eternity and Time") tackles another intersection of Aristotelian and
Plotinian thought in his consideration of *Ennead* 3.7, which surveys
the classic texts on the nature of time, including Aristotle's treatment
of the subject in the *Physics*. Strange provides a detailed analysis of
the arguments of this treatise. Plotinus's claim is to have given an
account of time that is superior to any of those offered by his predecessors.

In "Galen and the Logic of Relations," R. J. Hankinson examines
Galen's seminal work in the logic of relations. Galen recognized that
some forms of argumentation are not susceptible to analysis as either
categorical or hypothetical, e.g., A is equal to B, and B is equal to C,
therefore A is equal to C. Though it is difficult to assess Galen's originality, Hankinson does present a full analysis of the intricate account
of relational logic found in several of Galen's treatises. Arthur Madigan ("Alexander on Aristotle's Species and Genera as Principles") considers the greatest of Aristotle's ancient commentators, Alexander of
Aphrodisias. Madigan investigates Alexander's analysis of the sixth,
seventh, and eighth *aporiae* of *Metaphysics* 3, which concern species and
genera. While Alexander adheres to the Aristotelian doctrine that
what is real is individual, he appears not to have confronted the in-
consistency between this and two other Aristotelian tenets: what is
knowable is universal, and the knowable is real. In "Proof and Discovery in Aristotle and the Later Greek Tradition," Lawrence P.
Schrenk investigates the four "dialectical" methods offered by the
Greek commentators on Aristotle, namely, division, definition, demonstration, and analysis, in order to elucidate the relationship between
the process of discovering a thesis and its subsequent demonstration.
He surveys the development of these themes in both ancient philosophical and mathematical thought.

Leo J. Elders ("The Greek Christian Authors and Aristotle") offers
a comprehensive survey of the influence of Aristotle on Christian au-

thors. He begins with the state of Aristotelian studies in the first four centuries A.D., then traces his influence through the Christian apologists, theologians, and historians. While Christian authors were often hostile to Aristotle, Elders shows that numerous Aristotelian theses were also developed within this context on topics such as causation, analogy, and ethics. The Christian bishop Hippolytus in his *Refutation of All Heresies* seeks to attack a certain Basilides by showing that he is a follower of Aristotle. Ian Mueller, in "Hippolytus, Aristotle, Basilides," follows the Aristotelian themes in Hippolytus's criticisms: homonymy, self-thinking thought, genus and species, soul, and cosmology. He concludes that the "Aristotle" of Hippolytus and Basilides was only a corrupted version of the classical Aristotle. These misconstruals may have had their origin in authentic Aristotelian texts, but the episode reminds us of the misinterpretations that can accrue to an author over time. While Photius is best known for his role in ecclesiastical history, John P. Anton ("The Aristotelianism of Photius's Philosophical Theology") explores his philosophical adaptation of the Aristotelian account of substance. He shows how Photius's *Amphilochia* (in large part a commentary on issues raised by the *Categories*) reinterprets Aristotelian οὐσία along Christian Neoplatonic lines in order to be consistent with revealed theology. In "Averroes: The Commentator and the Commentators," Therese-Anne Druart makes the transition from Greek to Arabic philosophy in her discussion of Ibn Rushd or Averroes. She provides a valuable overview of Averroes as Aristotelian commentator by focusing on two questions: how did Averroes understand his task as commentator, and how did he view his relationship with earlier commentators? Averroes saw himself as correcting the Platonic excesses of his Arabic predecessors, and he consequently came to place greater importance on the Greek commentary tradition.

PART I

ARISTOTLE AND PLOTINUS

1   Plotinus and the Rejection of Aristotelian Metaphysics

LLOYD P. GERSON

It would not be quite accurate to claim that Aristotle's *Metaphysics,* like Hume's *Treatise,* "fell dead-born from the press, without reaching such distinction as even to excite a murmur among the zealots." First, there was no press. Second, the *Metaphysics* would not have been published as a book had there been a press. And finally, the *Metaphysics* was not completely ignored by Aristotle's school. Still, if one peruses Fritz Wehrli's monumental *Die Schule des Aristoteles* and notes the few scattered and desultory references to ontological or theological topics, one cannot resist forming the impression that the *Metaphysics* is pretty largely an academic failure.

Even Aristotle's formidable disciple and colleague Theophrastus, who himself actually composed a treatise on metaphysics, seems to write with a remarkably limited understanding of the work of his predecessor in this area.[1] Apart from a few references to book twelve, there is almost total silence regarding the central features of Aristotle's work as they are recognized today. There is nothing about the identification of first philosophy with wisdom and theology and a science of causes; nothing of the ἀπορίαι facing the construction of such a science; nothing of the doctrine of πρὸς ἕν equivocity or of the conclusion that being in the primary sense is separate form. Nor is there a word about the dialectical treatment of sensible substance in the central books of the *Metaphysics,* which has so exercised contemporary scholars. The list of the disap-

---

1. Theophrastus did not of course title his work μετά τὰ φυσικά, but he does describe it as dealing with first principles (Theo., *Met.* 4a1–2) and as distinct from physics (ibid., 2–4) and mathematics (ibid., 4b6–8). The first principles are apparently reducible to a unique first principle, i.e., god (ibid., 4b15). As Giovanni Reale, "The Historical Importance of the *Metaphysics* of Theophrastus in Comparison with the *Metaphysics* of Aristotle," appendix to *The Concept of First Philosophy and the Unity of the Metaphysics of Aristotle,* trans. John Catan (Albany: State University of New York Press, 1980), 364–91, shows, Theophrastus closely follows *Metaphysics* 12 in many respects. But apart from these and some less convincing parallels from *Metaphysics* 2, there is little awareness shown by Theophrastus of any connection between theology and a science of being *qua* being.

pearing doctrines could easily be expanded and reconfirmed by considering other philosophers both inside and outside the Lyceum.

We must not be tempted to account for this extraordinary state of affairs by supposing that Aristotle's successors regarded his metaphysical doctrines as too sublime for comment, for both Theophrastus and Strato, the first and second heads of the Lyceum after Aristotle, appear actually to have rejected the argument for the existence of an unmoved mover.[2] Strato's argument amounts to the claim that nature alone is sufficient to account for motion, a claim that must have been intended to recall Aristotle's own admission that if separate substance does not exist, then there is no special science of substance apart from physics (cf. Met. 6.1.1026a27–29). Since Aristotle adds that the putative science of separate substance is first philosophy and the science of being qua being, Strato's denial of the need for the hypothesis of an unmoved mover is nothing short of a rejection of the entire enterprise of the Metaphysics. And this from within the Peripatos!

If we look beyond the Lyceum to the tradition of Aristotelian commentaries, beginning with Alexander of Aphrodisias, we do indeed find something more like reverence for the words of the founder, but hardly any awareness at all of the problematic and crucial connection between the specific theological arguments in the Metaphysics and the science of being qua being. Though the extant corpus of Aristotelian commentaries includes four works on the Metaphysics, there exists not a single commentary by one hand on the entire work as preserved and edited by Andronicus of Rhodes in the first century B.C. Alexander's commentary ends at book five and is completed by an anonymous continuator; Themistius has a commentary, or more accurately a paraphrase, of book twelve alone; Syrianus comments on books three, four, thirteen, and fourteen; Asclepius halts his commentary at book seven. In the face of this modest harvest, one might well conceive the notion that the Metaphysics was doomed from the beginning to bear meager fruit.[3]

The dominance of Stoicism throughout the Hellenistic period explains in part the near oblivion into which metaphysics in general and Aristotle's work in particular were cast. A central principle of Stoic

2. For Theophrastus's criticism, see his Metaphysics 5b3–10, and for Strato, see the testimony contained in Cicero, Academica 2.38.

3. See Gérard Verbeke's "Aristotle's Metaphysics Viewed by the Ancient Greek Commentators," in D. J. O'Meara, ed., Studies in Aristotle (Washington, D.C.: The Catholic University of America Press, 1981), 114ff., for a useful summary of some of the basic interpretations in the commentators. Verbeke concludes that there is a consistent interpretation among the commentaries that may be aptly termed "Neoplatonic." We should distinguish, however, a Neoplatonic interpretation of Aristotle from a Neoplatonic refutation of Aristotle, as is to be found in Plotinus.

theoretical philosophy is the refusal—perhaps for methodological reasons as much as anything else—to countenance the existence of immaterial entities. Accordingly, physics becomes Stoic first philosophy, and theology becomes a branch of physics (cf. *Stoicorum Veterum Fragmenta* 2.42; cited hereafter as *SVF*). Within such a system there is little conceptual space for isolating being as a subject for investigation, and, especially, for raising Aristotelian ἀπορίαι regarding its nature. The evidence for this claim is to be found in the *corpus* of Stoic fragments, where a science of being *qua* being makes no appearance at all, not even as a dragon to be slain. It is as if it had never existed.[4] Considering that Stoics, and to a lesser extent Epicureans and Academic Sceptics, were the primary purveyors of theoretical philosophy throughout the Hellenistic period, it is hardly surprising that the doctrines of the *Metaphysics* simply lay dormant.[5]

The extent of the Stoic role in, so to speak, setting the philosophical agenda can be seen in the fragments of the works of the Middle Platonist Antiochus of Ascalon (ca. 130 B.C.–ca. 67 B.C.). Antiochus actually revolted against the Sceptical tradition that had developed in the Academy beginning with Arcesilaus in the third century B.C. and continuing down to Philo of Larissa, the teacher of Antiochus at the end of the first century. What is most important for my theme is that Antiochus aimed to show the fundamental harmony of the Old Academy, especially Plato, and the early Peripatetics, meaning none other than Aristotle.[6] So here was a true philosophical conservative, repelled

4. Zeno, Chrysippus, and Antipater are all reported to have written books titled Περὶ Ὀυσίας. Of course, these Stoics all identify οὐσία with matter. The few scattered references to τὸ ὄν, which identify it with body and make it a species of the genus τό τι, betray little more than a lingering memory of some Aristotelian terminology stripped of its argumentative context. The Stoic position was perhaps taken to follow immediately from the principle that immaterial entities cannot exist; hence, argument indicating the contrary can be safely ignored. F. H. Sandbach, *Aristotle and the Stoics* (Cambridge: Cambridge University Press, 1985), has argued the revisionary case that, for the Stoics, Aristotle was not rejected but largely unknown. But the lack of hard evidence, rightly insisted upon by Sandbach, is also explicable by the hypothesis that Aristotelian arguments, in metaphysics at least, were rendered irrelevant on the above principle.

5. Cf. Fritz Wehrli, *Die Schule des Aristoteles: Text und Kommentar* (Basel/Stuttgart: Benno Schwabe & Co., 1959), 10:95–128, who suggests in a *Ruckblick* over the material he has collected that the disintegration of the Peripatetic school was owing to its undogmatic and aporetic character as compared to its Academic, Epicurean, and Stoic rivals. He also suggests that conflict in doctrine between the *Metaphysics* and the early dialogues of Aristotle might account for diffidence or confusion on the part of his disciples: "der Zerfall der Schule hatte seine tiefste Ursache im Werke des Meisters selbst" (ibid., 96). Undoubtedly, there is much in what Wehrli has to say. One may also add the instability of the Peripatetic foundation owing to political reasons.

6. Cf. Cicero, *De finibus* 5.7. The evidence for the views of Antiochus is contained largely in Cicero and accordingly must be used with some care. There is little doubt concerning Antiochus's syncretizing approach and his embracing of Stoic assumptions. John Dillon, *The Middle Platonists* (Ithaca: Cornell University Press, 1977), chap. 2, has a most useful summary of what is known of the philosophical positions of Antiochus.

by Sceptical innovations and eager to avail himself of Peripatetic insights into the Platonic universe. It comes then as something of a shock to discover that when Antiochus is reported to be rehearsing Platonic doctrines of creation, the soul, and the gods, he does not interpret these in the light of the unmoved mover or anything resembling an Aristotelian doctrine of being, but rather in a thoroughly Stoic fashion.[7] Antiochus thinks that Aristotle is in harmony with Plato because Plato is in harmony with the Stoics. But the mighty Stoics interdicted metaphysics, and Antiochus feels himself therefore bound to ignore harmonies or disharmonies in matters metaphysical. Hence, his references to the gods are pure Stoicism, labeled in the syncretic fashion "Platonism."

I do not wish to give the impression that Middle Platonism is nothing more than a mislabeled collage of doctrines glued together by Stoicism. That is not the case. There were more or less "pure" Platonists, like Plutarch, who were actually critical of Stoic thought and who embraced an interpretation of immaterial being that is fundamentally Platonic. And there are others, such as Albinus in the second century A.D., who attempted something like a non-Stoic synthesis of Peripatetic and Platonic doctrine (in theology, at any rate). The *Didaskalikos*, a compendium of Platonic teachings, has for a century been attributed to Albinus. Recently, this has been challenged. Regardless of who the author of this work of Middle Platonism may be, it presents an Aristotelian theology that has been thoroughly excised from any ontological context.[8] Finally, I should mention the late second century A.D. so-called precursor of Neoplatonism, the enigmatic Numenius. Whether we call him a Middle Platonist or a Neopythagorean, it is evident from the extent of fragments of his works that he found congenial the blending of Aristotelian and Platonic theological ideas that was common in his time. I have uppermost in mind his apparent identification of the god "superior to οὐσία and form" with "the first νοῦς."[9] It is not difficult to see that such a conflation springs from the most elementary misunderstanding of Aristotle.

Perhaps I have said enough to convey the impression that the re-

---

7. Cf. Dillon, *Middle Platonists*, 81ff., for citation and discussion of the relevant texts.

8. On the theology of Albinus, see R. E. Witt, *Albinus and the History of Middle Platonism* (Amsterdam: Adolph Hakkert, 1971) (reprint of 1937 edition), 126–35. For the argument against the attribution of the *Didaskalikos* to Albinus and its proper attribution to Alcinous, see J. Whittaker, "Platonic Philosophy in the Early Centuries of the Empire," *Aufstieg und Niedergang der Römischen Welt* 36 (1987): 81–123.

9. Cf. fr. 16 and 17 of the edition *Numénius. Fragments* by Edouard Des Places (Paris: Societé D'Edition "Les Belles Lettres," 1973). See also the important discussion of the theology of Numenius by E. R. Dodds, "Numenius and Ammonius," in *Les sources de Plotin* (vol. 5 of Entretiens sur l'antiquité classique (Geneva, 1960), 12–16.

sponses to Aristotle's *Metaphysics* in the first half millennium after its composition are better characterized as uncomprehending and indifferent than as a rejection. The very complexity of the material pertaining to the construction of the science whose birth we are witnessing when we read the *Metaphysics* would militate against its easy assimilation into the tradition. It is not hard to imagine that before the edition of Andronicus of Rhodes there actually did not exist a perspicuous "package" of λόγοι that would convey to the interested reader an argument for a science that was at once theology and a science of being *qua* being. And subsequent to his edition, Platonism and Stoicism were too well entrenched to make the appreciation of such a science anything more than a theoretical possibility.[10]

I

With this background in mind it is nothing short of astonishing to see the resurrection of Aristotelian metaphysics in the *Enneads* of Plotinus. It is well known of course that Porphyry tells us in his biography of Plotinus (chapter 14) that the *Metaphysics* of Aristotle is concentrated in the *Enneads,* along with many other Peripatetic and Stoic doctrines. Porphyry's words "concentrated in" may be given some meaning by a glance at the *index fontium* of the great edition of Henry and Schwyzer, where about 125 references to the various treatises of the *Metaphysics* are listed. Every book of the *Metaphysics* is referred to, excepting book six. But the counting of references gives only a superficial impression. Aristotelian arguments are far more than scholarly window-dressing in the *Enneads.*

Plotinus is rightly called a disciple of Plato and defender of the Platonic heritage as he understands it. Plotinus's use of Plato, however, is frequently frustrating to the philosopher. Plotinus normally will cite Plato as *the* authority in support of one of his own doctrines. He will do so without either defending his interpretation of the Platonic text

10. Paul Moraux, *Der Aristotelismus bei den Griechen von Andronikos bis Alexander von Aphrodisias,* 2 vols. (Berlin and New York: Walter De Gruyter, 1973–74), provides an exhaustive study of Aristotle's influence among both his disciples and others in the period indicated by the title of his book. As far as the *Metaphysics* is concerned, it is almost as if it did not exist. For example, the single reference cited by Moraux to the identification of a science of wisdom with a science of being is two Pythagoreans writing sometime between the first century B.C. and the end of the first century A.D. (vol. 2, pp. 607, 632). It should be added that post-Plotinian metaphysics picks up the syncretic and uninformed tendencies of commentators prior to Plotinus, or, at least, Alexander. See Dominic J. O'Meara, "Le problème de la métaphysique dans l'antiquité tardive," *Freiburger Zeitschrift für Philosophie und Theologie* 33 (1986): 3–22, for some useful remarks, particularly on Syrianus and Proclus.

or defending his claim that a Platonic text so interpreted contains substantially the same doctrine as the one Plotinus himself is advancing. For example, Plotinus's interpretation of the first hypothesis of the second part of Plato's *Parmenides* is repeatedly used in defense of his postulation of a first principle of reality called "the One." But the dubiousness of this reading and its undefended use to express ideas of which there is no hint at all in Plato have impugned grievously both the so-called Neoplatonic interpretation of Plato and Plotinus's own philosophical reputation.

It is precisely in the interstice between the use of Plato as authority and the conclusions within Plotinus's own system that the importance of his treatment of Aristotle's *Metaphysics* is to be found. When Plotinus actually does argue for the basic tenets of his own system, he does so by arguing against Aristotelian principles. Plato's authority is appealed to only in support of conclusions resting on explicit argument. Accordingly, whether the authority is spurious or not is a question quite independent of the soundness of such argument. Plotinus's interpretation of Aristotle's *Metaphysics* is of course also not immune to criticism. There is little doubt, however, that Aristotle takes a position regarding the first principles of reality that is contradicted by Plotinus. The *Enneads* is the first and even up to the present day one of the very few attempts to appreciate Aristotle's arguments and to defeat them on their own ground. To see argument where before there had been mere slogans or abuse and mostly just sheer ignorance is certainly edifying.

When I say that Plotinus meets Aristotle on his own ground, I mean that in general Plotinus employs a metaphysical vocabulary that Aristotle would not find opaque in the slightest. More particularly and more surprisingly, Plotinus shares with Aristotle what is arguably the central insight in the *Metaphysics*, namely, that being is neither univocal nor purely equivocal. Plotinus expresses this agreement with the utmost lucidity: "In things in which there is a prior and a posterior the posterior gets its being [τὸ εἶναι] from the prior" (*Ennead* 6.1.25.17–18). If there is any doubt about the meaning of this assertion, it should be dispelled upon reading Plotinus's arguments, against the Stoics and in support of Aristotle, that being is not a genus and hence not univocally predicable of whatever has being (*Ennead* 6.1.1.18–19 and 25–28; 6.2.9.18–33).

Plotinus's recognition of the importance of this doctrine is not unprecedented, although it almost is. Alexander of Aphrodisias asserts it repeatedly in his commentary on the *Metaphysics* (cf. *In. Met.* 241.8–9, 21–24; 243.10–17; 246.10–13; and 643.3–5), a work Plotinus undoubtedly studied. What is remarkable is both Plotinus's evident engagement with Aristotle's ideas and his assent to a doctrine which is, at least on the surface, anti-Platonic.[11] As we move to the fundamental points of disagreement with Aristotle in the *Enneads,* Plotinus's acceptance of the πρὸς ἓν equivocity of being needs to be borne in mind.

It is possible to discern beneath the plethora of sometimes obscure argument a guiding strategy in Plotinus's refutation of Aristotelian metaphysics. This strategy has two parts. First, Plotinus aims to show that what Aristotle regards as the ἀρχή of all, the unmoved mover or 'thinking thinking about thinking,' cannot be the absolutely first principle. It cannot be absolutely first because it is not self-explaining. That is, it must have a principle or cause outside of itself. The second stage of the strategy is to demonstrate the existence of the true first principle and to deduce its properties, none of which can be possessed by Aristotle's god. It has been argued that Plotinus's substitution of the One as first principle in place of Aristotle's god is just an extension of the latter's approach: the unmoved mover taken to the *n*th degree, as it were.[12] I think this interpretation is quite seriously mistaken, and that in fact—apart from the details of Plotinus's own arguments, to which we shall turn presently—the attempt to dethrone the unmoved mover in favor of the One goes for the throat of Aristotelian metaphysics. Here briefly is why.

Aristotle argues that being is substance and that substance is primarily form.[13] The form of a sensible composite is separate "in notion," as Aristotle says (*Met.* 8.1.1042a29), but owing to the fact that

11. I say "anti-Platonic" because in the *Sophist* Plato says that τὸ ὄν is one of the μέγιστα γένη. Plotinus defends this doctrine without denying the equivocity of being by interpreting τὸ ὄν as referring to a nature rather than to being itself.

12. Cf. A. H. Armstrong, *The Architecture of the Intelligible Universe* (Cambridge: Cambridge University Press, 1940), who writes, "In [Plotinus's] conception of a First Principle and ground of existence higher than νοῦς and the Ideas, he is, as it has now become clear, not original but stands at the end of a tradition of which the dominant feature is the assimilation of Plato and Aristotle. . . . The One as a supreme source of being is really Aristotle's God carried to a yet higher degree of remoteness by identification with the αὐτὸ τὸ ἀγαθόν, and by the same identification brought into relation with the νοητά" (p. 12).

13. Of the four candidates for primary substantiality adduced by Aristotle—essence, universal, genus, and the substratum (*Met.* 7.3.1028b33–36)—the substratum as composite and the substratum as matter are eliminated at 7.3.1029a30–31, the universal is eliminated at 7.13.1038b35–39a2, and the genus is eliminated in 7.14. This leaves the substratum in the sense of form, and essence in those cases in which it is identical with form. For form as a τόδε τι, see 5.7.1017b24–26, 8.1.1042a29, 9.7.1049a35, and 12.3.1070a9–15. For form as οὐσία, see 7.7.1032b1–2, and 7.11.1037a27–30, b3–4. At 8.3.1043b2–4, he decisively eliminates the composite as primary, thus eliminating anything discussed in the central books of the *Metaphysics* as the primary subject of the science of being *qua* being.

its actualization is in an imperfectly actual composite, it is evidently not the sought-after unqualifiedly separate substance (cf. *Met.* 7.17.1041a7–9). What would be the sought-after primary referent of being is what the god of book twelve of the *Metaphysics* turns out to be. Now the conclusion to which the *Metaphysics* leads us is that being in the primary sense is what this god is, and that all other expressions of being are to be referred to the primary one. What "referred to" here means is "causally connected" as the characterization of first philosophy as a science of first causes indicates. What Plotinus agrees with and disagrees with in this summary is obvious. He agrees that being has a primary reference and derivative references, and that the latter are causally connected to the former.[14] But his argument that Aristotle's god is not the first principle of all amounts to the rejection of form—even unqualifiedly separate form—as the primary referent of being. If we add Plotinus's further agreement that Aristotle is right to identify substance primarily with form, then the conclusion is that being is not substance because being is not primarily form. Since the identification of being and substance is the central hypothesis in Aristotle's construction of first philosophy, it therefore seems quite false to characterize Plotinus's approach as merely a refinement of Aristotelian theology, leaving the science of being *qua* being untouched. It is, in fact, difficult to conceive of a more total rejection of Aristotelian metaphysics, short of the denial of the equivocity of being. Towards the end of this paper I shall return to some further implications of the rejection of the hypothesis that being is form. Now I should like to turn to the actual arguments Plotinus employs in behalf of his own metaphysical hypothesis.

II

In *Ennead* 5.6, titled by Porphyry "On the Fact That That Which Is Beyond Being Does Not Think and on What Is the Primary and What the Secondary Thinking Principle," Plotinus directly attacks the Aristotelian claim that the ἀρχή of all is thinking. The basic argument is both straightforward and powerful (5.6.1.1–14).[15] Thinking requires a distinction between thinker and object of thought (5.1.4.34–38). Hence, wherever there is thinking there is a duality. That which

14. At *Ennead* 6.1.3.5–6 Plotinus seems to agree with Aristotle on the priority of unqualifiedly separate οὐσία, which Plotinus calls "intelligible" οὐσία, to all other οὐσία. Plotinus can do this and assent to the equivocity of being without identifying οὐσία and being unqualifiedly.

15. Cf. *Ennead* 6.7.37, 6.7.37.12–13, 3.8.9.1–15, and 3.8.11.1–9.

is essentially dual cannot be absolutely primary, for duality has unity as its principle. Even if Aristotle is correct in holding that there exists an eternal substance which is thinking, this substance cannot be absolutely primary, for there is something upon which it depends, unity, which is its principle (5.6.3.1–4).[16]

What type of a distinction does Plotinus have in mind? It is surely not a distinction between two different entities, because Plotinus affirms in numerous places the substantial identity of mind and its objects (e.g., 5.3.5.21–28 and 13.13–14; 5.4.2.45–46; 5.5.1.19–23; 5.9.5.7–8 and 29–31; and 6.7.41.12–13). Nor could it be a distinction based in two different ways of conceiving of the same thing. If that were all Plotinus had in mind, his own first principle, which may be conceived under different aspects would be susceptible to the same criticism as Aristotle's god. Evidently, Plotinus means a distinction *within* one substance, something very like what Scholastics termed a real minor distinction. For example, a distinction between a substance and its accidents would be of this sort, and so too would a distinction between the principles of act and potency within a substance. It is Plotinus's contention that thinking and its intentional object are really distinct, and that the ontological complexity presupposed by such a distinction invalidates thinking as an absolutely first principle.

There are two questions raised by this argument. First, is Plotinus correct in holding that the thinking of god requires such a distinction. Second, assuming it does, is a god so characterized thereby disqualified as first principle?

Answering the first question involves the complicating factor that Plotinus does in fact believe that an eternal νοῦς exists, but that the contents of its thinking are Plato's forms; there is, of course, a distinction between thinking and objects thought on this view. It would grossly beg the question, however, to assume that this is the manner in which Aristotle must conceive of his god.[17] Aristotle goes out of his way to insist on the perfect unity of divine thinking and its content.

Why then is Aristotle wrong to identify thinking with primary being?[18] There are, I believe, at least three reasons. First, if god is

---

16. Plotinus adds elsewhere (*Ennead* 6.6.6.9–11) that there also must be a distinction between thinker and thinking, for reasons having to do with his doctrine of activity as secondary actuality. A discussion of this would, however, take us too far afield.

17. It is generally supposed that Plotinus followed Alexander of Aphrodisias (*On the Soul* 89.16–23) in identifying Aristotle's god with the active intellect which Aristotle discusses in *On the Soul* 3.5. The two passages which are taken to show this, *Ennead* 5.9.2.21–22 and 5.1.3.20–23, are certainly not conclusive. I do not think that Plotinus's criticism of the inadequacy of Aristotle's god as first principle relies on an interpretation of god as active intellect, whatever the merits of such an interpretation.

18. H. Seidl, "Aristoteles Lehre von der Noesis Noeseos des ersten, göttlichen Ver-

thinking and being in the primary sense, then thinking cannot be purely equivocal when attributed to god and to human thinkers. If thinking is essentially intentional, then it is difficult to see how god's thinking can be said to exclude the duality that follows from the existence of an intentional object distinct from the thinking itself. The only way we have of determining whether or not thinking is essentially intentional is by examining our own thinking, where, for Plotinus at any rate, thinking is evidently always thinking about something. Second, if thinking which is thinking about thinking is unqualifiedly a unity, then what is the difference between saying this and saying that thinking is thinking—an identity statement which is true even if god does not exist. But Aristotle has striven to prove the existence of god, which he then goes on to characterize as perfect thinking. This point perhaps pertains more to the duality of thinker and thinking than to the duality of thinker and thought, but it seems to me still to be relevant. Third, and relatedly, if god is pure form or οὐσία, as Aristotle holds, then to say that it is incomposite is to say that there is no real distinction between what it is and its being. If this were so, then being would be thinking, and we should not have the slightest idea how to characterize the being of things by definition bereft of thought. To attribute being to them would be self-contradictory. Hence, if being is not οὐσία then there is no reason to deny the compositeness of the primary thinker.

This last point brings us to the second question, namely, why, supposing that thinking is essentially composite, can it not be the absolutely first principle of everything. To begin with, I am certain that Plotinus never doubted for one moment that there must be some first principle or ἀρχή of all, and this for reasons which are not exclusively Plotinian or Platonic. The search for an ἀρχή of all is Presocratic in origin, perhaps as early as Anaximander. The underlying assumption of philosophical cosmology in its Presocratic form is the idea of explanatory adequacy. To give an explanation of a phenomenon is to adduce as cause that which itself is not in need of a similar explanation. Generalizing this principle, an explanation for the κόσμος is one which itself must be characterized in a way unlike anything within the κόσμος. Accordingly, insofar as the coming into being of anything presents itself as a datum in need of explanation, the explanation must

---

nunftwesens und ihre Darstellung bei Plotin," in *Aristoteles: Werk und Wirking*, ed. J. Wiesner (Berlin and New York: Walter De Gruyter & Co., 1987), 2:171–75, argues that Plotinus incorrectly conflates divine and human thinking in Aristotle, thereby invalidating his argument against Aristotle's god as a perfectly actual, undivided first principle.

itself be something that does not come into being, in short something that is an everlasting or eternal or necessary being. Atomism offers good evidence that this principle can be employed in a system that has no theological connotations whatsoever. Plotinus, as we shall see, has a very sophisticated adumbration of this principle to offer, but he does not question the assumption that there is some ἀρχή of all.

III

This being so, the demonstration of the essential compositeness of mind means that mind is disqualified from filling a role that must be filled, that of first principle. The all-too-facile argument for this, which Plotinus does in fact freely employ, is that duality implies unity as its principle, so that if an eternal duality—thinker and object thought—exists, then unity must exist (cf. *Ennead* 3.8.9.6–7; 6.9.2; 5.1.5.1–19; 5.6.3). Such an argument will undoubtedly appear to most as too Platonic, where "Platonic" is a pejorative term. But I think that Plotinus has a deeper argument, for which the above is merely an ellipse, and which does not depend on an apparent confusion of mathematics and metaphysics. It is an argument not directly concerned with the divine mind, though it encompasses this as well. It is a demonstration of the existence of a first principle of all, a first principle which cannot be what Aristotle supposes.[19]

In *Ennead* 6.9, titled "On the Good or the One," Plotinus offers an argument aimed at showing that the One must be posited to explain the being of anything you please. But it is an argument that is easily misconstrued. Plotinus is addressing the claim by Aristotle that "man and one man are the same thing" (*Met.* 4.2.1003b26–7).

Reason has informed us that if an individual loses its unity it is totally unable to be. We ought then to examine both in the individual and in general whether being and unity are the same. Now if the being of an individual is the multitude of its [parts], and it is impossible that unity is a multitude, then being and unity would have to be different. For man is a rational animal, so of course he has many parts, and these parts are tied together into a unity. But then man and unity are different, since one is made up of parts and one is indivisible. (*Ennead* 6.9.2.16–21)

Now Plotinus understood perfectly well that Aristotle did not claim that "being" and "one" mean the same thing. Plotinus is therefore not arguing that a conceptual distinction between being and unity must

---

19. Plotinus tells us that there are many demonstrations of the first ἀρχή and that the demonstrations are themselves a kind of ἀναγωγή to the One (*Ennead* 1.3.1.4–5).

be made where Aristotle did not make it. What he is claiming is that being and unity are more than conceptually distinct.

Plotinus tells us what, in this context, he means by "being," namely, the parts of the man as distinct from their unity. But he does not mean the parts as a disparate heap of limbs and organs; *these* are not the parts of a man. Like Aristotle, Plotinus holds that, say, a hand separated from the organic whole that is the animal is no hand at all. Moreover, if this is denied, then the disparate limbs and organs would each be one hand, liver, and so on, and Plotinus's argument would have demonstrated nothing at all. Rather, what Plotinus is getting at, I believe, is that an inventory or analysis of what a man is will give a list of parts, but none of these nor the entire list taken together is one, anymore than "the whale" as a subject of mammalian science is one. If the unity of the individual man were merely conceptually distinct from his being, then this unity would find its extensional equivalent in the list of parts or as the sum of the list. It is obviously not equivalent to one part of the list. Plotinus tells us, however, that what distinguishes being and unity is that the latter is indivisible. So unity cannot be the sum of parts either.

It begins to appear that Plotinus is trying to show that there is a real composition consisting of what the individual is and what makes it an individual, the latter designated as "unity." This is certainly an odd way of making the point that existence is really distinct from essence in any composite being. What I should like to do now is to try to show that this is indeed the point being made, and to mitigate the oddness somewhat.

Plotinus employs various forms of the verb εἶναι, including τὸ ὄν and οὐσία, equivocally, consistent with his acceptance of the Aristotelian doctrine of the equivocity of being. Plotinus also agrees with Aristotle that the primary referent of οὐσία or τὸ ὄν is noetic activity or νοῦς (cf. e.g., *Ennead* 5.4.2.44). But beyond νοῦς, and so beyond οὐσία, is the One. This makes all the difference to the meaning of the metaphysical language. For Aristotle identifies being with οὐσία, which in turn is identified with unqualifiedly separate form. Once οὐσία is removed as ἀρχή, it is no longer possible to say that being is unqualifiedly identical with οὐσία. For οὐσία receives something from above, from the One, and so it is not unqualifiedly self-sufficient, as Aristotle supposed being in the primary sense to be. Nominally, what οὐσία receives from the One is unity (cf. *Ennead* 6.10.15–17). But since the One is the first principle of all and perfectly one, it is most emphatically not to be identified with nonexistent unity, except in the precise sense of "existence" that refers to something possessed by everything else besides the One. For Aristotle, οὐσία in the primary sense has to do duty for form and the existence of form as well. Since, for Plotinus, οὐσία is not the ἀρχή of all or self-sufficient, οὐσία and τὸ ὄν, and finite forms of the verb εἶναι can be used alternately for what νοῦς is—its essence—and for its existence (cf. *Ennead* 5.4.6.2).

It would be possible and perhaps preferable to Plotinus's way to speak as follows. Οὐσία is not primary being, but primary finite being. Finite being, however, is a composite of essence and existence. Being in the primary sense is infinite being, in which there is no distinction whatsoever between essence and existence. Both in the case of an individual and in the case of νοῦς, essence is that which alone belongs to the subject; existence is superadded and derived from the ἀρχή of all, infinite being.[20]

As I say, perhaps this way of stating things would be clearer, but it is generally speaking not Plotinus's way. He is faithful to a vocabulary constrained by, among other things, an eccentric and to my mind perverse interpretation of the second part of Plato's *Parmenides*. Yet despite this, lucidity does prevail from time to time. For example, Plotinus does say that the One is the cause of the existence (εἶναι) of everything else and thus, because it is an ἀρχή, it is beyond existence (*Ennead* 5.3.17.11–14; cf. 5.3.15.12–13 and 28). In the same passage he also says that the One is productive of οὐσία, whereas in *Ennead* 6.6.10.15–17 he says that τὸ ὄν (meaning οὐσία) has its being from itself and its unity from the One. If the One produces οὐσία and if οὐσία can also be said to owe its being to itself, then it is obvious that Plotinus is speaking equivocally. The puzzle, if not the equivocity, disappears when we understand that what the One produces is οὐσία in the sense of existence and that what οὐσία or νοῦς is the cause of is οὐσία in the sense of essence. That is, we do not need to go outside essence to explain what it is, but its existence is not self-explaining. Hence, it has a qualified self-sufficiency. The One alone is unqualifiedly self-sufficient because it is uniquely self-caused (*Ennead* 6.8.14.42).

Since the One is the cause of the existence of everything else, and since Plotinus warns us explicitly that "the One" is just a misleading name for the ἀρχή of all (*Ennead* 5.5.6.26–30), it seems plainly wrong

20. Cf. *Ennead* 6.7.23.22–24, where Plotinus says that the One preserves (σώζει) all things in existence. It is true that at 3.6.6.13 we also read that νοῦς requires nothing for its own preservation. I think that weight of evidence, especially the texts cited in the following paragraph, requires that in these two passages we understand Plotinus to be addressing two different questions, one existential and the other essentialist. The second hypostasis, νοῦς, is self-sufficient with respect to intelligibility. It is not so with respect to its existence, even though its existence is eternal.

to insist that "the One" means unity *simpliciter*.[21] Rather, the One is the principle postulated to account for what an analysis of 'man' shows cannot otherwise be accounted for, namely, its existence.[22]

There is another way round leading to the same conclusion. Plotinus tells us that the One is unique. There cannot be two Ones (*Ennead* 5.4.1.15–21). If there were two, then neither would be the first principle, because that which they would have in common, oneness, would be the first principle. The argument for the necessary uniqueness of the first principle should be viewed in the light of Aristotle's argument, in book twelve of the *Metaphysics,* that "the primary essence" is unique because it is ἐντελέχεια (*Met.* 12.8.1074a31–38). Plotinus agrees with Aristotle that that which is absolutely primary must be conceived of in such a manner that it must be one in formula and in number, but he denies that primary οὐσία can fulfill this role (cf. *Ennead* 5.5.6.5–6; 5.3.17.11–14). His point here is distinct from that discussed earlier, namely, that the first principle must be absolutely simple. Even if Aristotle's god were the perfectly simple cognizer he holds it to be, it could not be first because it is not necessarily unique. In the light of the previous exegesis, I take Plotinus to be arguing that uniqueness is guaranteed only in that in which there is no real distinction between οὐσία (essence) and existence. Conversely, the impossibility of there being more than one thing in which this is so entails that in everything else such a real distinction is to be found.

IV

Plotinus's position is, in a way, a recovery of Eleaticism by means of the Aristotelian insight into the πρὸς ἕν equivocity of being. Parmenides had held that being is one, by which he meant to bring into question the truth of claims which presupposed the existence of plurality and change. Aristotle had imagined that the discovery that being was not univocal would accomplish the exorcism of Eleatic pretensions once and for all. Aristotle, though, had to allow that the primary

21. At *Ennead* 3.8.10.28–35 Plotinus claims that the One is (εἶναι) above all predicates (cf. 5.3.13). So to insist that the One is just unity seems counter to the text. What he means by saying that it is above all predicates is that predication requires composition and the One is perfectly incomposite. Further, at 6.6.18.42ff. he explicitly identifies the One with being and claims that it alone is self-sufficient.

22. At *Ennead* 6.9.1.27–28 Plotinus says that the more or less being something has the more or less unity it has. I take this to indicate that a conceptual distinction (as per Aristotle) may be retained for being and unity, over and above the analysis of being which yields a real distinction between essence and existence.

referent of being was unique, that being in the primary sense was identifiable with one nature only. This was surely something of a concession to Parmenides. And there the matter rested until Plotinus proceeded to analyze this nature further. What he discovered was that οὐσία cannot be what being is because οὐσία has being. Parmenides was at least on the right track when he implied that there could be no real distinction between what real being is and real being itself. He was right to rely on a little bit of linguistic coyness when, in describing the subject of true discourse, he employed a finite form of the verb "to be" without an explicit subject. But because he apparently had no inkling of the idea of equivocity, he could only describe discourse about being literally as the antithesis to discourse about anything else. He grasped the fundamental feature of the ἀρχή of metaphysical science, but he did not understand how to relate it to everything else.

According to Plotinus, a similar criticism may be made of Aristotle's god. I have elsewhere attempted to show that Aristotle both in the *Physics* and in the second book of the *Metaphysics* explored the notion that primary causality was efficient causality.[23] Nevertheless, insofar as we may take book twelve of the *Metaphysics* as his settled view, or at least as his conclusion in the light of the identification of being with substance, there is no doubt that god's causality is final causality.[24] How could it be otherwise when primary being is identified with form and separately existing form is identified with self-absorbed thinking? By contrast, efficient causes have their actuality outside of themselves. On this view, if there is some plausibility in the claim that the being of rational substances is illuminated by the life of the divine mind, there is no plausibility whatsoever in what should be the general conclusion of the *Metaphysics,* namely, that the primary referent of being

---

23. See my *God and Greek Philosophy,* London: Routledge 1990, chap. 3; and my "Causality, Univocity, and First Philosophy in Metaphysics ii," *Ancient Philosophy* 11(1991): 331–49.

24. J. Pépin, "La théologie d'Aristote," in vol. 3 of *L'attualità della problematic Aristotelica, Studia Aristotelica* (Padova: Editrice Antenore, 1970), 84–126, writes, "Sans doute cette causalité finale, principale manifestation du divin, n'exclut-elle pas à titre secondaire, une certaine intervention efficiente" (p. 125). Pépin cites *Metaphysics* 12.7.1072b14 where the world is said to "depend" (ἐξήρτηται) on god and *On the Heavens* 1.9.279a29 where the same word is used in referring to the world in relation to god and where efficient causality is evidently meant. But *On the Heavens* is a very early work with no metaphysical pretensions. It is precisely the new metaphysical hypothesis which identifies being with substance that occasions the reevaluation of the causality of god. Accordingly, a verbal similarity between the two texts cannot bear much weight. Beyond that, Pépin's claim, which has been anticipated by many scholars, does not seem to amount to more than an argument from "fittingness" which is not negligible, but which finally cannot stand against the force of the argument of the text.

illuminates the being of absolutely everything else owing to causal connectedness. Knowing that the blissful life of god is what we and the soul of the outermost sphere of the heavens aim to emulate hardly helps us to understand the being of, for example, the elements or artifacts. Aristotle's god is the metaphysical god who fails, owing to causal impotence as well as to entitative derivativeness.

Two features of the contrasting Plotinian picture need to be stressed above all others. First, the One, as we have seen, has a direct and explicit causal relation to absolutely everything else in the universe. The One is the cause of the existence of everything else. Second, this causal relation is a kind of efficient causality.[25]

Plotinus concludes that the first principle is an efficient cause as a result of the analysis of data that show that the existence of things needs explaining. Aristotle concludes that the first principle is a final cause as a result of an argument whose major premise is that motion is everlasting. Aristotle's first efficient cause cannot be unqualifiedly first because its causal activity is imperfect, that is, it is the actualization of a potency. An efficient cause therefore cannot be an uncaused cause, and an uncaused cause must operate other than as an efficient cause. Aristotle does indeed recognize an efficient cause of the existence of things, but this is in every case an efficient cause of the generation of something, such as a parent of an offspring.[26] He does not appear to have considered that the existence of that which has already been generated or of that which is ungenerable might be in need of an explanation.[27] Whether his identification of being with substance is the cause or the effect of this failure to have considered such a possibility, I have no way of knowing. But clearly enough, if being in the primary sense is unqualifiedly separate form, then there is no perspicuous efficient causal connection between this form and

25. Most frequently Plotinus will use some form of ποίησις to indicate the causality of the One. See for example *Ennead* 5.3.17.12. He also uses some form of γίγνεσθαι to indicate the relation from the side of the effect. See for example *Ennead* 5.5.51–52, 6.7.32.2.

26. When Aristotle uses the phrase αἴτιον τοῦ εἶναι he uses it generally in a metaphysical context to indicate the formal cause of a sensible composite. See for example *Metaphysics* 5.8.1017b15, 7.17.1041b26–29, 8.3.1043b13–14 (cf. 1043a2–3), 8.6.1045a8–b20; *Posterior Analytics* 2.1.90a9–11; and *On the Soul* 2.4.415b12–13. In the *Nicomachean Ethics* he uses the phrase to indicate the efficient causality of the generator of a sensible substance, for example, a father of children. See 8.11.1161a16; 12.1167a7; 9.2.165a23.

27. By contrast, compare Plotinus's claim (*Ennead* 3.7.6.53–54, that despite the fact that the universe does not have a beginning in time, it does have a cause of its existence (αἴτια τοῦ εἶναι).

sensible substances whose actuality is explained as the result of generation by another sensible substance.[28]

The question that starkly confronts us in the light of this exposition is what were Plotinus's reasons for claiming that that which is perfect and uncaused by anything else could have an actuality outside of itself. How could the One be an efficient cause? Plotinus's bare-bones answer is that all activity is essentially productive. The One can no more withhold its production than fire can keep from radiating heat.[29] Why conceive of actuality in this way? Unfortunately, the text is far from helpful on this point. However, if the primary effect of the One's causal activity is indeed the existence of everything else, including that which does not come into existence, then it would seem that causing existence is not bringing about a change (*Ennead* 5.1.6.21–25). It is not the actualization of a potency in something else, but that for which there is no more appropriate term than "creation." In Aristotelian change, the actuality of the agent is in the patient and extensionally equivalent to the actualization of its potency (cf. *Physics* 3.3.202a13ff.). That is why efficient causes need potency, and actualize it when they are producing their effects. Plotinus does not view the existence of things (as opposed to their coming to be) as the actualization of a prior potency. Hence, the existence radiating from the One is not the actualization of a potency.[30] To put this point in a slightly different way, since the existence of everything composite is owing to a cause outside of itself, and since this existence is not the actualization of a potency, the first cause *must* have an actuality outside itself which cannot be the actualization of a potency because there is no potency to actualize. So, what is true for the primary ἐνέργεια must hold for all ἐνέργειαι since these participate in the primary. That the primary cause must be an ἐνέργεια follows from the Aristotelian principle that

28. *Metaphysics* 12.7.1072b14 has heaven and nature "depend on" (ἤρτηται) an ἀρχή. Alexander of Aphrodisias, *In. Met.* 266.10 is more expansive in saying ἤρτηται τὸ εἶναι (cf. 244.20–21). But as Verbeke observes, "it is hard to say what exactly Alexander has in mind" ("*Metaphysics* Viewed by the Commentators," 118 n. 40).

29. Plotinus makes a distinction between an activity τῆς οὐσίας and the activity ἐκ τῆς οὐσίας. See *Ennead* 5.4.2.27–33, 2.9.8.22–25, 4.5.7.51–55, and 6.2.22.24–28). As the first passage indicates clearly, the use of the term οὐσία here is not intended to exclude the distinction from applying to the activity of the One, which is strictly speaking "beyond οὐσία."

30. Plotinus does in fact say that the One is the δύναμις of all things, although not in the way that matter is δύναμις. See *Ennead* 5.1.7.10, 5.3.15.33–35, 3.8.10.1, 6.7.32.31, and 5.4.1.36. Briefly, what Plotinus means by this jarring locution is that the One is virtually what everything else is because it is owing to its power or fecundity that everything else exists and because a cause contains within itself its effects.

the primary cause must be perfect. That the primary cause must be an efficient cause follows from the fact that the existence of every composite is only thus explained. That the primary efficient cause can also be a final cause follows from further principles regarding the nature of composite being whose examination is outside the scope of this paper.

The notion of activity as necessarily productive is the core of Neoplatonic metaphysics, by which I mean the characteristic that sets Plotinus apart from Aristotle, from later creation metaphysics such as that of Aquinas, and, it needs to be stressed, from Plato himself. For though Plotinus of course identifies the One with the form of the good in the *Republic* and with the subject of the first hypothesis of the second part of the *Parmenides,* there is not the slightest evidence that in either case Plato conceived of a first principle as cause of the existence of everything else. The form of the good is explicitly identified as the cause of being and truth in the forms alone (*Rep.* 6.508e3–6, 509b6–8). And though it is at least questionable how Plato conceived of the being of the forms, there is no doubt at all that analysis of the entitative composition of the sensible individual by Plotinus is not supported by any Platonic text. As for the *Parmenides,* I think that an impartial reading of Plotinus's favorite text can only lead one to conclude that Plotinus saw there what he wanted to see and not what was really there.[31]

We must not go too far in the direction of separating Plotinus from his revered master. Of course, there are many features of Platonic metaphysics which, if I might use a somewhat ambiguous expression, stimulated the thinking of Plotinus. In his conception of the second and third hypostases, νοῦς and ψυχή, he is attempting to conform his thinking to Plato at many points. Even here, though, there is a story to be told about originality in interpretation which cannot be understood without bringing Aristotle into the discussion. What I wish to insist upon here is that Plotinus's rejection of Aristotelian metaphysics is not to be dismissed as based on nothing more than nostalgia for the groves of Academe. It is based, first of all, on a close, discerning, and sympathetic reading of the *Metaphysics* that, as we have seen, was

31. E. R. Dodds, "The *Parmenides* of Plato and the Origin of the Neo-Platonic 'One'," *Classical Quarterly* 22 (1928): 129–42, provides the starting-point for modern interpretations of the origin of Plotinus's first hypostasis. Dodds is most concerned to argue that there is ample evidence in Greek philosophy—including Speusippus and the Neopythagorean Moderatus, as well as Plato's *Parmenides*—to support the refutation of an "oriental" origin of Plotinus's idea. He emphasizes, however, both the remarkable originality of Plotinus and his transformation of the *Parmenides.*

practically unprecedented. The best evidence of this is that Plotinus adopts Aristotle's metaphysical terminology and what is arguably his central insight, namely, the equivocity of being. Finally, I think that what needs to be said as plainly as possible is that whereas Aristotle's central metaphysical hypothesis—the identification of being with substance—was rejected by many because it was ill understood, it was rejected by Plotinus because he understood it all too well.

2   Plotinus on the Nature of Eternity and Time

STEVEN K. STRANGE

Plotinus's treatise on eternity and time, *Ennead* 3.7 in Porphyry's edition of his master's works, has been among the most widely read of his treatises, not only due to its intrinsic philosophical interest and historical importance, but also because it is one of the most accessible and self-contained of Plotinus's writings. Unlike most of Plotinus's treatises, *Ennead* 3.7 does not at first seem to presuppose on the part of the reader either an extensive knowledge of the inner workings of Plotinus's metaphysical system or an intimate familiarity with specific issues of scholastic controversy in the first centuries A.D. It takes the form of a detailed philosophical commentary on the fundamental texts about eternity and time from the classical period of Greek philosophy. These are texts that even now retain their central interest for us: Plato's distinction between eternity and time in the *Timaeus* (37c–39a), Parmenides' argument for the timeless nature of being that lies behind Plato's distinction (B8.1–22), and Aristotle's account of the nature of time in the *Physics* (4.10–14). Nevertheless, despite its relative popularity, this treatise, like the rest of Plotinus's writings, presents great difficulties which still stand in the way of an adequate understanding of it. Commentators on the treatise tend to be content with repeating what they take to be Plotinus's *doctrines* about the nature of eternity and time, without any real attempt to come to terms with his *arguments* for them.[1] But properly understanding a philosopher does not consist

---

1. References to the *Enneads* will be to Henry and Schwyzer's *editio minor*. The following discussions of the treatise will be cited by the author's last name only: Werner Beierwaltes, *Plotin: Über Ewigkeit und Zeit (Ennead 3.7)* (Frankfurt am Main: Klostermann, 1967); Émile Bréhier, trans., *Plotin: "Ennéades"* 2nd ed. (Paris: Les Belles Lettres, 1956), vol. 2, introduction to *Ennead* 3.7, pp. 123–26; G. H. Clark, "The Theory of Time in Plotinus," *Philosophical Review* 54 (1944): 337–48; Karen Gloy, "Die Struktur der Zeit in Plotins Zeittheorie," *Archiv für Geschichte der Philosophie* 71 (1989): 303–26; Andreas Graeser, "Zeitlichkeit und Zeitlosigkeit: Bemerkungen zu Plotins Unterscheidung zweier 'immer' (III.7)," *Philosophisches Jahrbuch* 94 (1987): pp. 142–48; Jesús

merely in learning the catechism of his positions: a philosopher, especially a deep and difficult systematic thinker like Plotinus, cannot really be understood apart from his arguments, which allow us to see the philosophical reasons for holding the views that he does. It seems worthwhile, therefore, to try to trace the overall outlines of the argument of *Ennead* 3.7 in the hope of elucidating Plotinus's views about eternity and time.

I. *ENNEAD* 3.7 AND PLOTINUS'S PHILOSOPHICAL METHOD

It will be impossible fully to appreciate the arguments of *Ennead* 3.7 without first coming to understand Plotinus's conception of how one goes about arguing for a philosophical position. Indeed, I think that the failure to get clear about his methodology has contributed significantly to misunderstandings of Plotinus's work in general.[2] There is less excuse for this in the case of our treatise than there is with most of Plotinus's work, for it is here that Plotinus makes his most self-conscious remarks about what he takes to be proper philosophical method.

Plotinus takes the proper method of philosophy to be what I will call a *dialectical* method, in a sense that has become familiar from recent work on Aristotle's methodology. Indeed, it seems to me that Plotinus is quite self-conscious in adopting Aristotle's philosophical method, as he understands it, to his own practice. As is now widely recognized, Aristotle's method of investigating any subject is characteristically to survey first the views of "the many," i.e., commonly accepted opinions, and those of "the wise," i.e., the views of previous

---

Igal, trans., *Plotino, "Enéadas"* (Madrid: Gredos, 1982–87), vol. 1–2, and especially the general introduction (vol. 1, pp. 74–77); Hans Jonas, "Plotin über Ewigkeit und Zeit: Interpretation von *Enn.* III.7" in A. Dempf et al., eds., *Politische Ordnung und menschliche Existenz: Festgabe für E. Voegelin* (Munich: Beck, 1962), 295–319; Peter Manchester, "Time and the Soul in Plotinus, III.7 [45], 11," *Dionysius* 2 (1978): 101–36; J. E. McGuire and Steven K. Strange, "An Annotated Translation of Plotinus *Ennead* III.7, On Eternity and Time," *Ancient Philosophy* 8 (1988): 251–71; John F. Phillips, "Stoic 'Common Notions' in Plotinus," *Dionysius* 11 (1987): 33–52; Richard Sorabji, *Time, Creation and the Continuum* (Ithaca, N.Y.: Cornell, 1983), chaps. 8–10. Beierwaltes's book is a text and translation of the treatise with introduction and commentary, and Jonas's article also provides a useful paraphrase of the entire treatise. Sorabji unfortunately deals only with the doctrine of eternity.

2. The best treatment of Plotinus's methodology is Thomas A. Szlezák, *Platon und Aristoteles in der Nuslehre Plotins* (Basel and Stuttgart: Schwabe, 1979), chap. 1, pp. 14–51, which presents useful criticisms of previous discussions. Szlezák however commits the common error of taking Plotinus to claim only to be an interpreter of Plato (cf. n. 21 below). The same is true of Jean-Michel Charrue, *Plotin: Lecteur de Platon* (Paris: Les Belles Lettres, 1978); see pp. 17–18. See also Phillips, on whose discussion cf. nn. 16–18 below, and Alain Eon, "La notion plotinienne d'exégèse," *Revue internationale de philosophie* 24 (1970): 252–89.

philosophers, on the subject; to compare and contrast these *endoxa*, the authoritative or reputable opinions, noting their agreements and disagreements with one another; and then to use these agreements and disagreements and his own dialectical ingenuity and techniques (discussed in the *Topics*) to develop the salient philosophical puzzles or *aporiai* that arise about the subject matter. The final stage of the inquiry is then to resolve these puzzles by drawing the requisite distinctions in order to show how the various authoritative views, or as many of them as possible, can be reconciled with one another, and their apparent difficulties and contradictions minimized.[3] What is crucial is that this last stage is supposed to be sufficient: no further justification is taken to be required for the distinctions that one draws except that they are what is needed to resolve the conflicts among the authorities. Thus, in the *Nicomachean Ethics*, Aristotle is willing to say that if we manage to do this, "enough will have been shown" (δεδειγμένον ἂν εἴη ἱκανῶς; *NE* 1145b6), and even that the resolution of the puzzles amounts to discovery (ἡ γὰρ λύσις τῆς ἀπορίας εὕρησις; *NE* 1146b7–8), presumably the discovery of the truth about the matter under investigation.

There is a well-known difficulty about how Aristotle's reliance on this dialectical method in his treatises is supposed to fit with his official view of theoretical understanding based on the explicitly nondialectical notion of demonstration of the *Analytics*. Presumably he thinks that if a dialectical investigation has been properly conducted, the distinctions that are indicated to resolve the salient puzzles will reflect or embody the proper principles of the subject matter in question.[4] Plotinus, however, need not have been disturbed by this problem: he could just have followed the Academic tradition in assuming, probably correctly, that Aristotle in his treatises is merely employing the method of dialectical argumentation he had learned in Plato's Academy.[5] This

---

3. There has been much good work in recent years on Aristotle's methodology, but the classic treatment of Aristotle's use of the dialectical method remains G. E. L. Owen, "*Tithenai ta phainomena*," in S. Mansion, ed., *Aristote et les problèmes de méthode* (Louvain: Presses Universitaires, 1961), reprinted in G. E. L. Owen and Martha C. Nussbaum, eds., *Logic, Science and Dialectic* (Ithaca: Cornell, 1986). On Aristotle's dialectical method, see also J. D. G. Evans, *Aristotle's Conception of Dialectic* (Cambridge: Cambridge University Press, 1977). T. H. Irwin, *Aristotle's First Principles* (Oxford: Clarendon, 1988), among other scholars, wishes to distinguish different types of dialectical inquiry in Aristotle. I follow the ancient commmentators in treating Aristotle's dialectic as a unitary method applicable to all areas of philosophical inquiry. In any case it sems safe to assume that Plotinus read Aristotle in this way.

4. Cf. *Topics* 101a35–b4, where Aristotle asserts that dialectic provides the proper way to the principles of any science. See also *Metaphysics* 3.1, 995a28–31.

5. Cicero in various passages (*De finibus* 5.10, *Tusculan Disputations* 2.9, *De oratore*

would be enough to persuade Plotinus, as a committed Platonist and defender of what he takes to be Plato's views, that the philosophical method practiced and encouraged by Aristotle was the correct one. In any case, the method that Plotinus adopts as his own is very close to that of Aristotle. As I will argue, this can clearly be seen both from Plotinus's methodological remarks in *Ennead* 3.7 and from his actual procedure in the treatise.

Plotinus begins the first chapter of *Ennead* 3.7 with some remarks on the great difficulty of the concepts of eternity and time. We—he seems to mean "we Platonists"—are always going around talking as if we understand what eternity and time are, as features, respectively, of the intelligible and sensible worlds (as Plato had argued in *Timaeus* 37c–38b).[6] We speak as if we possessed a clear impression of what they are (ἐναργές τι παρ' αὐτοῖς περὶ αὐτῶν ἐν ταῖς ψυχαῖς ἔχειν πάθος νομίζομεν; *Ennead* 3.7.1, 4–6). But in fact we do not, as becomes apparent as soon as we try to make our concepts of them explicit.[7] Nevertheless, rather than investigating these concepts further in order to get clear about them, Plotinus says, we are generally satisfied just to parrot the relevant texts of those he calls "the ancients" (οἱ παλαιοί), i.e., the philosophers of the classical period,[8] even though we under-

---

3.80) credits Aristotle with using (and even, wrongly, with inventing) the method of arguing on both sides of the given question, a clear allusion to the initial aporetic stage of Aristotelian dialectical inquiry. Cicero's focus is on this because of its similarity to the method of Academic scepticism, which was a development from the dialectical method practiced in the older Academy. The Academic sceptics were, like the Socrates of Plato's early dialogues (and the Aristotle of the *Topics*), more concerned with refuting theses and raising *aporiai* than in solving them, while it is the solution of the *aporiai* that makes dialectic a positive method of inquiry for Aristotle. Positive Aristotelian dialectic, however, has clear Platonic antecedents as well: consider for instance the way that the Eleatic Stranger in the *Sophist* solves the puzzles he has raised about being and not-being by employing the distinction between absolute and relative not-being. Note that Plotinus identifies the highest sort of dialectic with the dialectic of the *Sophist* (cf. *Ennead* 1.3.4 and 6.2).

6. It is important to notice that Plotinus assumes that his readers will be Platonists who will share his assessment of Plato as preeminent among the philosophers of the classical period: cf. *Ennead* 5.8.4, 54–56, where it is taken for granted that "we" will wish to be worthy of the appellation (προσηγορία) "Platonist." Plotinus appears to be writing for his own students, and perhaps for circulation to other noted Platonists such as Longinus (Porphyry, *Life of Plotinus* §§19–20), not for general publication. This accounts for his neglect in most of his treatises to defend fundamental Platonist assumptions such as the theory of Ideas.

7. The opening of *Ennead* 3.7.1 is very reminiscent of Augustine's remarks at *Confessions* 11.14 init. about the difficulty of defining time, especially "quid est ergo tempus? si nemo ex me quaerat, scio; si quaerenti explicare velim, nescio."

8. The expression οἱ παλαιοί (i.e., φιλόσοφοι), "the ancient philosophers," seems to have been used in an almost technical way in the Platonic tradition as early as Antiochus of Ascalon in the first half of the first century B.C. (cf. Cicero *De finibus* 5.23) to denote

stand these texts in different and often contradictory ways (3.7.1, 7–13). Plotinus considers such an attitude to be quite unphilosophical; it is perhaps this sort of reproach he had in mind when he referred to his famous contemporary, the Platonist Longinus, as "a scholar, but certainly no philosopher" (φιλόλογος μὲν ... ὁ Λογγῖνος, φιλόσοφος δὲ οὐδαμῶς; Porphyry, *Life of Plotinus* 14.19–20). To be sure, Plotinus goes on to say that we should think that at least some of the ancient and blessed philosophers have discovered the truth about these matters[9]—I will have more to say about this claim shortly—but he declares that it is incumbent upon us to investigate which of them has done so, and how we ourselves can also reach a correct understanding of them. This means that we will have to work through their views in order to fully understand and evaluate them: as in Aristotle, this is the job of dialectic. We examine their views, however, not for their own sake but to gain an understanding of the subject for ourselves— Plotinus makes it clear later in the treatise that he has no interest in the history of philosophy (ἱστορία) for its own sake (3.7.10, 9–11).

The opinions of the ancient philosophers seem to play the same sort of role for Plotinus as do the *endoxa* of the wise for Aristotle. What corresponds for Plotinus to the other source of Aristotelian *endoxa*, the opinions of the many? This becomes apparent from Plotinus's remarks at the beginning of his discussion of time in chapter seven of the treatise. He says there that if it had been the case that none of the ancient and blessed men had said anything about the subject of time, we would then be obliged to develop our own account of it, but that in doing so we would need to make sure that our opinion fit with (ἐφαρμόζειν) "the conception [ἔννοια] we possess of it" (3.7.7, 14).[10] This is a reference to the theory of "common conceptions" or "natural conceptions" (κοιναὶ ἔννοιαι or φυσικαὶ ἔννοιαι—often conflated in post-Hellenistic usage with the "preconceptions," or προλήψεις, of Epicurus), a theory which seems to have been originally formulated

---

Plato, Aristotle and their contemporaries in the Old Academy. Cf. also John S. Kieffer, *Galen's Institutio Logica* (Baltimore: Johns Hopkins, 1964), 130–33. Porphyry at least was willing to extend it to include the early Stoics (see e.g., *De Abstinentia* 3.1.5), and given the contents of *Ennead* 3.7 Plotinus may be using it this way too. He obviously means it to include Parmenides as well.

9. Compare what Plotinus says at *Ennead* 2.9.10.12–14: the Gnostics "dare to disparage what ancient and divine men have spoken well and in accordance with truth"— a reference to Plato and others who had discussed the nature of intelligible reality, cf. *Ennead* 2.9.6, 26–28 and 37–38.

10. For the distinction between ἱστορία and the investigation of ἔννοιαι, which corresponds to Aristotle's distinction between the views of the wise and the views of the many, see also Porphyry, *Against Boethius on the Soul, apud* Eusebius *Preparatio Evangelica* 14.10.3, where what is at issue is the immortality of the soul.

in Stoicism, but which by Imperial times had become common philosophical currency among the various schools.[11] Common conceptions are beliefs that are shared by all (or nearly all) human beings about the contents of our concepts of things,[12] and the Stoics agreed with Aristotle (e.g., *NE* 1098b28–29) that such commonly held beliefs, while they could be confused, could not be completely false or off the mark, and hence that they can provide a reliable guide for inquiry.[13] Alexander of Aphrodisias (*In Met.* 9.19ff.) straightforwardly identifies natural conceptions with Aristotle's opinions of "the many";[14] Platonists tended to identify them with the objects of recollection (cf. Alcinous, *Didaskalikos* §4, 155.23–30 Hermann). Presumably the reason that they cannot be false is that, since they are shared by everyone, they must arise naturally in human beings, and Nature, as Peripatetics, Stoics, and Platonists could all agree, does nothing in vain.[15] Plotinus would agree with this too, and he followed earlier Platonists in

11. Plotinus, like Plutarch, speaks only of ἔννοιαι in this connection, cf. Robert B. Todd, "The Stoic Common Notions: A Re-examination and Reinterpretation," *Symbolae Osloenses* 48 (1973): 61–62. The classic discussion of the theory of common conceptions is A. Bonhöffer, *Epictet und die Stoa* (Stuttgart: Enke, 1890), 188ff., which should however be compared with the criticisms of F. H. Sandbach, "*Ennoia* and *Prolepsis* in the Stoic Theory of Knowledge," *Classical Quarterly* 24 (1930): 44–51; reprinted in A. A. Long, ed., *Problems in Stoicism* (London: Athlone, 1971). A wealth of material on the theory and its background is provided by Klaus Oehler, "Das Consensus omnium als Kriterium der Wahrheit in der antiken Philosophie und der Patristik," *Antike und Abendland* 10 (1961): 103–29, and Ruth Schian, *Untersuchungen über das "argumentum e consensu omnium"* (Hildesheim: Olms, 1973). For Plotinus's use of common conceptions as criteria, see Phillips's article and H. J. Blumenthal, "Plotinus and Proclus on the Criterion of Truth" in Pamela Huby and Gordon Neal, eds., *The Criterion of Truth: Essays Written in Honour of G. Kerferd* (Liverpool: 1989), and for the notion of fitting our ἔννοιαι or προλήψεις in particular, cf. the material from Epictetus presented by Bonhöffer with Epicurus, *Kuriai Doxai* §§37–38; Alcinous, *Didaskalikos* 156.19–21 and 165.10, Hermann; Plotinus, *Ennead* 5.3.2, 12, and other passages cited by Phillips (p. 46, n. 34).

12. The fourth-century Neoplatonist Sallustius characterizes them as "those conceptions to which all men will assent if questioned properly" (κοιναὶ δέ εἰσιν ἔννοιαι ὅσας πάντες ἄνθρωποι ὀρθῶς ἐρωτηθέντες ὁμολογήσουσιν; *Concerning the Gods and the Universe* 1.2). Galen, *On the Best Sect* §2, *ad fin.* identifies common conceptions with what is self-evident to the mind (1.107, Kühn); cf. A. A. Long, "Ptolemy on the Criterion," in Huby and Neal, eds., *The Criterion of Truth,* 161 (= J. Dillon and A. A. Long, eds., *The Question of "Eclecticism"* [Berkeley: California, 1988], p. 200).

13. Cf. Aristotle, *Met.* 993a30–994b4 and *NE* 1172b36–1173a1: ἃ γὰρ πᾶσι δοκεῖ, ταῦτ᾽ εἶναι φάμεν ("What seems so to everyone, we say is true"), and for later Greek thought, Malcolm Schofield, "Preconception, Argument, and God," in Schofield et al., eds., *Doubt and Dogmatism* (Oxford: Clarendon, 1980), 294ff.

14. For Alexander's view see also R. W. Sharples, *Alexander of Aphrodisias On Fate,* 18. Alexander may have influenced Plotinus's adoption of Aristotle's methodology.

15. On this point, cf. Michael Frede, "Stoics and Skeptics on Clear and Distinct Impressions," in M. F. Burnyeat, ed., *The Skeptical Tradition* (Berkeley: U. of California Press, 1983), 84 (= Frede, *Essays in Ancient Philosophy* [Minneapolis: Minnesota, 1987], 168), and Jonathan Barnes, "Aristotle and the Methods of Ethics," *Revue internationale de philosophie* 34 (1980), 506–10.

assimilating common conceptions to the inborn notions that are our confused earthly reminiscences of the Ideas.[16]

But while our common conceptions or shared ordinary notions can provide reliable guideposts for our inquiry, in that any statement that conflicts with them has no chance of being true, they are unclear and can as they stand provide no insight into the nature of things.[17] We must therefore use philosophical analysis to help us understand things that we already have some awareness of, but are unable to define for ourselves adequately without reflection.[18] Here Plotinus insists that we

16. Cf. *Ennead* 5.3.3, 6–9 on the κανών or standard of goodness in the soul with Alcinous, *Didaskalikos* §4, 156, 19–21, Hermann. Platonists of course did not think that an empiricist account of the origin these notions could be given: cf. Cicero, *Tusculan Disputations* 1.57–58, *Didaskalikos* §25, 177.45–178.12, Hermann, and Plutarch *apud* Olympiodorus *In Phaed.* 156.1–14. All three of these passages connect common conceptions with recollection. The role of recollection in Plotinus's epistemology is somewhat controversial. H. J. Blumenthal, *Plotinus' Psychology* (The Hague: Nijhoff, 1971), 96–97, among other scholars, thinks that genuine Platonic recollection has been replaced in Plotinus by the notion of the undescended intelligence, so that texts which mention recollection can only be paying lip service to Plato's theory. Phillips distinguishes between a sort of recollection that deals with common conceptions (Plotinus's "imprints" [τύποι] in the soul), as in *Ennead* 5.3.2–3, and another sort involving direct knowledge of Ideas (ibid., 1.2.4): see n. 18 below. I am unconvinced by attempts to find important differences between Plotinus's view of recollection and common conceptions and that of the tradition. In fact he seems to appropriate the traditional view as his own; this accounts for his not saying more about the subject. Plotinus's more complex psychology no doubt makes for some differences, but they should not be overemphasized.

17. Plotinus connects our preanalytic grasp of eternity and time, which presents us with the initial illusion of ἐναργεία or clarity, with that produced by "means of more concise [or cursory] conceptual apprehensions" (ὥσπερ ταῖς τῆς ἐννοίας ἀθροωτέραις ἐπιβολαῖς, 1.4: for ὥσπερ marking an example rather than a comparison, see Sleeman-Pollet, *Lexicon Plotinianum* 1161.26–30). Phillips (p. 41 n. 29) follows Beierwaltes in taking an ἀθρόα ἐπιβολή to be a direct intuition of the nature of something, and hence as providing a clear and distinct notion of it. This is not correct: *Ennead* 1.8.1.40 and 5.5.10.8 show that Plotinus means by an ἀθρόα ἐπιβολή what we would expect from the use of the term in Epicurus's *Letter to Herodotus* (Diogenes Laertius 10.35), namely a "general view" of something that in the case of a complex object can fail to represent clearly all of its features. Hence the ἀθρόα ἐπιβολή of something can give rise to a confused perception or idea (as also true in the case of the πρωτὴ ἐπιβολή of the nature of soul at 6.2.4, 21–24). Beierwaltes cites for his view of ἀθρόα ἐπιβολή O. Becker, *Plotin und das Problem der geistigen Aneignung* (Berlin: De Gruyter, 1940); but note that Becker (p. 15) is quite aware of the basic meaning of the term. In the case of *simple* objects of apprehension, such as Ideas (4.4.1, 19–20, cf. 6.3.18, 11–12) or the One (3.8.9, 21), there is of course no implication of inadequacy in the grasp afforded by an ἀθρόα ἐπιβολή. Cf. also McGuire and Strange, p. 266 n. 13.

18. Other sources speak of the process of clarifying our preconceptions as "articulation" (διαρθρώσις) of them: cf. Anon. *In Theaet.* 23.1ff., Epictetus *Diss.* 2.11.13–18, 2.17.5–9 (other passages in Bonhöffer, *Epictet*, cited in 189 n. 11 above), Plutarch, *De comm. not.* 1059bc (reading, with Wyttenbach, διαρθρώσας), and Porphyry, *De Abst.* 1.31.2 and *Ad Marc.* §10. Note that the Porphyry passages make clear that properly articulating conceptions is what leads to knowledge of Ideas. If this is Plotinian, as I assume it is, it would explain the connection between the two sorts of recollection noted by Phillips (see n. 16 above).

must respect the opinions of the ancients, that is, we must control our analysis by reference to the views of the wise. In the passage of *Ennead* 3.7.7 just cited he goes on to say that as it is, i.e., since the ancient philosophers *have* said something about the nature of time, we must not seek to develop our own account of it without first examining the previous views about it in order to see if our account will be in agreement with any one of them (εἴ τινι αὐτῶν ὁ παρ' ἡμῖν λόγος συμφώνως ἕξει; 3.7.7, 15–17). Presumably our account will have to be in agreement with at least one of them, since Plotinus has already indicated that he assumes that at least some of the ancient philosophers will have reached a correct understanding of the nature of time.

There are two ways in which Plotinus's dialectical method, while closely resembling it and surely based on it, differs from Aristotle's. The first is the pride of place that Plotinus is prepared to grant to the opinions of the ancient philosophers over those of the many[19]—hence what may be called Plotinus's scholasticism. Common conceptions play a role in Plotinus's method analogous to that of the views of the many in Aristotle.[20] As we shall see, Plotinus employs common conceptions as a standard to which positions taken in the dialectic are required to conform. But unlike Aristotle, he does not dialectically investigate the content of common conceptions themselves, probably because, as natural conceptions and the objects of recollection, their truth is taken to be guaranteed. But the most striking difference from Aristotle is that Plotinus accords a preeminent status among previous philosophers to those he takes to have been genuinely wise. Aristotle notoriously shows no special reverence for any of his predecessors: he seems arrogant enough to think that he is capable of reaching a deeper level of understanding than any of them had. Plotinus on the other hand appears antecedently committed to the belief that Plato, above all other figures in the history of philosophy, has attained to a godlike degree of understanding. On such a view, our task is to try to understand Plato, not to transcend him.

Plotinus, then, is a committed Platonist, and presents himself as an exponent of Platonist philosophy.[21] How can this apparently anteced-

19. But Aristotle too occasionally favors the views of the philosophers over those of the many: cf. *EE* 1214b34–1215a4.

20. Cf. Todd, "Stoic Common Notions," 61 (cited in n. 11 above). The use of common notions as principles in dialectic may go back to Socrates: cf. Xenophon, *Memorabilia* 5.6.15, where they are apparently referred to as τὰ μάλιστα ὁμολογούμενα, "the things most of all agreed upon."

21. But it should be clear from his gibe at Longinus in *Life of Plotinus* §14 that he does not see himself merely as such. It is wrong to take the famous passage at *Ennead* 5.1.8.10–14 as a claim to be merely an exegete of Plato; Plotinus is only claiming there

ent commitment to Plato's doctrines be seen as anything other than dogmatic and undialectical? Certainly Plotinus never allows his dialectical inquiry to call into question the truth of Plato's views. He cites Plato's texts almost scripturally, the way that until recently some contemporary philosophers used to cite Marx or Wittgenstein.[22] The problem for Plotinus is how to *understand* Plato's doctrines, which are *ex hypothesi* held to be true, for Plotinus concedes that Plato is sometimes unclear and even apparently self-contradictory (cf. 4.8.1, 27–28; 4.4.22, 11–12). But this is because he is trying to express the nature of intelligible reality, which Plotinus thinks is very difficult to grasp and still harder to explain clearly to others in words even if one does understand it.

I think that Plotinus's Platonism can be defended to some extent from a charge of unphilosophical dogmatism if we understand it to be a *hypothesis* that he adopts in order to escape from this impasse. The defense might go something like this. It is our task as philosophers to try as hard as we can to understand the hidden intelligible nature of reality. This is very difficult, especially for us in our present fallen condition. But Plato's doctrines, though obscure, seem to provide a reliable guide for our investigation: they are obviously deep, they have stood the test of time without being refuted, no other philosopher's opinions appear to be better. Therefore, we should assume that they are true: they express, however obscurely, a true understanding of the nature of things. Plotinus may be seen as assuming that Plato was a *sophos*, a wise man; he had achieved or at least come close to the understanding of the nature of the One or the Good that on Plotinus's reading he alludes to in the *Republic* and describes obscurely in the second part of the *Parmenides*. Therefore, since Plato possessed an adequate understanding of the truth, what he says about it must be true, however hard to interpret his statements may be.[23]

that the doctrine of the three hypostases is implicit in Plato (see my review of M. J. Atkinson, *Plotinus's Ennead 5.1: On the Three Principal Hypostases* in *Philosophical Review* 95 [1986]: 101). At *Ennead* 6.2.1, 4–5 and 6.2.3, 1–2 it is said to be a condition upon the inquiry that what we say should agree with Plato (compare Plutarch, *De An. Proc.* 1013b, where the criterion, following Eudorus, is said to be plausibility, τὸ πιθανόν, and agreement with Plato).

22. Cf. David Sedley, "Philosophical Allegiance in the Ancient World," in Miriam Griffin and Jonathan Barnes, eds., *Philosophia Togata* (Oxford: Clarendon, 1989), 102–03. Sedley's article is extremely illuminating on the notion of belonging to an ancient "school" of philosophy. Against the widespread view of Plotinus as a dogmatist, see R. Ferwerda, "L'incertitude dans la philosophie de Plotin," *Mnemosyne* 33 (1980); 119–27.

23. On this "circle of justification" in Plotinus's method, see also Eon, *La notion plotinienne*, 263 (cited in n. 2). Compare Plotinus's attitude toward Plato with the Stoics' reverence for Socrates: according to them, he if anyone had made progress toward

Our task is to try to reach a similar understanding for ourselves. It would of course follow from the fact that we understand a true theory of some subject that we understand that subject. Plato, however, never gives us a developed theory or complete view of any subject, only hints of such a theory, which we must then try to fill in by the dialectical investigations of the views of other philosophers who may have had wise or helpful things to say about the subject, insofar as their statements can be brought into line with what Plato says about it. Doing this may even help us to better understand what Plato himself says. For we do not assume that we can tell at the outset what it is that Plato is saying: we begin by assuming that his doctrines are true, but not that we know what they mean.

For the question of the nature of eternity and time, these other philosophers are Parmenides and Aristotle, respectively, whom Plotinus clearly takes to be authorities on these matters, though not as reputable as Plato, nor to be preferred to him.[24] His investigation of the nature of eternity and time thus amounts to exegesis and commentary on Plato's words about eternity and time in the *Timaeus,* in light of a dialectical investigation of the theories of other philosophers that aims to see how far these can be brought into line with what Plato says in the *Timaeus,* an investigation controlled throughout by appeal to our shared conceptions.

II. THE NATURE OF ETERNITY

The fundamental presupposition of Plotinus's investigation of eternity as well as that of time is Plato's statement at *Timaeus* 37d that time is the moving image (εἰκών) of eternity. Plotinus takes this to imply that eternity and time, whatever they may turn out to be, will be analogues of one another, so that their defining and characterizing properties will stand in relations of analogical correspondence to each other.[25] Further, since Plotinus also assumes, following the *Timaeus* (30c–31b), that the sensible cosmos of becoming as a whole is an image of the intelligible world of being, the world of Ideas which he identifies with the 'animal itself' of the *Timaeus,*[26] it follows that eternity stands

---

wisdom (Diogenes Laertius 7.91); cf. also A. A. Long, "Socrates in Hellenistic Philosophy," *Classical Quarterly* 38 (1988): 150–51.

24. Plotinus criticizes Parmenides and Aristotle in *Ennead* 5.1.8–9 for their disagreements with Plato's view of the nature of the intelligible world.

25. See especially *Ennead* 3.7.11, 45–62, where Plotinus makes the correspondence between the properties of eternity and time explicit. The characteristics of time reflect those of eternity because time is derived from eternity.

26. Cf. for example *Ennead* 6.2.22, 36–38.

in a relation to intelligible being that is similar to the relation that time has to sensible becoming, so that, for example, Being can be understood to exist in some sense *in* eternity, as becoming exists *in* time.

I will not undertake to discuss in detail Plotinus's treatment of eternity. I want, rather, to bring out some features of his main lines of argument, especially as they pertain to his later discussion of time, and to try to clear up a few misunderstandings of them. Richard Sorabji[27] has recently argued, in my view correctly, that this treatise contains the first clear articulation of what was later to become the classical doctrine of eternity as an eternal 'now,' which appears in Boethius (*Consolatio* 5, prose 6) and through him influences the medievals.[28] Sorabji also argues that the classical doctrine has been thought to be incoherent for the wrong reasons (though he has his own doubts about its coherence). I agree with him that the charge of incoherence need not be taken to have been proved. I will indicate briefly why I think this is so in the course of my comments on Plotinus's arguments.

Plotinus considers the nature of eternity in chapters two through six of *Ennead* 3.7, before turning to the nature of time in chapters seven through thirteen. He takes up eternity first because Plato had declared that time is an image of eternity, and a good way to understand the features of an image is first to understand its original.[29] His

27. Sorabji, chaps. 8–9.

28. Boethius is indebted to Plotinus's discussion of eternity particularly for his notion of the nontemporal uses of "now" (νῦν) and "always" (ἀεί). This is not to imply that Boethius has read *Ennead* 3.7; he seems rather to be dependent on some work deriving from it. Plotinus, for instance, would never countenance speaking of the *spatium* of eternal life, as does Boethius (*loc. cit.*). See n. 45 below, on E. Stump and N. Kretzmann's conflation of the views of eternity of Boethius and Plotinus. This is an area where work remains to be done.

29. This follows from his understanding of the paradigm-image relation. Surprisingly, it is implied by Beierwaltes (pp. 214–15, perhaps under the influence of Aquinas, *Summa Theol.* 1a10.1 *resp. init.*), that according to Plotinus one can *only* know an image by first coming to know the corresponding original. But Plotinus in fact denies this (*Ennead* 3.7.1, 20–24), saying that it would be possible also to investigate the nature of the original by first investigating its image, then passing to consideration of the original by a method he calls ἀνάμνησις or recollection. Beierwaltes seems to think that if one were to proceed by the latter method one would not come to *know* the image before understanding the original, since to know it is to know its cause. (See Beierwaltes p. 149 for his comment on *Ennead* 3.7.1, 16–24.) However Platonic this argument may seem, I doubt it is Plotinian, and it is certainly not present in the text: cf. *Ennead* 3.7.1, 21–22, which speaks of contemplating the essence of time, τὸν χρόνον ὅς ἐστι, before contemplating eternity. Bréhier's introduction to the treatise (p. 123) curiously exhibits the opposite mistake of thinking that Plotinus holds that one can only come to know a paradigm through its image. The issue is more adequately discussed by Jonas, pp. 295–96 and 311–12; see also Phillips, p. 46.

goal is to determine precisely what the property or properties of intelligible Being are in virtue of which we say that it is eternal and that it exists in eternity.[30] He sets out to investigate what eternity is according to those thinkers who declare it to be something different from time (3.7.1, 17–18), i.e., those who hold that it is something other than mere everlasting duration. These thinkers are Plato and Parmenides, with perhaps a bow to Aristotle's description of eternity in *On the Heavens* 1.9 (279a23–28; cf. *Ennead* 3.7.3, 19 and 3.7.4, 42–43). In fact, Plotinus's discussion of eternity is more a commentary on Parmenides than on Plato, though Plato himself is of course dependent on Parmenides B8 at *Timaeus* 37e.[31]

Plotinus finds himself at a loss for suitable candidate definitions of eternity to examine via his dialectical method, for eternity is not an object of everyday experience and hence not an ordinary notion about which there could be suitably authoritative common beliefs, and nothing that could count as a definition of eternity had been offered by the ancients. Indeed Plato, at *Timaeus* 37d, seems to have been the first to use the term αἰών in a way that does not denote any stretch of time. Plato however says very little about eternity and does not offer a definition of it. What he does say about eternity in the *Timaeus* can be summarized in the following three points, each of which Plotinus takes as fundamental for his discussion of the nature of eternity: (1) Eternity is a feature of the intelligible world, conceived as the paradigmatic animal itself. From *Tim.* 38c1–2 it appears that Plato is using the word αἰών not in a technical philosophical sense, but in its ordinary meaning in the Greek of his day, to refer to the lifespan of the animal.[32] (2) Eternity "remains in unity" (μένοντος αἰῶνος ἐν ἑνὶ), while time exhibits a regular motion, "proceeding according to number" (κατ' ἀριθμὸν ἰοῦσαν) as its image (*Tim.* 37d6). (3) Eternity admits of no description involving tenses other than the present (*Tim.* 38ab). This last derives from Parmenides' argument for the timeless nature of Being, which both Plato and Plotinus identify with their intelligible world of Ideas. So even though Parmenides does not mention eternity by name, Plotinus quite naturally takes him to be talking about it.

---

30. I agree with Jonas (p. 297 n. 3) that no distinction is intended between αἰώνιος and ἀΐδιος at *Ennead* 3.7.3.2: the latter term is introduced here as a synonym of αἰώνιος because it has a less clumsy abstract form ἀϊδιότης, "eternality."

31. See the table of correspondences between Plotinus's language in *Ennead* 3.7.3–6 and that of Parmenides B8 given by Beierwaltes (p. 178) which however is not complete. Chapter 3 of the treatise in particular concerns the timelessness of Being of Parmenides B8.

32. On this point, cf. Andre-Jean Festugière,"Le sens philosophique du mot AIΩN," *La parola del passato* 11 (1949): 172–89, reprinted in his *Études de philosophie grecque* (Paris: Vrin, 1971).

With no actually proposed definitions of eternity to consider, Plotinus instead begins his discussion in *Ennead* 3.7.2 by raising puzzles about two possible candidate definitions of it that he apparently invents himself.[33] These are suggested by the assumption that time is the image of eternity, Plato's condition (2), with its implication that eternity should therefore stand in a relation to the intelligible cosmos that is analogous to the relation of time to the sensible cosmos, itself an image of the intelligible animal itself. Possible definitions of time therefore ought to be analogous to possible definitions of eternity. Following this principle, Plotinus uses the proposed definitions of time he will consider later, which he takes from Aristotle's *Physics* 4.10, to generate possible definitions of eternity. Thus, eternity might be taken to be identical with intelligible substance itself, i.e., the whole of intelligible reality, as time was thought by some to be identical with the heavenly sphere (*Physics* 218b1), since each contains all the items belonging to their respective realms. Alternatively, eternity might be identified with intelligible rest or stability—αὐτόστασις, the Idea of rest (*Ennead* 3.7.2, 36)—as time was identified by some early thinkers with motion (*Physics* 218b10–11).

Neither of these proposed characterizations of eternity should be immediately ruled out as implausible. Plotinus himself wants to insist that intelligible entities must have their existence in some sense *in* eternity, just as all sensible things exist in time. The latter he takes to be part of the common conception of time, and the former is assumed to follow from it together with the principle that time is the image of eternity. But eternity cannot just be taken to be the whole of which the Ideas are parts, as physical things are parts of the body of the universe. Rather, eternity must be grounded in a property that applies to the Ideas in some other way, for intelligible substance as a whole and each of its parts, i.e., each of the Ideas, must be eternal in precisely the same sense (3.7.2, 10–15 and 17–19). This would not be the case if eternity was merely intelligible substance itself, for then the other Ideas could only be eternal by participation in it, and thus only derivatively.[34] The second candidate definition, that eternity is just the stability or fixity of the Ideas, seems close to what is probably Plato's

33. Contrast Bréhier, p. 125, who assumes that Plotinus is here dealing with actual predecessors' views.

34. Plotinus is careful later to specify precise senses of the terms "eternity" and "eternal" in an attempt to make this condition come out true: the fundamental property is that of eternality (ἀϊδιότης), which is predicated of the intelligible world as a whole (as are beauty and truth, *Ennead* 3.7.4, 7–12), while "eternity" denotes this property taken together with its subject, like Aristotle's examples of "snubness" and "snub" in the *Metaphysics* (*Ennead* 3.7.5.15–18; cf. 3.1–3).

actual line of thought in the *Timaeus* passage where he stresses the contrast between the unchanging nature of the Ideas and the constant flux of sensible becoming.[35] Plotinus, however, refuses to accept such an interpretation of the *Timaeus*: he rightly insists that there must be something more to the eternity of the Ideas than their mere stability if eternity is going to be something different from time (cf. 3.7.2, 32–33), for rest or changelessness just as much as motion will be measured by time.

How does Plotinus think he can distinguish the eternal mode of being of the Ideas from that of merely temporally unchanging essences? We should be clear about what is at stake here. The Ideas, for Plotinus, as for the Plato of the *Sophist* and the *Statesman,* seem intended to ground not only the truth but also the necessity of universal judgments about the natures of things. That is, if "S is P" is such a judgment, then it is supposed to be necessarily true because S and P correspond to Ideas that stand in what the *Sophist* calls a relation of "communion" (κοινωνία) with one another (*Soph.* 257a; cf. 250e) that is not a merely external relation and that cannot be otherwise than it is. The reason it cannot be otherwise is that Ideas are the sort of things that do not admit change. But *why* do they not admit change? Why is it impossible for their natures to be otherwise than they are? This seems a legitimate question, but if Ideas are merely stipulated as what is unchanging (as for instance at *Tim.* 27d), there can be no non-trivial answer to it, and in particular no answer that connects this feature of the Ideas with their nature as the objects of understanding and the causes of phenomena. All that can be said is that this is just how Ideas are. Perhaps Plato himself was content with this,[36] but it seems pre-

---

35. The same proposal is considered in *Ennead* 4.4.15, lines 8–11 and rejected in *Ennead* 4.4.16. For this view of Plato's thought in the *Timaeus*, see G. E. L. Owen, "Plato and Parmenides on the Timeless Present," *The Monist* 50 (1966), reprinted in his *Logic, Science and Dialectic* (cited in n. 3 above); and John Whittaker, "The 'Eternity' of the Platonic Forms," *Phronesis* 13 (1968): 131–44. For criticisms of this view see Leonardo Tarán, "Perpetual Duration and Atemporal Eternity in Parmenides and Plato," *The Monist* 62 (1979): 43–53, and especially Richard Patterson, "On the Eternality of the Platonic Forms," *Archiv für Geschichte der Philosophie* 67 (1985): 27–46. In all essentials I accept Whittaker's view of the passage: the key point is that Plato sees existing in time as coextensive with undergoing change, and in fact considers existing in time to involve undergoing a change, namely becoming older ("becoming older and younger than oneself "; *Tim.* 38a2–5). Hence something will have eternal existence if and only if it is eternally unchanging in all respects. The weakest aspect of this interpretation is that it does not adequately account for Plato's remark that eternity "remains in unity," condition (2) in my text, and it is not surprising that Plotinus places particular stress on this condition in laying out his stronger interpretation of the *Timaeus* passage.

36. Festugière, "Le sens philosophique," 183 (cited in n. 32 above), claims that the answer is provided by the fact that for Plato the Ideas are by definition unchanging

ferable to be able to give a principled reply to the question, and this is what Plotinus's theory of eternity, as we shall see, allows him to do.

With this in mind, let us turn to Plotinus's positive account of eternity in chapters three through six of our treatise. Here Plotinus attempts to derive the defining characteristics of eternity as the proper mode of being of intelligible reality by reflecting upon a number of considerations:[37] (a) the conditions on eternity he finds in Plato's *Timaeus*; (b) Parmenides' arguments in B8 for the timeless nature of Being; (c) his own account of the fundamental logical structure of the intelligible world, based on the μέγιστα γένη of Plato's *Sophist*; (d) conditions drawn from the dialectical investigations of the two candidate definitions of eternity in chapter two; and finally (e) further considerations, adumbrated in chapter four, concerning the relative perfection or completeness of the intelligible world vis-à-vis the sensible, namely, that the intelligible world, as what is Being in the full or perfect sense, must be a perfect whole, and thus in complete possession of all of its parts (which are not parts of extension or duration, but rather consist in the multiplicity of the Ideas themselves).[38] The details of his arguments are somewhat obscure.[39] The characteristics

essences, i.e., they are distinguished from sensibles precisely by being fixed, not in flux. He is perhaps right that this is Plato's answer, but it depends crucially on this particular way of making the Ideas-sensibles distinction, a way that is notoriously fraught with difficulties, and which I do not think that Plotinus would want to endorse. But Plotinus, because his conception of eternity is stronger than Plato's, has available to him the better answer that I present in the text. Cf. also Patterson, "On the Eternality," 36 (cited in n. 35 above), and Aristotle *Met.* 1088b23–24. An interpretation of Plotinus's motives similar to mine is given by Igal, "Introducción general" (pp. 74–75).

37. For a similar argument proceeding by reflection upon what the characteristics of intelligible reality would have to be, see Plotinus's derivation of the μέγιστα γένη of Plato's *Sophist* as the categories of the intelligible world in *Ennead* 6.2.8–9. Especially remarkable is Plotinus's insistence in both texts that the desired characteristics be ἐνορώμενα (3.7.3.6 and 4.3; 6.2.7, 1), that is, features that are "seen" upon reflection to be necessary aspects of the concept of intelligible reality. On this, cf. Andrew Smith, "Potentiality and the Problem of Plurality in the Intelligible World," in H. J. Blumenthal and R. A. Markus, eds., *Neoplatonism and Early Christian Thought: Essays in Honor of A. H. Armstrong* (London: Variorum, 1981), 107.

38. Intelligible reality is completely partless, yet somehow contains a multiplicity: see, e.g., *Ennead* 2.4.4, 11–12: ἀμερὲς μὲν γὰρ παντελῶς πάντη αὐτό, μεριστόν δὲ ὁπωσοῦν. The multiplicity affirmed by Plotinus of the intelligible world is to be identified with the multiplicity of its constituents. Cf. the following note.

39. His first line of argument, leading up to the initial characterization of eternity in §3, draws upon (c) and (d), and appears to be an argument by elimination (cf. also McGuire and Strange, p. 252). Eternity, as a feature of the intelligible world as a whole, must have some connection with the five μέγιστα γένη of the *Sophist* which are the constituents of that world (note that *Ennead* 3.7 immediately follows in the chronological order of Plotinus's writings the treatise on categories, 5.1–3, which contains his most detailed discussion of these "categories of the intelligible"). But the argument of chapter

of eternity that he ends up with are the following (cf. especially 3.7.3, 36–38; 3.7.5, 25–28).[40]

Eternity is:

1. A sort of life (ζωή)—for Plotinus, this means a kind of conscious or intentional activity
2. An activity that is essential to the intelligible realm (cf. ἐν τῷ εἶναι at 3.7.3, 37)
3. Present all together (ὁμοῦ πᾶσα, 3.7.3, 37) as a complete whole[41]
4. Not deficient in any respect, i.e., possessing perfect being (πλή-ρης, 3.7.3, 37, and 3.7.4 *passim*)
5. Without any sort of extension (ἀδιάστατος, 3.7.3, 37; cf. 3.7.3, 15)[42]
6. Not admitting past or future—which follows from (3) and (4)
7. Infinite (ἄπειρος, 3.7.5, 36)

Plotinus takes these characteristics to be connected especially closely with three of the μέγιστα γένη of the intelligible world, namely, *motion* (which he identifies with Aristotelian ἐνέργεια or activity), *rest*, and *sameness*. They are not logically independent of one another; in particular, (7) is supposed (cf. 3.7.5, 25–28) to be a consequence of (3)–(6). Hence, not all of (1)–(7) can belong to the *definition* of eternity. Plotinus connects (5) with Plato's description of eternity as "remaining in unity."

The intelligible world is essentially alive for Plotinus because it is an infinite active intellect or divine mind (νοῦς) whose acts of thought are identical with the Ideas, and since it is a pure act, they are in turn

---

2 has established that eternity is not the οὐσία of the intelligible world, but rather a state of this οὐσία. (It is ultimately defined as the state of intelligible substance considered as being in a certain state or κατάστασις, namely ἀϊδιότης; 3.7.5, 14–18.) Hence it can only involve motion, rest, sameness, and difference (κίνησις, στάσις, ταυτότης, and ἑτερότης). Difference is then excluded at 3.7.3, 11–12. The grounds for this are probably that the intelligible world is a single thing whose internal differences are due solely to its multiplicity of powers or δυνάμεις (3.7.3, 6–7), and this is not relevant to its eternality (cf. also 4.4.15, 7–9, where ταυτότης is associated with eternity and ἑτερότης with time). The eternity of the intelligible world can therefore only reside in the sameness (identified with its lack of extension or διάστασις) and stability (στάσις) of its life (ζωή, which is identified with κίνησις).

40. See also Plotinus's description of εὐδαιμονία as eternal life in 1.5.7.20–31, and Sorabji's discussion (p. 113).

41. An allusion to Parmenides B8.5: ὁμοῦ πᾶν.

42. *Ennead* 1.5.7, 23 adds the Parmenidean phrase "neither more nor less" (cf. Parmenides B8.44–45), glossing this as the claim that it is measured by no interval (μῆκος). This is connected with the complete partlessness of intelligible reality, which is nevertheless somehow divisible (cf. n. 38 above).

the same as it, on the Aristotelian principle that actual intellect is the same as its objects. Given this conception of the nature of the intelligible, it is not unreasonable for Plotinus to take its proper mode of being to be a kind of life, which he identifies with the genus motion (κίνησις) of Plato's *Sophist*. (That this is to be identified with the life of the intelligible world Plotinus takes to be the indicated by *Sophist* 248e6–249a2.) Following Aristotle (cf. *Met.* 12.7.1072b26–27), Plotinus identifies this life with the activity or ἐνέργεια of νοῦς. The crucial feature of this life that distinguishes it as eternal rather than merely changeless is that it is wholly present to itself, and is therefore without any sort of duration or extension.[43] What this means is that there are in no sense distinct moments, phases, or parts of this life (cf. 3.7.3, 19–20). If there were, it would not all be present at once: some of it would be in one part of itself and some in another, and hence its being at any point of itself would be imperfect, lacking some "part" of itself. This would imply a need to move toward perfection, and thus change and time (3.7.4, 15–28). All of it is simultaneously present, so to speak, at the unique single moment of eternity.[44]

This is notoriously an extremely difficult concept to grasp. It has often been claimed to be incoherent. It is said, for instance, that it is impossible to conceive of any sort of life, even a timelessly eternal one, apart from duration[45] or change.[46] Plotinus would reply that this does

---

43. No such conception need be attributed either to Parmenides or to Plato; cf. Whittaker, "Eternity" (cited in n. 35 above), and Sorabji, pp. 98–112. It had however been found in them before Plotinus: cf. e.g., Plutarch *De E* §20 *init.* and Whittaker, "Ammonius on the Delphic E," *Classical Quarterly* n.s. 19 (1969): 185–92.

44. Cf. also *Ennead* 4.4.1.15: ἀλλ' ἔστιν ἕκαστον πάρον. Jonathan Barnes offers a similar interpretation of Parmenides' notion of the timeless now, based on a reading of B8.19–20 which resembles Plotinus's: see his *The Presocratic Philosophers*, 2nd ed. (London: Routledge and Kegan Paul, 1982), 193–94; cf. *Ennead* 3.7.3.27–34. Barnes insists, however, that Parmenides' νῦν must be taken as a temporal moment, though one stripped of any connection with past and future. Plotinus would not agree: see below on his non-temporal sense of "now." (Note that Barnes thinks that such a conception of the eternal now is internally coherent.) Plotinus's forerunner Numenius, like Barnes's Parmenides, conceives of eternity as an eternal temporal present (fr. 5.6–9, Des Places). Plotinus clearly means to reject Numenius's view: cf. Dominic J. O'Meara, "Being in Numenius and Plotinus: Some Points of Comparison," *Phronesis* 21 (1976): 128 n. 5.

45. Cf. Aquinas *Summa Theol.* 1a10.1 *resp.* 2. Cf. also William Kneale, "Time and Eternity in Theology," *Proceedings of the Aristotelian Society* n.s. vol. 61 (1960–61): 87–108; Graeser, p. 142 n. 3; and Eleanor Stump and Norman Kretzmann, "Eternity," *Journal of Philosophy* 78 (1981): 429–58. For similar reasons, Pierre Aubenque, "Plotin philosophe de la temporalité," *Diotima* 4 (1976): 83, denies that Plotinus conceives of eternity as timeless at all, but rather as sempiternal or everlasting, a view rightly rejected by Graeser (loc. cit.). Stump and Kretzmann interpret the classical notion of eternal life as a *totum simul* found in Boethius, which they take to be the same as Plotinus's conception, as what they call a "timeless duration," which though a duration contains no order or succession of events, and every portion of which is present to every other.

not follow for the life of νοῦς or intellect, which is a pure activity or ἐνέργεια. He thinks that such an activity, since it already contains within itself its goal or τέλος, can be instantaneous and need not therefore in and of itself be in time.[47] He seems to be right at least in that nothing in Aristotle's conception of activity *requires* that activities involve duration. At *Ennead* 6.1.16, 16ff. he gives as an example the case of an instantaneous act of seeing (an Aristotelian example, cf. *Met.* 1048b23 and *NE* 1174a14–15), and in *Ennead* 1.5 he argues that the happiness of pure contemplation, as an activity, cannot increase over time, because, not being essentially something extended, it is not the sort of thing that can be measured by time—in fact, it is the same as eternal life (1.5.7, 26–30).

One might also be disturbed by Plotinus's repeated use of temporal language in describing eternity. He is quite prepared to speak of eternity as existing "now" (νῦν; cf. Parmenides B8.5), and he quotes with approval Aristotle's folk-etymological derivation of αἰών, "eternity",

---

Whether or not this represents Boethius's conception, it is certainly not Plotinus's, whose claim that eternity is completely ἀδιάστατος (unextended) is clearly intended to exclude any sort of duration. Stump and Kretzmann note Plotinus's use of the term ἀδιάστατος (p. 431 n. 6), but remark that since "in the rest of *Enneads* III.7 . . . Plotinus goes on to derive duration from his definition [of eternity]," that it is not to be taken seriously. But this claim cannot be supported from Plotinus's text, nor do they attempt to do so. (On this point cf. Sorabji, p. 113.) In addition, their interpretation seems to miss a key step in Plotinus's argument: the unextendedness of eternal life is supposed to follow directly from the complete co-presence of that life to itself, which is just the denial of real distinction of parts within it, which any sort of duration, if this is to be more than an empty word, must possess. (For further elucidation of the details of their view, see Paul Fitzgerald, "Stump and Kretzmann on Time and Eternity," *Journal of Philosophy* 82 (1985): 296–73, and their "Reply to Fitzgerald," *Journal of Philosophy* 84 (1987): pp. 214–20.) Stump and Kretzmann are unwilling to grant that a notion of nondurational eternal life is coherent, because they think that the concept of life necessarily involves that of duration (p. 446). But this seems just to be a confusion resulting from reimporting temporal concepts into the notion of eternal life, as if the eternal now to be part of a life must have a future. Plotinus, as we have seen, identifies eternal life with Aristotelian ἐνέργεια, which does not require anything beyond itself. And the only sort of multiplicity Plotinus allows in the intelligible world is a multiplicity of δυνάμεις or powers (identified with the Ideas; cf. *Ennead* 3.7.3, 7), which need involve no real distinctions.

46. This accusation is made by A. H. Armstrong, "Eternity, Life and Movement in Plotinus's Accounts of Noῦς," in *Le néoplatonisme: Colloques internationaux du Centre National de la Recherche Scientifique (Royaumont, 9–13 juin 1969)* (Paris: CRNS, 1971), 69–74 (cf. Sorabji, p. 114); see also H. J. Blumenthal "*Nous* and Soul in Plotinus: Some Problems of Demarcation," in *Plotino e il Neoplatonismo in Oriente e in Occidente*, Accademia Nazionale dei Lincei, Problemi attuali di scienza e di cultura, no. 198 (Rome: Accademie Nazionale dei Lincei, 1974), 203–19. On the problem posed by Plotinus's occasional talk of potency in the intelligible world, see Smith, "Potentiality" (cited in n. 37 above), and *Ennead* 6.8.1, 11–13, where Plotinus explicitly recognizes the difficulty.

47. Cf. *Ennead* 6.1.16, 14–15: ἡ λεγομένη ἐνέργεια οὐ δεῖται χρόνου, and McGuire and Strange, pp. 252–53.

from ἀεί ὄν, "always existing" (*Ennead* 3.7.4, 42; cf. Aristotle, *On the Heavens* 279a27; and Porphyry *Sententiae* §44, 58, 7–9 Lamberz). But "now" and "always," it will be claimed, contain an implicit reference to other times beside the present: "now" indicates the present in contrast with other times, and "always" means "at all times, not only now." Plotinus's reply is that he is using these terms here in extended senses—extended by analogy—and that hence they should not be understood as carrying with them their normal logical baggage. "Now," for example, is being used in a way that explicitly contrasts with its ordinary use to indicate the present that joins the past to the future. Plotinus's notion of the eternal now has been carefully stripped of its association with past and future times, and is merely used to signify that the whole of an eternal being's life is present to it at once, analogously to the way that a bit of one's life is present to one in the temporally present moment. (Plotinus clearly believes that Parmenides B8.5 refers to an eternal, not a temporal now.[48]) At *Ennead* 3.7.6, 21–36), Plotinus himself makes the point that "always" is used of eternity in an extended sense (οὐ κυρίως).[49] This use can be misleading, he says, if it is not understood to mean, not that what is eternal goes on existing, but that it cannot not exist. Certainly he could have wished that Plato had been more cautious in the way he had used ἀεί of his eternal Ideas at *Timaeus* 38a3 without any sign of qualification.

If there is no duration or distinction within the life of eternity, then it is not logically possible for an eternal entity to undergo change or be otherwise than it is (cf. 3.7.5, 1–12). That would require another moment of its existence besides the present one in which it could be otherwise, and there are no such moments available. His conception of eternity thus gives Plotinus a clear way of explicating the difficult notion of the necessary being of the Ideas, without merely stipulating that they be unchanging essences. This view of eternal life is certainly paradoxical, but it has not been shown that it is incoherent or untenable. Plotinus's theory of eternity is an excellent and on its own terms largely successful example of his approach to the deeper metaphysical problems of Platonism.

---

48. Cf. above, n. 44, on Barnes's interpretation of Parmenides B8.5.

49. For the two senses of ἀεί, see also *Ennead* 3.7.2, 28–29 and 5.8.12, 17 (where the "always" of time is said to be an image of the "always" of eternity), and Graeser's article.

III. THE DIALECTICAL INVESTIGATION OF TIME

Plotinus begins his dialectical investigation of time (3.7.7, 17 ff.) with a division of previous accounts of it into those that had treated it as a kind of motion or change (κίνησις); those that had taken it to be a subject of motion, i.e., the heavenly sphere; and those that had defined it as something that belongs to motion, i.e., a property or attribute of motion. This is an attempt to rationalize Aristotle's discussion of previous accounts of time at *Physics* 4.10.218a30–b20. According to this scheme, all previous accounts of time were agreed that it was somehow connected with motion—that is, *physical* motion, change in bodies[50]—and such universal agreement ought on Plotinus's methodological principles to reflect a fact about the nature of time. Indeed, he remarks that our conception of time reveals it to be something that, like motion, is never the same and always in flux (3.7.7, 20–22). He follows Aristotle (*Physics* 4.10.218a30–b20) in rejecting that time could itself be any sort of physical motion or a subject of motion. Two of the arguments he gives for this are apparently original. The first is that time cannot itself be a motion because it is that in which motion occurs,[51] and must therefore be different from motion. That a container is distinct from what it contains is treated by Plotinus as a common conception, and indeed it appears as an assumption in the second, dialectical part of Plato's *Parmenides* (138b2–3). A later passage of our treatise shows that Plotinus takes the other premise of this argument, that all physical motion is in time, to be a part of our common conception of time (3.7.8, 45–47; cf. 3.7.10, 6).[52] The second argument is that motion can stop or cease but time cannot (3.7.8, 6–8). Presumably this also involves a reference to common conceptions or intuitions about time.

Since time can be neither motion nor what is in motion, we are left with the remaining accounts which treat it as something belonging to physical motion. Plotinus considers in detail the Stoic and Peripatetic versions, which further agree in defining time in terms of the quantitative aspect of physical motion. (He dismisses the Epicurean definition of time as the παρακολούθημα or "accompaniment" of motion

50. Plutarch attributes to Pythagoras the view that time is the World Soul, the cause of celestial motion (*Platonic Questions* 1007b; this is the sense, whatever the text). Plotinus knows nothing of this attribution. "Aetius" and Simplicius think the identification of time with the sphere of the outer heaven mentioned by Aristotle is Pythagorean: cf. Ross's remarks on *Physics* 4.10.218b1.

51. On being 'in time' as occupying time or being subject to measurement by it, cf. *Physics* 4.12.221a13–18 and a26–b23.

52. Aristotle endorses this view at *Physics* 4.14.222b30–31.

at 3.7.10, 1–8 as being obviously inconsistent with our conception of time as the container of motion.) The Stoics had defined time as the extension (διάστημα) of motion, or of the motion of the universe.[53] This means time is the proper extension of motion, itself thought of as a particular kind of continuous quantity, i.e., as just so much motion (cf. τὸ πολὺ τῆς κινήσεως, at 3.7.8, 37).[54] Here the Stoics may have been following the lead of Speusippus, who had defined time as the quantity that is proper to motion (τὸ ἐν κινήσει ποσόν, Plutarch *Platonic Questions* 1007 B [= Speusippus, fr. 53 Lang]). Plotinus's refutation of the Stoic definition takes the form of a trilemma. If they mean to identify time with the motion itself, considered as an extended quantity, this collapses back into the view just refuted, that time is a motion. If they mean that time is an extension that inheres in motion, the way magnitude inheres in physical body, then their definition will be inconsistent with our conception of time as that in which motion occurs: time on this view would be *in* the motion rather than the other way round. Only if they mean that time is a sort of extension that lies outside the motion and contains it, in the way that spatial extension contains bodies, will this fit the conception of time. But if so, they have not yet made clear the nature of this sort of extension.

If the view that time is the extension of motion means anything other than that it is the extended motion itself under some description, it is difficult to distinguish it from the Peripatetic conception of time as the measure or number of motion derived from Aristotle's *Physics*. Plotinus's elaborate discussion of this conception in chapter nine of the treatise amounts to a dialectical criticism of Aristotle's discussion of time in *Physics* 4.11–14. It is clear, however, that Plotinus is working here with material and arguments drawn from the previous Peripatetic commentary tradition of the *Physics*. This can be seen by comparing his discussion with the relevant passages of Simplicius's *Physics* commentary. As we will see, Plotinus is aware of the views of Alexander of Aphrodisias, and this suggests he may have been using here Alexander's lost commentary on the *Physics*, which is probably Simplicius's main or only source for the pre-Alexandrian tradition as well.[55]

---

53. Chrysippus's reported definition of time as τὸ παρακολουθοῦν διάστημα τῇ τοῦ κόσμου κινήσει (*Stoicorum Veterum Fragmenta* 2.509) does not associate him with the Epicurean view, as Paul Henry and H.-R. Schwyzer suggest in their apparatus at *Ennead* 3.7.7.26. The term παρακολουθοῦν is apparently intended to mark the ontological dependent status of time as a λεκτόν: it is something that supervenes upon bodily motion.

54. Hence A. H. Armstrong in the Loeb translation of the *Enneads* is not right to translate διάστημα as if it referred to the distance covered by the motion.

55. Certainly Plotinus knew and often worked from Alexander's commentaries,

Rather than examining Plotinus's arguments against the Peripatetic conception one by one, it will be convenient instead to consider how he responds to the most obvious difficulties with Aristotle's account of time. These difficulties were clearly seen by the earlier Peripatetic commentators and will have been known to Plotinus through Alexander's commentary or other sources.

Aristotle defines time as the number (or measure[56]) of motion according to the successive order or 'before and after' that it contains (*Physics* 219b1–2). We perceive this before and after through our awareness of a succession of moments or 'nows' in the course of the motion. Time is supposed to be somehow the measure of the motion thought of as an extended quantity bounded by the first and last of these nows, as the underlying subject of the motion takes time in getting from one to the other. Aristotle seems aware that this definition is obscure, and in attempting to clarify it in *Physics* 4.11–14, he gets himself into a number of well-known difficulties from which it is unclear how he is to be extricated. The four most important difficulties were noted by the Peripatetic commentators before Plotinus:

1. What motions or type of motion is it of which time is supposed to be the measure? This puzzle was raised already by Aristotle's pupil Eudemus (Simplicius, *In Phys.* 717.6–14). If Aristotle intends time to be the measure of motion in general, then this will include not only regular or uniform (ὁμαλής) motion[57] but irregular and disorderly motion as well. But by definition irregular motion presents no repeatable units by which it can be measured (cf. *Ennead* 3.7.9, 5–6), hence it can only be measured by comparing it with simultaneous regular motion. Time in the strict sense will therefore be the

---

among others, as Porphyry informs us in *Life* 14.10–14. Moreover, *Ennead* 3.7.10.12–13 seems to contain a reference to Alexander as "he who says [time] is the measure of the motion of the All" (see n. 58 below on Alexander's interpretation). It is more likely that Plotinus is here using Alexander's commentary on the *Physics* than his brief treatise *On Time*, which is extant in Arabic and Latin versions. An English translation of this work by F. M. Zimmermann is presented and discussed by R. W. Sharples, "Alexander of Aphrodisias *On Time*," *Phronesis* 27 (1982): 58–81. On the distinction between this work and Alexander's commentary on the *Physics*, see pp. 67–68.

56. Strato of Lampsacus (*apud* Simplicius, *In Phys.* 789.2–9; cf. Simplicius *In Cat.* 346.14ff. and 351.4–8 [I owe the latter references to R. W. Sharples]) objected that since time is a continuous quantity and recognized as such by Aristotle, that he should have stuck to calling it a measure instead of a number, which is a sort of discrete quantity. Plotinus agrees with this criticism: see *Ennead* 3.7.9, 12 and 17–31. Aristotle perhaps calls time a number because he has in mind the account of time in Plato's *Timaeus*, where time is a motion that proceeds according to number.

57. Cf. *Ennead* 3.7.9, 31–34, where, following Aristotle (*Physics* 8.6.260a17–19), Plotinus identifies the primary uniform motion with that of the outer heavenly sphere, but ignores the problem of how we can even know that any motion is regular or uniform, i.e., proceeding at a constant rate, without some *independent* measure of time. Aristotle is aware of this difficulty: cf. Edward Hussey, *Aristotle's Physics Books III and IV* (Oxford: Clarendon, 1983), 174.

measure of *regular* motion, since the measure of this sort of motion will be what measures the other sort of motion as well. Regular motions can however be faster or slower than one another, and hence will involve different measures of time. Which of these measures will be time in the primary or strict sense, according to the Aristotelian definition? Here the commentators are obviously thinking of the different temporal measures provided by the cycles of the various heavenly bodies, the day, month, year, and so forth, the different "measures of time" of *Timaeus* 39c–d. Aristotle could answer that it does not matter which of these one picks as the basic unit of measurement for time: since they stand to one another in fixed and definite ratios, any of them could in principle serve as the fundamental unit. Alexander quite plausibly held, however, that the primary unit of measure of time was given by the heavenly motion with the shortest natural unit, i.e., the swiftest motion. He was therefore led to identify time with sidereal time, the number of the motion of the outer sphere of the fixed stars.[58] Plotinus remarks that this seems the best solution to the problem (3.7.9, 32–35).[59]

2. What sort of number or measure is it that Aristotle has in mind as constituting time? In *Physics* 4.11–12, Aristotle says repeatedly that it is the number that is counted or measured, and not that which we use to count (*Physics* 219b5–9, 220b8–9). This distinction is taken by the commentators to be the same as the distinction between arithmetical or "monadic" number, composed of abstract units (*Met.* 1083b17; cf. Plato *Philebus* 56d–e) and concrete number, i.e., a number of objects of a given type, in this case units of motion or of time.[60] Aristotle illustrates this distinction in *Physics* 4.14 with the example of the numbers seven and ten as opposed to seven or ten dogs or horses (223b4–6, 224b12–15). The problem with Aristotle's claim here is that if time is the concrete or *numbered* number of motion, there will then necessarily be a different time (since there is a different number) for each distinct motion, even those which occur simultaneously. For Aristotle is committed to the view that different motions are really distinct from each other just in virtue of having distinct goals or τέλη. It appears that Alexander's predecessor Aspasius even wanted to change the text at *Physics* 219b6–7 in order to make Aristotle say there that time is *numbering* or abstract number, not numbered number (cf. Simplicius, *In Phys.* 714, 31–715, 13), and Alexander seems to have followed him in this.[61] As we shall see, Plotinus exploits this difficulty for his own purposes.

58. Cf. Alexander, *On Time*, chap. 10 (Sharples, "Alexander," 64; cited in n. 55 above), but there is no reason why he could not have said this in the *Physics* commentary as well. As Sharples notes (p. 69), Alexander bases this interpretation on *Physics* 4.14.223b18–20. The same view is proposed by Fred D. Miller, Jr., "Aristotle on the Reality of Time," *Archiv für Geschichte der Philosophie* 56 (1974): 136.

59. Though it is the solar, not the sidereal day that is commonly used as the basic unit of time measurement, probably because it is the one that most obviously suggests itself to our senses. (Cf. *Tim.* 46e–47a.)

60. So also Hussey, *Aristotle's Physics*, 151 and 176ff. (cited in n. 57 above). The latter usage is quite natural in ancient Greek, and we too can speak of a "number" of persons. For this same distinction in Plotinus, cf. *Ennead* 6.1.3, 25–27 and 6.6.16, 2. It is perhaps this distinction that Strato had in mind in insisting against Theophrastus that time is a measure that is essential to motion, not accidental to it (Simplicius *In Cat.* 346.14ff.).

61. Cf. Sharples, "Alexander," 79 n. 45 (cited in n. 55 above).

3. It is hard to see how Aristotle can explain how one and the same time can be simultaneously present everywhere (cf. *Physics* 219b10, 220b5–6), which Plotinus takes to be part of the common conception of time, unless he is willing to make time numbering number.[62] Aristotle seeks to account for this by arguing for the sameness of simultaneous nows at *Physics* 4.14.223b1–12, and returns to the issue in an appendix to this chapter at 224a2–17. What he seems to want to say there is that simultaneous motions share the same time because they share the same now (219b10–12)—not however *numerically* the same now, since on his official account particular nows have to be localized to particular motions, but the same now in being or in species.[63] This does not seem to suffice for what he wants, since the common conception is that the present time is numerically the same everywhere (as Aristotle appears to concede at 220b5–6), and time is on his definition a concrete number of nows. Hence he is forced to say that different simultaneous motions share the same now in the same way that seven horses and seven dogs share the same number, but this is to make time abstract or numbering number (cf. 220b8–9), and he thus contradicts his earlier insistence that time is a concrete number of nows.[64] This provides the motive for Aspasius's "emendation" at 219b6–7.

4. What is the nature of the relation between time and the soul that perceives it? Alexander held that all the above difficulties could be resolved if we understand the time that is marked off by nows to be numbering number, as suggested by *Physics* 220b8–9 (cf. Simplicius, *In Phys.* 729, 9–12), and consequently followed Aspasius's alteration of the text of 219b6–7. In accordance with his view of abstraction,[65] Alexander held that time in this sense, as abstract or numbering number, exists in thought, i.e., in the soul that perceives time, while the before and after in motion, which is what time numbers or measures, exists outside the soul in the movement of the heavenly sphere. Thought measures time by marking off the periods of the regularly repeating motion of this sphere, e.g., by successive sunrises or sunsets. This line of interpretation is clearly tailored to fit what is notoriously the most difficult and recalcitrant passage in Aristotle's discussion of time, namely *Physics* 4.14.223a21–29, which makes the claim that time cannot exist without soul to number it.[66] Plotinus has what seems the obvious objection to this: if time is the measure of the ordered succession in physical motion and this exists outside the soul, why does soul actually have to measure it before time can

62. In light of the theory of relativity, this might be seen to be a virtue of Aristotle's account, but the fact remains that he wants to defend the thesis that one and the same time is simultaneously present everywhere, because this is what everyone believed.

63. Sarah Waterlow [Broadie], "Aristotle's Now," *Philosophical Quarterly* 34 (1982): 111, tries to defend Aristotle on this point by defining what she calls a 'when' as "a point of temporal coincidence" between items or nows in the successions of different simultaneous motions. 'Whens' would thus be equivalence classes of nows. But I fail to see that Aristotle's official theory leaves him with any noncircular way of defining the notion of temporal coincidence.

64. Cf. Hussey, *Aristotle's Physics*, p. 160, ad 220b5.

65. See A. C. Lloyd, *Form and Universal in Aristotle* (Liverpool: Francis Cairns, 1981), 55ff.

66. On Aristotle's inconsistencies on this point, see G. E. L. Owen, "Aristotle on Time," in Peter Machamer and Robert Turnbull, eds., *Motion and Time, Space and Matter* (Columbus: Ohio State University Press, 1976), 23 (= Owen, *Logic, Science and Dialectic*, 313, cited in n. 3 above).

exist? That, Plotinus says, is like claiming that a physical magnitude cannot be the size it is unless someone happens to measure it (*Ennead* 3.7.9, 68–75 and 80–82). Plotinus suggests that this objection will stand regardless of whether time is taken to be numbering number or numbered number, and hence presents it as a dialectical counter against Aspasius's proposal that time is to be identified with numbering number. Even if Alexander can meet this objection, Plotinus thinks he has still established dialectically that time must be something ideal or in the soul, since the only remaining way to save Aristotle's theory involves conceding that time depends upon soul for its existence. Alexander's view takes care of the problem about the unity of a simultaneous time by defining simultaneous times as those that are *perceived* to co-occur: their nows are one and the same in the soul of the perceiver. On Alexander's interpretation, then, time becomes something ideal because it is a matter of the *perception* of the before and after in physical motion.[67] In one passage Aristotle himself seems to concede that time is ideal in an even stronger sense. He notes that we do not need to perceive any physical motion at all in order to be aware of the passage of time: all that is required is that we be aware of a movement in our thought (219a4–8). Hence the existence of time need not be dependent on the existence of *physical* motion at all.

It is clear that Plotinus is aware of all these difficulties with Aristotle's account, and he uses them to raise puzzles of his own. However, his interest is not so much in refuting the theory as in understanding where and how it fails, so that he can improve upon it and avoid its pitfalls. He had already raised the difficulty about how to account for simultaneous motions in his discussion of the Stoic view of time (3.7.8, 29–30). In examining the Peripatetic view he contents himself with the remark that if time is something existing in motion, it will not be everywhere, but only in the motion it is in (3.7.9, 46–48; cf. our discussion of difficulty [2] above). He focusses instead on the related problem of whether time is numbered number or numbering number. He agrees with Alexander and Aspasius that it must be taken to be numbering number, but thinks that this too leads to problems. For one thing, he claims, we need to specify *how* this number measures motion (3.7.9, 45–46). If the Peripatetics claim that this takes place in virtue of the soul using it to measure motion, Plotinus will agree, but will protest that this does nothing to help *define* time (3.7.9, 83–84). For why should the definition of time include any reference to *physical* motion at all if there is psychic motion going on in the soul?[68] We have seen that Aristotle sometimes seems to concede that there

---

67. *Physics* 4.11.219a33–35 perhaps shows that this is not as far from Aristotle's thought as Sharples thinks it is (Sharples, "Alexander," 69; cited in n. 55). Cf. Gloy, pp. 303–04: "Aristoteles Theorie ist nicht verständlich ohne die Unterscheidung eines an sich seienden Substrats der Zeit, das sich an der Bewegung findet, und einer Explikation und Definition der Zeit, die auf das Konto der zählenden Seele geht."

68. Plotinus seems to have taken this argument from Galen: cf. n. 82 below.

can be time without physical motion. Moreover, numbering number does not itself exhibit any temporal order, so where does the temporality of the order of time come from? Why should it be thought that the fact that it is *number* that is used to measure motion by itself gives rise to time (3.7.9, 12–17 and 53–55)? Here Plotinus sets a dilemma. Either the order of succession that is contained in motion must *already* be a temporal order before it is measured or counted, and Aristotle's definition of time turns out to be circular (cf. 3.7.9, 57–62), or the fact that number numbering motion is time is due to its being soul that does the measuring. But how can this be, Plotinus asks, unless soul is somehow the cause of time (3.7.9, 79–80)?[69]

Plotinus's dialectical investigation has now cleared the way for his own full-blown idealist theory of the nature of time. All earlier physicalist views of the nature of time have now been refuted, along with physicalist interpretations of Aristotle's theory of time; as we will see, Plotinus thinks that the purified version of Aristotle's theory that his arguments leave standing is compatible with the truth about the nature of time.[70] He thinks his arguments have freed time from any essential links to the material world, while leaving it firmly attached to the soul; they have even suggested that the soul must be considered the cause of time. It remains for him to sketch in the remaining chapters of the treatise (3.7.11–13) an account of how soul generates time, and to show how this account accords both with common conceptions and with Plato's texts.

IV. THE POSITIVE ACCOUNT OF TIME

Plotinus's account of how the soul generates time is presented in *Ennead* 3.7.11. It is first introduced in the form of a rather odd and halfhearted myth, almost a parody of Platonic myths. The mythical trappings are apparently supposed to indicate that the account is not to be taken literally, for it is presented as an account of how soul first brought time into being, yet Plotinus certainly does not think that time ever literally had a beginning. What Plotinus is trying to express in this passage is rather the causal relation he sees as holding between the soul and time, the fact that soul generates time, and his saying that the soul existed "before" time is a clear if metaphorical way of

69. This argument only shows that soul is a necessary condition for the existence of time. However, Plotinus takes the Peripatetics to have already conceded that time is independent of physical motion.

70. See below, p. 51, on Plotinus's ultimate assessment of Aristotle's view at *Ennead* 3.7.13, 9–18.

48   STEVEN K. STRANGE

putting the point that the soul, as the cause of the being of time, is ontologically prior to it.

According to Plotinus's myth, in the beginning time did not exist, except as an Idea in the intelligible world.[71] But there also existed in the intelligible world what Plotinus calls an "officious nature" (φύσις πολυπράγμων; 3.7.11, 15)[72] which wanted to be able to rule itself. This power set itself in motion;[73] time came into being along with its motion, and so "we" made time (3.7.11, 14–18). In the succeeding lines, Plotinus immediately goes on to provide an interpretation of his own myth. The soul in the intelligible world contains "a certain unquiet power" (τις δύναμις οὐκ ἥσυχος; 3.7.11, 21), because of which it seeks to create something on its own, something more than what it possesses "already" in virtue of being a member of the intelligible world. This "unquiet power" of the soul is apparently its faculty of ὄρεξις or desire, as comparison with Ennead 4.7.13 (beginning) and 4.3.7.1–8 seems to indicate (cf. also Ennead 6.8.2, 30–33), and the association of the "fall" of the soul from the intelligible realm with its desire to rule itself recalls the account of the fall of the soul in Ennead 5.1.1, 1–22.[74] However, it is impossible that the soul can really come to possess anything of its own outside the intelligible world since that world already contains the totality of being. Hence to satisfy its desire, the soul is forced to make for itself a world of appearance of its own, in the only way it can, in the image of the world it already knows, the world of Ideas. The world it makes for itself is the sensible world. Now, according to Plotinus, the essential feature of the soul that serves to distinguish it from intellect or νοῦς is that whereas intellect is able to think many, indeed all, of its thoughts at once, soul must think discursively, one thought at a time (cf. 5.1.7, 42–43; 5.3.17, 23–24). Hence the fallen soul, which has separated itself from νοῦς, cannot think the entirety of true being all at once (cf. 3.7.11, 20–23, inter-

71. Cf. Ennead 5.3.6, 14–16 on the ἡουχία or quietude of unfallen soul as it exists in intellect.
72. This translation of φύσις πολυπράγμων is taken from Clark, p. 350.
73. On the syntax of line 14, cf. Manchester, p. 117 n. 41, and McGuire and Strange, n. 102.
74. Cf. especially the reference to newly fallen souls delighting in their new-found autonomy (τὸ αὐτεξούσιον) at Ennead 5.1.1, 5, as well as the other parallel passages on the fall of the soul collected by Jonas, pp. 315–17. The soul's "unquiet power" of ὄρεξις seems to be identical with the φύσις πολυπράγμων of line 15; cf. Manchester, p. 120. The reference of the feminine pronoun at line 27 is the soul itself, the possessor of this power, in its role as proximate Demiurge of the sensible world: contrast Manchester, p. 116 n. 37. Aristotle sometimes says that the most general classification of faculties of soul is into νοῦς and ὄρεξις (e.g., On the Soul 3.10. init.); this is probably relevant to Plotinus's claim that the "fall" of the soul from the realm of νοῦς is due to the manifestation of its ὄρεξις.

preting *Timaeus* 37d3–4), but must think of it part by part, and must think images of being, not being itself. Hence the soul's conscious activity is not all at once as is that of νοῦς, but is extended and successive (cf. 3.7.11, 35–43): it is rather what Plotinus calls "discursion" (διέξοδος).[75] Therefore the stages of the soul's life are constantly different and successive, as one of its thoughts leads to another, and this defines and generates temporal succession as a construction out of the process of discursive mental activity. Moreover, the inner conscious activity of the soul is also what generates the physical universe itself: this is why the universe and all its motions occur in succession and within time (3.7.11, 27–36; cf. 3.7.12, 24–25).[76] Time is therefore constituted by the life of the soul (a *non-physical* sort of motion), which is itself an image of the eternal life of intellect: the analogical correspondence of their features is argued in detail in 3.7.11, 45–62. Time can thus be defined as "the life [ζωή] of the soul in progressive movement from one stage of life [βίος] to another" (3.7.11, 43–45). On this view the dated linear succession of events derives from the psychological succession of thoughts: the 'now' of time is the present moment of consciousness.

Plotinus says that "we" made time (3.11.18): presumably "we" are here identified, as is common in the *Enneads*, with the individual rational soul. This seems inconsistent with the doctrine of *Ennead* 4.4.15–17, according to which it is the World Soul, not our souls, which generates time.[77] But the closing passage of our treatise (3.7.13,

75. Cf. *Ennead* 3.7.13, 43 with, e.g., 4.3.12, 28. In the earlier treatise, 4.3–4, Plotinus describes the conscious life of undescended soul as not involving discursive thought: he is driven to do so by his eschatology and his conception of the eternal bliss of the divine cosmic souls. Undescended soul nevertheless differs from intellect in retaining the *potential* for thinking discursively (4.4.1). The distinction of soul and intellect as what thinks discursively or step by step as opposed to what thinks everything at once is fundamental to Neoplatonism. This fact is only highlighted by Proclus's innovation of recognizing a higher level of soul capable of thinking some but not all forms at once (Marinus, *Life of Proclus* §27, *init.*).

76. For this doctrine, see the first few chapters of *Ennead* 3.8. The earlier *Ennead* 4.4.17 gives an apparently different account of the source of discursion and temporal succession in terms of the practical need for incarnate soul to focus on different intentional objects. This seems inconsistent with the account of 3.7.11 in that it presupposes the existence of the physical universe.

77. Cf. *Tim.* 37–38 with Plotinus *Ennead* 4.4.15, 11–14; Igal, "Introducción general," 76–77. Igal proposes to reconcile these texts by identifying time not with the activity of discursive thought but with the outer activity of the lower aspect of the World Soul. This however would fail to account for all rational souls sharing one and the same time, which is one of Plotinus's main concerns in the treatise (see below on *Ennead* 3.7.13, 66–69). Igal also raises a further difficulty concerning Plotinus's view on whether souls are located in time in the way physical things are. *Ennead* 4.4.15, 11ff. seems to suggest that our souls are "in a way" in time, while the position of 3.7.11 (a later treatise) is

66–69) makes clear what Plotinus has in mind here: he is speaking of the *hypostasis* Soul as the generator of time.[78] "We" can be identified with the hypostasis Soul in virtue of Plotinus's doctrine of "the unity of soul," namely, that all individual souls, while remaining distinct from one another, are yet somehow also numerically one (cf. *Ennead* 4.9).[79] At *Ennead* 3.7.13, 66–69, this doctrine is appealed to in order to account for the common conception that the same time is simultaneously present everywhere. The view of *Ennead* 3.7.11–13 may indeed mark a development in Plotinus's views on the origin of time from those presented in *Ennead* 4.4, but since the World Soul and our souls are not here distinguished, it is still possible that the activity of the World Soul is to be given a preeminent role in the account of time, since it is still the soul that is responsible for the celestial revolutions that define time.[80]

Plotinus attempts to confirm his claim that the soul is responsible for the being of time in chapter twelve (3.7.12, 4–25) by means of a thought experiment. Time, Plotinus argues, cannot be conceived to exist without the soul, as Aristotle indeed seems to concede, but the soul can be conceived to exist without time if it withdraws completely from its activity of discursive thought and returns to the unextended life of intellect. Since the ceasing of soul's discursive activity would abolish time, it must be this that generates time (3.7.12, 15–22).[81] Now Alexander had claimed that Aristotle's view that time cannot exist

---

that no soul is in time, since soul produces time. But note that the time-producing soul of *Ennead* 3.7.11, 30 is said to 'temporalize' itself (ἑαυτὴν ἐχρόνωσεν). The last passage of *Ennead* 3.7.13 (53ff.) is precisely a discussion of why Plotinus's theory does not entail that the soul is strictly *in* time: cf. 4.4.15 *fin.*, where the same view is upheld.

78. So Jonas, pp. 309–10, n. 17; cf. McGuire and Strange, n. 103.

79. On the unity of soul doctrine, cf. H. J. Blumenthal, "Soul, World-Soul, and Individual Soul in Plotinus," in *Le néoplatonisme*, 55–63 (cited in n. 46 above). I do not think, however, that the doctrine is as dangerously incoherent as Blumenthal appears to suggest. Part of the difficulty in Blumenthal's account of the matter comes from failing to distinguish the lower soul which informs bodies, and which is not really individual for Plotinus, since it is an emanation from the World Soul, from what Plotinus often calls "our" soul, i.e., the rational soul, which is individual and *distinct* from the lower soul. The appeal to the doctrine in *Ennead* 3.7 shows its importance for Plotinus; it also plays an important role in his theory of participation in *Ennead* 6.4–5.

80. Roland Teske, "The World-Soul and Time in St. Augustine," *Augustinian Studies* 14 (1983): 75–92, has seen the fundamental importance of the doctrine of the unity of souls for Plotinus's theory of time, as well as its influence on Augustine's view of time in *Confessions* 11. Contrast Gloy, p. 304, who thinks Plotinus's doctrine is that the World Soul, not individual soul, is the generator of time, and that the crucial difference from Augustine's "subjectivist" view lies in this point.

81. Reading ἐπεὶ οὐδ' ἂν ἡ σφαῖρα αὐτὴ εἴη, ἧ οὐ πρώτως ὑπάρχει χρόνος at *Ennead* 3.7.12.16–17 with Igal (cf. McGuire and Strange, p. 270 n. 110).

without soul's activity was consistent with his own view that time is the number of the motion of the outermost heavenly sphere, since the soul of this sphere is the cause of its motion, which is in turn the cause of all other physical motion. Eliminating soul would therefore eliminate all motion as well (Simplicius *In Phys.* 759.18ff.; Alexander, *On Time* §16). Plotinus refutes this with the claim that we can imagine the rotation of the heavens could stop without the inner activity of the soul stopping: in that case soul would measure the state of rest of the universe just as it had formerly measured its motion, i.e., by using time (3.7.12, 17–19). Time would therefore, *pace* Alexander, still exist.[82]

Plotinus claims that the main point on which the Peripatetic theory of the nature of time had gone astray was in taking time to be essentially a measuring concept. He thinks that time is not a measure, but is a quantity that only comes to be measured accidentally, by comparison with regular or uniform physical motion. Remarkably, he wishes to believe that this is what Aristotle had actually meant to say, and that he had come to be misunderstood because of his obscurity and the fact that he was writing for students who had heard his lectures (3.7.13, 9–18). Plotinus's point is that the process of thinking and its associated subjective time is a continuous uniform process, not naturally articulated into units by which it could be measured (cf. 3.7.12, 1–4). Indeed, it is a familiar fact of experience that we often cannot tell just subjectively how long something takes, without, e.g., looking at a clock. The purpose of the regular heavenly motions, as Plato had said in the *Timaeus* (47a) is to reveal the existence of time to our senses, but time is something imperceptible in itself (3.7.12, 25–33). Rather, the soul's activity measures itself by picking a simple unit of regularly repeated motion, e.g., the sweep of a watch's second hand or the movement of the stars, to use as a standard of comparison. Plotinus thus manages to sidestep the problems about time measurement that beset other idealistic theories of time, such as Locke's and Berkeley's, which attempt to hold onto Aristotle's notion of time as essentially a measuring concept.[83]

Plotinus can claim to have argued for his theory of time in the proper dialectical manner, by showing that it provides a more ade-

---

82. This argument is certainly not original with Plotinus, for it is opposed by Alexander in *On Time* §5. It seems originally to be due to Galen: cf. Sharples, "Alexander," 72–78 (cited in n. 55 above) and Simplicius, *In Phys.* 708.27 ff.

83. See J. D. Mabbott, "Our Direct Experience of Time," *Mind* 60 (1951), reprinted in part in Richard Gale, ed., *The Philosophy of Time: A Collection of Essays* (New Jersey: Humanities Press, 1968), 304–21.

quate account of the phenomena of time than any other that had been proposed. He is able to account for the common conception that the same time is simultaneously everywhere by pointing to the soul and its life, which is time, as simultaneously present everywhere. Simultaneous times are also the same in the souls of all perceivers, since all souls, as Plotinus claims, are in a sense one and the same soul (3.7.13, 66–69). Time is connected with motion because it is the motion that is the life of the soul, which is the cause of all physical motions.[84] Though the discursive conscious life of the soul is not itself in time, since it is identical with time, all physical motion is in time because it is simultaneous with some stretch of time (this is illustrated by the example of a man walking, at 3.7.13, 53–66). Hence Plotinus's theory, he thinks, meets the crucial conditions for a philosophical account of time. Finally, he thinks his theory, unlike others, provides a clear analysis of the difficult concept of temporal succession. Aristotle had tied this to the ordered succession of the before and after in physical motion. But, as we have seen, Aristotle had been unable to distinguish clearly between two sorts of succession, the kinetic and the temporal (cf. 3.7.9, 56–63). Moreover, he had been left with no easy way to explain how the movement of thought could be in time, and this had apparently led some of his followers to deny that subjective or psychological time was real (cf. 3.7.13, 30–40).[85] A similar insistence that time has primarily to do with measuring physical motion has led some contemporary philosophers to speak paradoxically about the "myth of passage" and to deny the reality of subjective time. Plotinus claims that all these difficulties can be solved if we realize that psychic motion is more real than physical motion, and that the succession it contains is metaphysically the cause both of temporal succession and of the succession in physical motion.

This is a view of time that perhaps few of us will find sympathetic. Like the rest of Plotinus's metaphysics it is radically idealist. But whatever we may think of it as a philosophical theory, it should at least be admired for the care and ingenuity with which it is argued. In a rigorously dialectical manner, Plotinus examines on their own terms and independently of any presuppositions of his own all the physicalistic theories of time that were available to him, and shows that even by their own lights they are incapable of saving the phenomena of time. He then tries to show how his own view, derived from a deep and original reading of Plato, can solve the puzzles raised by all other

84. This is of course the doctrine of *Phaedrus* 245–46 and of *Laws* 10.
85. Cf. McGuire and Strange, p. 270 n. 124.

theories. His arguments thus amount to a dialectical demonstration of his own theory, which is all he thinks is available in such matters. Plotinus's doctrines may seem odd to us, but his method is that of a true philosopher.[86]

86. Versions of this paper were read at the University of Texas at Austin, Princeton University, Duke University, to the ancient philosophy seminar at The University of Chicago, and at Georgetown University, as well as at the Catholic University of America. I am grateful to the audiences on those occasions, and to Ted McGuire and Ian Mueller, for their help, and particularly to Tom Beauchamp, Bill Blattner, and R. W. Sharples for written comments.

PART II
ARISTOTLE AND LATE GREEK THOUGHT

3   Galen and the Logic of Relations

R. J. HANKINSON

Historians of logic are generally aware that the discovery of the fourth figure of the syllogism was attributed by Arabic sources to Galen,[1] although how secure that attribution is remains a matter of dispute.[2] Less widely known, although both more interesting in its content and more secure in its ascription, is his pioneering treatment of the logic of relations.[3] At the beginning of the *Institutio Logica*,[4]

1. See *pro* the ascription N. Rescher and A. Marmurra, *Galen and the Syllogism* (Pittsburgh: 1966); *contra*, see W. Kneale and M. Kneale, *The Development of Logic* (Oxford: 1962), 183–84. Kneale and Kneale offer an explanation of how such a development might have been ascribed to Galen: He is known to have elaborated a theory of complex syllogisms (ones involving three premises and a conclusion, and four terms, considered as combinations of moods in basic syllogistic) in which there were four figures, combined as follows: (where "I," "II," and "III" represent the three traditional syllogistic figures) I + I, I + II, I + III, II + III. He apparently rejected the combinations II + II and III + III, although the reasons for this are obscure, and clearly valid examples of both types are possible, such as the combination of Camestres and Cesare: AaB, AeC, BaD |- CeD (where "AaB" abbreviates "A belongs to all B," and "AeB" abbreviates "A belongs to no B") for II + II, and Datisi and Disamis (AaB, CiB, DaC |- AiD) for III + III (see Kneale and Kneale, p. 184 for a possible explanation of this). I. M. Bochenski, *Ancient Formal Logic* (Amsterdam: 1957) merely remarks without comment that Galen explicitly rejects the "fourth 'Galenic' figure" (p. 105); see n. 2, above.

2. Rescher, in *Galen and the Syllogism*, takes it as established—but the case is far from clear. In particular, the proponents of the genuineness of the attribution need to explain how it can be that Galen himself says, in his only surviving complete text on logic, the *Institutio Logica* (ed. K. Kalbfleish [Leipzig: 1896], English translation and commentary by J. Kieffer, *Galen's "Institutio Logica"* [Baltimore: 1964]; German translation and commentary by J. Mau, *Galen: Einführung in die Logik*, Deutsche Akademie der Wissenschaften zu Berlin, Veröffentlichung, no. 8 [1960]), that there can only be three syllogistic figures (*Inst. Log.* 12.1; cf. Bochenski, *Ancient Formal Logic*, 105 n. 1), particularly in view of the fact that *Institutio Logica* is a relatively late work, in which several of his other logical texts are cited. Had Galen originally, in his hot youth, promiscuously espoused the fourth figure, but later returned to the path of orthodox rectitude, one might have expected him to mention it. In view of the fact that Galen wrote a (lost) work entitled *On the Number of the Syllogisms* (which is also mentioned in *On His Own Books* [19:43, Kühn; cited hereafter as *Lib. Prop.*]) one might readily imagine how, given Galen's reputation for logical innovation, the "invention" of the fourth figure could have been falsely ascribed to him, particularly if the work discussed someone else's claim that there was a fourth figure.

3. Kneale and Kneale dismiss it in a paragraph (*Development of Logic*, 185). Bochenski

Galen writes: "Furthermore, there is another third species of syllogism useful in demonstrations, which I call relational; however Aristotle and his followers try to force them into the class of categorical syllogisms" (*Inst. Log.* 16.1). The other two "species" of syllogism are the categorical syllogisms, which Galen deals with in an orthodox Aristotelian manner, finding fourteen valid moods in three figures (*Inst. Log.* 8–11), and the hypotheticals (ibid. 4.6–7, 14), which are Stoic in origin (although Theophrastus worked on the logic of conditional inference in the Peripatos, and may have elaborated a mood-structure for hypothetical syllogistic).[5]

Galen's treatment of the material culled from the Peripatetics is generally traditional and unoriginal. In regard to the Stoic legacy, Galen has more to say. He remarks that the third Chrysippean indemonstrable is demonstratively useless (*Inst. Log.* 4.4–6; 14.3, 8).[6] He does so on the grounds that the form of the conjunction does not of itself indicate whether the conjoined items are accidentally or necessarily linked (ibid. 4.4–5)—and hence the negated conjunction that

---

gives it half a page, and concludes by saying: "it is easy to see that the results of Galenus' research into the logic of relations are rather poor" (*Ancient Formal Logic*, 105). Some work has recently been done on this topic, however; see Jonathan Barnes, "Uma terceira espécie de silogismo: Galeno e la logica das relações," *Análise* 2 (1985): 35–61.

4. See n. 2 above; a new edition and translation of this work is being prepared by Jonathan Barnes and Michael Frede.

5. See Jonathan Barnes, "Theophrastus and Hypothetical Syllogistic," in W. W. Fortenbaugh et al., eds., *Theophrastus of Eresus* (New Brunswick: 1985), 125–41.

6. The indemonstrable can be stated as follows,

[III]　(1) not-(A & B)
　　　 (2) A
so　　 (3) not-B

Cf. Sextus Empiricus *Outlines of Pyrrhonism* 2.157–58, and *Adversus Mathematicos* 8.223 ff.; and Diogenes Laertius 7.79; see also H. von Arnim, *Stoicorum Veterum Fragmenta*, 4 vols. (Leipzig: 1905–24), 2:241–45. The other four indemonstrables, to which the Stoics thought all valid arguments could (in some sense) be reduced, are:

[I]	(1) if A then B		[IV]	(1) A or B
	(2) A			(2) A
so	(3) B		so	(3) not-B
[II]	(1) if A then B		[V]	(1) A or B
	(2) not-B			(2) not-A
so	(3) not-A		so	(3) B

There is no scholarly orthodoxy on the precise interpretation of the status of the indemonstrables in Stoic logical theory, nor upon the nature of the reductions to them supposedly effected by the *themata* (there were apparently four: we can reconstruct with confidence only two of them). On these issues see B. Mates, *Stoic Logic* (California: 1961); Ian Mueller, "An Introduction to Stoic Logic," in J. Rist, ed., *The Stoics* (California: 1978); Michael Frede, "Stoic vs. Aristotelian Logic," in *Essays in Ancient Philosophy* (Oxford: 1987); and Michael Frede, *Die Stoische Logik* (Göttingen: 1974). It is of course a commonplace that [IV] is only valid for "or" construed exclusively; Galen's reaction to this will be discussed below.

forms the major premise of the third indemonstrable will sometimes indicate a merely contingent separation between the two conjuncts, as in "it is not both the case that Dion is walking and Theon is talking" (ibid. 4.4; 14.7), while others, such as, "Dion is not both at Athens and on the Isthmus" (ibid. 4.4, 14.4), do indicate "whole or complete conflict" (ibid. 14.3–8).

Moreover, his treatment of inclusive disjunction, which he calls παραδιεζευγμενον or "paradisjunction" (ibid. 5.1 ff., 15.1 ff.), is of much independent interest, and exhibits his keen logical sense. The Stoics, of course, treated disjunction as being properly exclusive (and hence genuine disjsunctions should be necessarily true, and exhaustive— they should cover the whole of logical space). Galen realizes that this by no means exhausts the available ordinary language senses of "or" (this is just as true in classical Greek as it is in modern English), nor the available valid arguments constructible disjunctively (the treatment here parallels that of conjunction, but I shall not follow that out here). All of these indicate a keen interest in the structure of logic, as well as a not inconsiderable logical sense. Galen was clearly no mean logician.

However, it is with the "third species" of syllogism that Galen's major claim to both novelty and importance in the history of logic rests.[7] Galen holds quite explicitly that certain forms of argument are simply unsuited to treatment in either the categorical or the hypothetical manner; the types of argument he has in mind are, as he himself says, relational in structure. Galen then anticipates the famous examples supplied by de Morgan and others in the nineteenth century of evidently valid arguments that are unformalizable in categorical syllogis-

7. It is worth noting at this point that Galen's language of genus and species is a little loose, at least if the text of the following passage of *Institutio Logica* 18.8 is correct: "all these syllogisms must be said to belong first to the genus of relational syllogisms, but secondly in species they are constructed according to the force of an axiom" (τῷ γένει μὲν ἐκ τῶν πρός τι ῥητέον, ἐν εἴδει δὲ κατ' ἀξιώματος δύναμιν συνισταμένους). As Galen elsewhere twice remarks that "nearly all syllogisms derive their construction from the validity of the universal axioms that are set over them" (ibid. 17.1, 7), one would expect the genus-species relation to be the other way about. Perhaps the text should be emended, either by simply transposing "genus" and "species," or by deleting "in species": the former is unlikely both paleographically and semantically (you don't in general discuss *genera* after species), the latter reduces the μὲν to a redundancy (as well as being unacceptable on other grounds). Jonathan Barnes (review of *Die Fragmente zur Dialektik der Stoiker* by K. Hülser, *Classical Review* 39 [1989]: 264) writes that "the text is certainly corrupt," and suggests reading ἐν εἴδει δὲ κατ' ἀναλογίαν κατ' ἀξιώματος, which gives a good sense, and removes the oddity from the passage. If this is right, then the claim that Posidonius is the real originator of theory of relative syllogistic is rendered groundless (for Posidonius, see n. 10 below), and that too would be helpful to my thesis. It must be stressed that Barnes's emendation is, while seductive, at best speculative.

tic ("all horses are animals; therefore, all horses' heads are animals' heads"), examples which eventually provided the impetus for Frege to develop his revolutionary new method of treating inference and formal validity in his *Begriffschrift* of 1879.

Just how revolutionary Galen really was is difficult to determine. Very little survives of Greek logic after Aristotle (although Galen's period and that immediately following his lifetime are better represented than most), and it is consequently far from easy to judge just what is original and what simply the retailing of a contemporary commonplace (it is worth repeating in this regard how serious a loss to the history of logic is the disappearance of Galen's own fifteen-volume treatise *On Proof*,[8] as well as his commentaries on the Peripatetic *Analytics*, Aristotle's *Categories* and *On Interpretation*, and sundry other logical works).[9] He at least appears to claim originality for the name "relational" (see above), and that is perhaps enough to allow us to claim on Galen's behalf the first articulated recognition that here was a genuinely separate *class* of formally valid inferences. Galen was the first to argue that, in spite of the efforts of the Peripatetics, one simply could not force the deductions of the geometers and the mathematicians into the rigidly inflexible forms of Aristotelian logic.[10]

That mention of geometers and mathematicians is not casual. Galen himself tells us that it was only a reflection on the sureness of "arithmetic and calculation on the geometrical model" that prevented him from falling into a Pyrrhonian *impasse* (ἀπορία): "I was schooled in these things at the outset by my father, who had learned them from

8. For a collection of fragments and a reconstruction of its contents, see I. von Müller, *Über Galens Werk vom wissenschaftlichen Beweis* (Munich: 1895).

9. We know of the existence of these works from quotations and references in the rest of Galen's *oeuvre*, as well as citations in his catalogue (*Lib. Prop.*, 41–42).

10. Posidonius, of whom generally Galen had a high opinion (see *On the Doctrines of Hippocrates and Plato* [5:390, Kühn; hereafter *PHP*], where he is described as "the most scientifically knowledgeable ἐπιστημονικός of the Stoics"), is sometimes thought to be the precursor of much of what Galen says in the *Institutio Logica*, and he is credited (*Inst. Log.* 18.8) with labelling certain arguments as being "conclusive in virtue of an axiom" (quite which arguments depends of course on whether or not you accept Barnes's emendation; see n. 7 above). It seems on balance probable that much of what Galen says is original, not least because he himself claims to have changed his mind as a result of later logical insights (*Inst. Log.* 17.1). See Kieffer, *Galen's "Institutio Logica,"* 128, for a careful discussion of the issue. See also Barnes, review of *Die Fragmente* (cited above in n. 7), where he takes issue with Hülser for treating the whole of *Institutio Logica* 17.1–18.8 as being Posidonian (Hülser prints it as fr. 1094; cf. Edelstein and Kidd, eds., *The Fragments*, vol. 1 of *Posidonius* [Cambridge: 1972], fr. 191); Barnes is surely right here. *PHP* has recently been edited with a translation and commentary by P. H. De Lacy as vol. V 4 1 2 of the *Corpus Medicorum Graecorum* (Berlin: 1977); the series will be cited hereafter as *CMG*.

his father and grandfather. And as I saw that not only were predictions of eclipses evidently accurate, but also how sundials and water-clocks were calibrated, and all the other things of this sort worked out on the architectural model, I considered the geometrical model to be superior for use in demonstrations" (*Lib. Prop.* 19.40).[11] He goes on to remark that, in spite of their manifold disputes and differences, self-contradictions even, the best philosophers all agree in praising geometrical proof. For Galen, the type of inference used in geometry and arithmetic is paradigmatically the *best* sort of argument and the most secure type of proof, and, not unimportantly, it is of direct and practical use. Galen, after all, was a practicing doctor. He is interested in the type of inference that will be of use to a medical man (which is one reason why he rejects the third indemonstrable: it is not that it is *invalid* as such, it is simply that it can do no genuine work in discovery).[12] But his interests in logic are not confined to its practical applications. He holds too that a thorough grounding in proof-theory is a prerequisite for anyone who wants to reason well and clearly. In order to do science, we must be able to do logic.[13]

So what are we to make of his treatment of relational syllogisms? First of all, Galen is at pains to emphasize the generality and ubiquitousness of the procedure. In the first chapter of the *Institutio Logica*, when discussing the basic form of inferences of a type that are such as to commend themselves to any ordinary person who contemplates them, Galen makes use of the following argument:

11. Galen's father, Nicon, was an architect (see *On the Diagnosis and Cure of the Passions of the Soul* [5:40–41, Kühn]; *Lib. Prop.* [19:40, Kühn]; *On Good and Bad Nutritional Humours* [6:755, Kühn]; *On the Therapeutic Method* [10:561, 609, Kühn], and Galen regularly exalts the type of knowledge available to people like him over the sterile and petty disputes of the school philosopher; cf. in particular *On the Diagnosis and Cure of the Errors of the Soul* (5:63ff., Kühn).

12. Although the reason why it cannot is formal: discovery on the basis of argument requires necessary connections and disjunctions, and the third indemonstrable does not (at least as it is elaborated by the Stoics) deal exclusively in them (see Frede, "Stoic vs. Aristotelian Logic," 118). It should be noted here that it is a mistake to assimilate the Stoics' first and second indemonstrables ([I] and [II] of n. 6 above) straightforwardly to *modus ponens* and *modus tollens* respectively, where the latter schemata make use of conditionals materially interpreted. There *were* people in the ancient world (Philo of Megara is their archetype) who adopted a material reading of the conditional (see Sextus, *Outlines of Pyrrhonism* 2.110); the Stoics adopted something much closer to a relevance account of the truth-conditions for the conditional (the so-called Chrysippean conditionals: see ibid. 2.111), and hence their logic approximated (in some respects at least) to modern relevance logics. This fact is of enormous importance; the details are, however, obscure.

13. This belief is expressed innumerable times throughout Galen's work: but see compendiously the short treatise *That the Best Doctor Be Also a Philosopher* (1:53–63, Kühn).

(A)   (1) Theon is equal to Dion
      (2) Philon is equal to Dion
so   (3) Theon is equal to Philon

That argument (although it may appear to bear the surface form of the Aristotelian syllogism) makes use of a particular two-place relation, "is equal to," which has no place in syllogistic. Its validity, Galen asserts (*Inst. Log.* 1.5) rests on the following statement, which he calls an "axiom," or "a proposition carrying conviction in itself to the intellect."[14]

(Ax1) Things equal to the same thing are equal to one another

In a modern notation this would read

$$(Ax1^*)\ (x)(y)[(Ez)(x = z\ \&\ y = z) \rightarrow x = y]$$

The ordering of the terms in [A] is mildly significant; as it stands, it emphasizes both the transitivity and the symmetry of the equality relation. Consider the treatment of Alexander of Aphrodisas:

Thus it is not the case that in the case that if A is equal to B and B is equal to C, then it follows of necessity that A is equal to C, that this is already a syllogism. It *will* be syllogistically concluded if, adding a further universal premise to the effect that [P1] "things equal to the same thing are also equal to each other," we compress the two assumed premises into one which is equivalent to the pair of them, namely: [P2] "A and C are equal to the same thing"; for thus it follows syllogistically that [P3] A and C are equal to each other.[15]

(P1) looks like (Ax1); so what is at issue between Galen and Alexander?[16] First of all, Galen holds that [A] is valid as it stands, while Alexander thinks that is not, but that there is a syllogistic argument parallel to it which is valid and which makes use of the same material. Second, there is a problem with the form of (P1). If the argument is to be syllogistic (where "syllogistic" means "corresponding to one of the fourteen syllogistic moods analyzed by Aristotle"),[17] then it has to

14. Although Galen notes the indeterminacy in the use of the term "axiom" (ἀξίωμα) at *Inst. Log.* 1.5, and as we shall see below, his own usage occasions some problems.

15. Alexander of Aphrodisias, *In. An. Pr.* in *Commentaria in Aristotelem Graeca*, ed. Wallies (Berlin: 1883), 344.

16. Alexander of Aphrodisias, by general consent the greatest of the Greek commentators on Aristotle, was a younger contemporary of Galen—an Arabic tradition has it that they quarrelled violently, although it is not recorded that the nature of logic was one of their bones of contention. Galen himself, in his *On Prognosis*, ed. V. Nutton, vol. 5 of *CMG* (Berlin: 1977), 14.627–29, records a violent dispute with one Alexander of Damascus, but it seems that this Alexander is not to be identified with the Peripatetic (see Nutton's commentary, ad loc.).

17. At this point it is worth noting that Frede ("Stoic vs. Aristotelian Logic," 110–

fit one of the canonical forms of the syllogism. As it stands $\langle\{(P_1), (P_2)\},$ $(P_3)\rangle$ is not couched in the appropriate form: the premises do not consist of terms suitably conjoined with quantity-operators and the 'belonging to' relation. In order to get it to look like a syllogism in Barbara, we need to rewrite it as follows:

[B]   (P₁B) All pairs of objects such that each member of the pair is equal
            to some third object are such as to be equal to one another
        (P₂B) A and C are a pair of objects such that each member of the
            pair is equal to some third object
so   (P₃B) A and C are such as to be equal to one another

Thus do "Aristotle and his followers try to force them into the class of categorical syllogisms."

Even then there are loose ends and problems. [B] is horribly inelegant and top-heavy in the structure of its predicates. In order to fit the canonical form of Barbara ("All B's are C's; all A's are B's; so all A's are C's"; or more accurately "C belongs to all B, B belongs to all A; so C belongs to all A"), the "term" B has to be read as "pairs of objects such that each member of the pair is equal to some third member," while the "term" C turns out to be "such as to be equal to one another." These unwieldy items seem a far cry from the intuitively plausible candidate predicates such as "animal" and "mortal" that usually clothe Barbara's slender form. Furthermore, syllogistic form demands that the pair "A and C" be read as a single conjunctive subject in both the minor premise (P₂B) and the conclusion (P₃B), yet it has to be decomposed, and its components taken separately, in the predicative parts of both (P₂B) and (P₃B). Finally, and from our point of view most importantly, the middle term of the original argument, the thing to which A and C are individually equal and which consequently guarantees their mutual equality, has dropped out of sight altogether in [B]. It has disappeared into the general "some third object" which is a *part of* the "middle term" of the argument expressed in "syllogistic form," and not the middle term itself. Furthermore, it appears to import a further variable, "some third object," into the heart of what is itself supposed to be a variable. The simple fact is that syllogistic cannot handle arguments with multiple generality.

16) argues strongly for the claim that syllogistic, as it was understood by Aristotle himself, was not confined to the fourteen valid moods (plus the modal moods) analyzed explicitly in the *Prior Analytics,* and makes the crucial claim that a syllogism was an argument, and not an argument-schema. But whatever one says about that, it seems clear that the subclass of valid arguments which constitute syllogistic cannot, for the later Peripatetics any more than for their master, be construed broadly enough to include valid inferences involving multiple generality. The doctrine of terms is what is responsible here.

Alexander's "reformulation" is an attempt to disguise that unpalatable truth.

Suppose that we replace the variable "some third object" with a particular, in this case "B," the "middle term" of the original argument. Then we will be able to construct the following syllogism:

[B*]   (P1B*) All pairs of objects such that each member of the pair is equal to B are such as to be equal to one another
        (P2B*) A and C are a pair of objects such that each member of the pair is equal to B;
so   (P3B*) A and C are such as to be equal to one another

That avoids the problem of multiple generality within the premises at the expense of compromising the complete generality of the argument itself; for, since "B" turns up within the predicates of (P1B*) and (P2B*), [B*] will generate a conclusion only in respect of some one particular object B. We therefore will need to have separate and distinct syllogisms of equality for every object in the universe. Alexander's solution is logically emasculate.

Let us return to Galen's own treatment. Argument [A], he claims, is valid in virtue of its being dependent upon an axiom, where an "axiom" is some conceptually self-evident general truth. The axiom in question is of course one of Euclid's common notions.[18] Elsewhere, Galen makes use of this and other Euclidian common notions as exempla for his theory of demonstration (see in particular *de Methodo Medendi* 10:36 ff., Kühn),[19] but the ambit of "axiom" as Galen intends it here is broader than simply that of the foundational geometrical commonplaces. Rather it is any proposition that commends itself directly and without inference to the intellect as being obviously true, ἐναργῶς φαινόμενον (the scope of Galen's notion of φαινόμενον is broader than simply that of perceptual appearances).[20] (Ax1) is an example of the type, but so are the following.

(Ax2) Nothing occurs without a cause (*de Methodo Medendi* 10:36, Kühn; cf. p. 37).[21]

18. *Elements* 1, Common Notion 1.
19. I discuss the passage in detail in my translation and commentary of Galen's *On the Therapeutic Method, Books 1 and 2* (Oxford University Press, 1991).
20. As indeed it frequently is in Greek. For the history of the concept in Aristotle, see G. E. L. Owen, *"Tithenai ta phainomena,"* reprinted in Barnes, Schofield, and Sorabji, eds., *Science,* vol. 1 of *Articles on Aristotle* (London: 1975), and in G. E. L. Owen and Martha C. Nussbaum, eds., *Logic, Science and Dialectic* (London: 1986). For the history of the concept in the Peripatetics in general, see Sextus, *Adversus Mathematicos* 7.224.
21. This axiom is an ancient commonplace, and forms the cornerstone to Galen's own theory of science. At *PHP* 5.390–91, he claims that "it is a point of agreement among just about every philosopher" apart from the Epicureans. Cf. ibid. 544, where

(Ax3) It is necessary that everything be either affirmed or denied (ibid., 37)

(Ax2) is clearly a claim in metaphysics, while (Ax3) is a logical or
semantical principle. Axioms, then, are for Galen categorically pro-
miscuous; and that is only to be expected if they are supposed to be
behind every valid demonstration (not necessarily, of course, every
valid inference).

Immediately before the passage of *de Methodo Medendi* where Galen
cites (Ax2) and (Ax3) as being axioms, he gives an example of a particular proof in geometry to illustrate his general claim that most
contemporary scientists, in their ignorance of the principles of demonstration,

> behave like a man who tries to measure a sphere, cube, cone, cylinder, or
> something else of that sort, without knowing any geometrical or computational
> theory, unarmed with either cubit-, span-, or foot-rules, and who then gets
> angry with those who want him to put up a demonstration or shut up. Thus
> anyone who asserts that the area of a right-angled triangle, in which one of
> the sides enclosing the right angle is five feet long (as it might be) and the
> other twelve feet long, is not thirty feet but forty feet, without having any
> demonstration of this, would seem to be ridiculous. For the same reason, anyone
> who makes an assertion of some kind that he is unable to back up with a dem-
> onstration seems equally ridiculous. (*de Methodo Medendi* 10:32–33; Kühn)

Galen fills out his illustration of the area of the triangle. His filling is
schematic and sketchy, but it affords an idea of what he has in mind.
Take a right-angled triangle whose sides enclosing the right angle are
of five feet and twelve feet. The area of the triangle is consequently
thirty feet. How do we prove this? First of all by showing it rests on
two prior propositions

   (1) the area of a rectangle with sides 5′ and 12′ is 60′

and

   (2) the area of a right-angled triangle of sides 5′ and 12′ is half
   that of the rectangle constructed with the same sides

then by progressing to the higher-level, more general propositions of
which these particular propositions are special cases. Ultimately, one

---

the claim is even stronger: it is "one of the things everyone agrees upon." Other causal
axioms Galen subscribes to include: "that which is changed takes on a form similar to
that which causes the change" (ibid. 566–67); "it is impossible that when two bodies
come together they should not both act and be acted upon" (ibid. 567); "everything
comes to be from something existent" (*de Methodo Mendendi* 10:36, Kühn); "nothing
comes to be from nothing" (ibid. 37).

will arrive at axioms from which all the other propositions are derivable as theorems, and whose truth is self-evident (at least to someone who understands the meanings of the terms). This is the procedure known as ἀνάλυσις, and it is that of Euclidean geometry.[22] Galen does not spell out exactly what the higher-order propositions are upon which (1) and (2) rest, but it is not difficult to supply them. Eventually one will arrive at the general area axiom for triangles

(Ax4) The area of any triangle = half (base × height)

from which (1) and (2) can be deduced in this particular case, and of which they can be seen to be instances.

The important thing here is the generality of the procedure: what the logical investigator needs to do is to establish axioms at the highest level of generality possible such that they are appropriate to the procedure in question. This is important as a piece of logical theory: what Galen is urging us to do is to treat his axioms as meta-theorems for deduction.[23] The meta-theorems allow us to see why the deduction works in each particular case. If we consider the theorem concerning the area of the triangle on the syllogistic model suggested by Alexander, effectively we will have to treat each set of dimensions as being a special case: we will be able to go no further than (2) in our analysis. Thus, what should appear as a multiplicity (indeed an infinite multiplicity) of instances of an absolutely general axiom (Ax4) will turn up, on the Peripatetic scheme, as a disorderly set of quite distinct theorems. And this is grossly to misrepresent the proper logical structure of geometrical inference.

The problem of course is directly occasioned by the fact that Peripatetic syllogistic, given the rigidity of its formal structure of copula and terms, cannot tolerate premises with multiple generality. Galen insists, quite rightly, that to adhere to that form is to leave logic hamstrung.

Before we return to the argument of the *Institutio Logica* 16, and see how Galen makes good his case against both Stoic and Peripatetic treatments of relations, let us reinforce what has been established so far with a brief examination of some more texts in which Galen asserts that the validity of an inference rests upon an axiom.

In his monumental *On the Doctrines of Hippocrates and Plato* (see n. 10 above), in which he attempts to demonstrate the substantial agree-

22. For the Greek geometrical concept of ἀνάλυσις, see R. Robinson, "Analysis in Greek Geometry," in *Essays in Greek Philosophy* (Oxford: 1969); and K. J. J. Hintikka and U. Remes, *The Method of Analysis* (Dordrecht: 1974).
23. I owe this insight to the paper of Barnes, cited in n. 3 above.

ment on all important questions of his two great idols, Galen frequently makes use of the notion of an axiom in this sense. In his extended and brilliant criticism of the Stoic doctrine of the location of the intelligence, Galen takes the Stoics (Zeno, Diogenes of Babylon, and Chrysippus are singled out) to task for their failure to produce their arguments for the cardiac location of the intelligence in sufficiently perspicuous form—precisely, they fail to enunciate the axiom upon which their argument depends (*PHP* 5.211–62). I shall not here analyze Galen's refutation as such,[24] but it turns on showing first of all that the Stoic argument depends upon an axiom, and second that the axiom in question is false.[25]

Characteristically, Galen considers that Plato made use of this method in his proof of the tripartition of the soul at *Republic* 4.436–41, when he enunciates his *Principle of Noncontradiction*:

(PNC) It is evident that the same thing will not consent to do or undergo opposite things at the same time, in the same respect, and in relation to the same object. (*Rep.* 4.436c; quoted at *PHP* 5.798)[26]

What unites these diverse cases is the belief that, as he puts it at *Institutio Logica* 17.1: "Nearly all the syllogisms derive their construction [σύστασις] through the validity of the universal axioms that are set over them. Since I only came to realize this later, it is not written either in my commentaries *On Demonstration*[27] or in *On the Number of the Syllogisms*."[28] The exact force of the "nearly all" at the beginning is unclear;[29] Kieffer writes: "How seriously to take the qualifier is a question. It seems best to take it as a mark of caution, and to assume that

24. I do treat this topic in my "Greek Medical Models of the Mind," in S. Everson, ed., *Psychology* (Cambridge University Press, 1991); and "Galen's Anatomy of the Soul," *Phronesis* 36 (1991).

25. Or rather the axiom in question, "All that is sent through something is sent out of the parts continuous with it," is ambiguous. The ambiguity resides in the apparently innocent "is sent out of," that can be read in either (*a*) a causal or (*b*) a positional sense. In case (*a*), which is the sense the Stoics need to ground their argument, it means "by the agency of," in which case the axiom is false; (*b*) gives a sense which is possibly true, but has not got the logical leverage to deliver the conclusion the Stoics want. See *PHP* 5.244–46, and cf. 256–57. The actual argument is given three separate formulations at *PHP* 5.241–43, attributed to Zeno, Diogenes, and Chrysippus respectively; the first version goes as follows: "[*a*] Speech passes through the windpipe. [*b*] If it were passing from the brain, it would not pass through the windpipe. [*c*] Speech passes from the same region as discourse. [*d*] Discourse passes from the mind. Therefore [*e*] the mind is not in the brain" (ibid., 241). I present a detailed analysis of these arguments in my "Greek Medical Models of the Mind" (cited in n. 24 above).

26. It is slightly misleading to label this as the "principle of noncontradiction," but that need occasion no particular problems here. Cf. Aristotle, *Met.* 4.3.1005b18–21.

27. For this lost text, see n. 7 above.

28. See n. 2 above.

29. Cf. *Institutio Logica* 17.7; and see n. 7 above.

Galen means all syllogisms with which he is acquainted, not that he is aware of exceptions to the rule" (Kieffer, *Galen's Institutio Logica*, 123). Kieffer thinks that, whatever one makes of the qualifier, the role of the axioms must extend beyond the ambit merely of the relational syllogisms; he holds that Galen would treat the basic moods of the categorical syllogism (i.e., those of the first figure), as well as some at least of the Chrysippean indemonstrables as axioms for the arguments that exhibit that form.[30]

If that is right, then clearly the notion of an axiom in this sense is close to that of a meta-theorem—an articulating principle of the logic itself. But some at least of the axioms we have examined do not look much like meta-theorems, and there seem to be enormously more of them for relational arguments than for either of the other types. Perhaps that simply shows that logic is a lot vaster than had previously been imagined. At all events, it is not clear that Galen has a lucid doctrine on this subject. Kieffer may well be wrong to think that axioms are supposed to apply in the case of the basic patterns of Aristotelian and Stoic syllogistic (these patterns will be *self-evidently* valid). Since there are indefinitely many distinct relational patterns as opposed to a small and limited stock of traditional categorical and hypothetical syllogisms, Galen's "nearly all" is readily explicable.[31]

However that might be, it seems that at the very least Galen has exposed a serious inadequacy in Peripatetic logic. I want finally to turn to a close analysis of the chapters of the *Institutio Logica* that deal directly with relations to see how this pans out. After the first relational argument, [A], of *Institutio Logica* 16.1, Galen offers a sequence of examples, involving numerical operations, and matters of proportion (cf. *Inst. Log.* 18.1, 5–7); and all of them are such that

the construction of the demonstrative syllogism will be by virtue of a conditional axiom [κάτα δύναμιν ἀξιώματος ... συνημμένου], both for numbers and for other things that belong to the category of relation; ⟨for also in these cases⟩ the syllogism will depend on one of the axioms, e.g., [Ca] "⟨if⟩ Sophroniscus is the father of Socrates, Socrates is the son of Sophroniscus," and conversely [Ca*] "if Socrates is the son of Sophroniscus, then Sophroniscus is the father of Socrates." The minor premises of the above propositions are obvious. This syllogism will be expressed hypothetically as [C] "[a] if Socrates is the son of Sophroniscus, then Sophroniscus is the father of Socrates; but [b] Socrates is the son of Sophroniscus; so [c] Sophroniscus is the father of Soc-

30. See in this context Mau, *Galen: Einfürung in die Logik,* 55–56.
31. At all events, it seems that *some* patterns of inference must be regarded as basic, since the axioms themselves exhibit particular logical forms (generally conditional); thus (for instance) one would have to treat the first Stoic indemonstrable as the "axiom" lying behind any axiom in conditional form—but what could be the axiom for that? Shades of what the tortoise said to Achilles.

rates." In categorical premises, the construction of the argument will be more forced [βιαιότεϱον]; yet here too it is clear that {the argument goes through} with the assumption of some such universal axiom [καθόλον τι' ἀξίωμα] as [D] "[Ax6] ⟨the man whom someone has as a father, of him he is the son;⟩ [b] Lamprocles ⟨has⟩ Socrates ⟨as a father⟩; [c] so Lamprocles is the son of Socrates." Similarly syllogisms used in the discussion of any form of relation will derive the conviction of their construction and their probative force from a general axiom [γενικὸν ἀξίωμα]. (ibid. 16.10–12)

First of all, my diacritical marks: "⟨. . .⟩" indicates a lacuna in the Greek text; I have supplied and translated the supplements of Kalb-fleisch, which are accepted without comment by Kieffer. The mark "{. . .}" indicates a supplement I have made myself—the Greek of the sentence is as it stands grammatically deficient. The crucial supple-ment is what I have labelled "[Ax6]": there is no textual warrant for the text as it is supplied. And one thing stands out: as it is presented, [D] is not an argument in categorical syllogistic. If we were to supply the following as the missing "axiomatic" premise:

[Da] Whoever has Socrates as a father is the son of Socrates[32]

then the argument can indeed be represented as a syllogism in Bar-bara (or rather Barbara supplemented to allow for premises contain-ing proper names). But [Ax6] cannot form part of such an argument, for it is multiply general. The case is exactly analogous to that of argument [B] as Alexander handles it.

Furthermore, the substitution of [Da] for [Ax6] has the advantage of making the categorical case parallel to the hypothetical one, and of showing how treating these arguments as though they were individual cases misrepresents the general force of inferences of this type—it mistakes their logical form. For, again analogously to the case of [B], we will need a separate and quite distinct justification for every indi-vidual case of the father-son relationship (or, to make Galen's clearly invalid—not to say sexist—case valid, of the parent-child relationship).

However, it might be objected, Galen does say that in categorical syllogistic the argument will be "more forced" (βιαιότεϱον, whatever that means); and it is not obvious how the argument using [Da] (as opposed to [Ax6]) might be construed as being "more forced" than [C], while [Ax6] clearly does seem in at least some sense "more forced."[33] Furthermore, Galen explicitly says that the argument re-quires the addition of "a universal axiom" (καθόλον τι ἀξίωμα). If he

32. And thus in place of Kalbfleisch's supplement ὄν τις πατέρα ἔχει, υἱός ἐστί τούτου reading something like ὅς Σωκράτην ἔχει πατέρα, υἱός ἐστί Σωκράτους.

33. Frede writes in this context: "It is . . . this disregard for the actual formulation of arguments which allows the Peripatetics to classify all sorts of arguments as categor-

is using "axiom" in anything like the sense in which he elsewhere holds that arguments generally rely for their validity on some general axiom (*Inst. Log.* 17.1, 7), it looks as though [Ax6], Kalbfleisch's original supplement, fits the bill better than [Da].

On the other hand, [Ca] is described as an ἀξίωμα immediately above, and while Galen thinks it inappropriate to give the name "axiom" to all declarative sentences although "you mustn't quarrel [sc. with those who do], but having learned their custom, accept them as speaking according to their own fashion"; ibid. 1.5), nonetheless, as we have already seen, any proposition "which carries conviction of itself to the intellect" (ibid. 1.5; cf. *Methodo Medendi* 10.36) will count for Galen as an ἀξίωμα; and evidently both [Ax6] and [Da] fit the bill here. Furthermore it seems from the structure of the argument that [Ca] (on its first appearance) is supposed to be the ἀξίωμα for the argument both in its hypothetical and in its categorical forms. (It is worth noting at this point that Galen will on occasion express the same argument in a number of different ways, hypothetical and categorical. Cf. *On Semen* 4.609–10, Kühn, where he sets out the same argument concerning parental resemblance in five different ways, two of which he apparently describes as "hypothetical," one as "categorical," the remaining two being undesignated—but his practice is a trifle slapdash in this case.)[34]

---

ical syllogisms which in our view have very little resemblance to an Aristotelian syllogism, e.g. [Frede then reproduces argument [D], with [Ax6], without comment]. . . . For even Galen, who usually sides with the Peripatetics against the Stoics, says with reference to certain arguments that the Peripatetics 'do violence' to them to have them classified as categorical syllogisms" (Frede, "Stoic vs. Aristotelian Logic," 109).

34. The arguments are as follows:

"Hypothetical":

[I]   if offspring can resemble either parent, then the cause of the resemblance
        must be common to both;
        offspring can resemble either parent
so   the cause of the resemblance must be common to both

[II]   if the offspring resemble their parents because of a common cause, then
        either they resemble them because of the nature of the semen, or because
        of the nature of the menstrual fluid
        but there is no common menstrual fluid
so   they resemble them because of the nature of the semen

"Categorical":

[III] since offspring can resemble either parent, they possess some common cause
        which makes them resemble either parent
        for the resemblance of the offspring to the parent comes about in respect of
        the cause

Unassigned:

[IV]   the resemblance of offspring to their parents comes to be either as a result
        of the semen, or as a result of the menstrual fluid
        it doesn't come to be as a result of the menstrual fluid
so   it comes to be as a result of the semen

Consequently, I am inclined on balance to think that my [Da] rather than Kalbfleisch's [Ax6] is the appropriate supplement to Galen's mutilated text. Perhaps [Da] is "more forced" simply because it is a less natural form of locution than [Ca]. However, in the course of his exposition, Galen still ought to have made use of, and referred to, [Ax6], or its hypothetically expressed equivalent

[Ax6*] if anyone is the father of someone else, then that person is their son

It is clear that at the highest level of generality, *this* is the axiom which underlies and supplies the validity to the particular argument concerning Socrates' relationships in its full generality. Consequently, this is the axiom that Galen should have fixed upon as being what is basic to both the hypothetical and categorical formulations of the argument, and the one which they both fail, in their irreducible particularity, to exhibit.

Perhaps a statement of that sort was originally to be found in Galen's text. Logic corrupts more easily than almost any other form of ancient writing, and it would be easy both to explain the disappearance and to supply a suitable run of text that would have Galen show how [Ca] and [Da] both depend upon [A6*] and [Ax6]—which, properly interpreted, are simply alternative formulations of the same proposition.[35] Nonetheless, such a supplement would be purely speculative, and I shall not offer one, even *exempli gratia*.

[V]   if all resemblances of offspring come about as a result of the semen, it is
      necessary that the female produce semen, since many children most closely
      resemble their mothers

This list is puzzling in many ways. For one thing, the arguments are not even informally equivalent; they make use of different premises, and establish their conclusions on the basis of different assumptions; secondly, [II] is not valid as it stands (it requires supplementing with the conclusion of [I], but this is not a serious difficulty); while thirdly, strictly speaking neither [III] nor [V] are arguments at all—this is particularly striking in view of the fact that [III] is supposed to be the only example of the argument put categorically; furthermore, [III] is not expressed in anything like the form of categorical syllogistic. What this shows, I think, is that Galen considers an argument to be "categorical" in at least one sense just in case it makes no use of an explicitly conditional premise. In this sense, even [IV], which is in the form of the fifth Chrysippean indemonstrable, turns out to be categorical (although cf. *Inst. Log.* 3–4, where the fourth and fifth indemonstrables are clearly ranged under hypothetical syllogistic). What all this shows at the very least is that one must be careful of reading too strict a formal set of concepts into all Galen's talk of "hypothetical" and "categorical."
    A similar example of Galen's willingness to treat arguments indifferently in both hypothetical and categorical form is to be found at *On the Composition of Simple Drugs* (11:499–501, Kühn).
    35. And if the latter claim is Galenic, then it is perhaps not too much to see him as a precursor of the conditional treatment of universally quantified propositions—to see him, that is, as recognizing that (*a*) "All As are Bs" is formally expressible as (*b*) "take anything you like, if it's an A, then it's a B," but not too much weight can be placed on that—whatever else may be true, Galen had no inkling of the function of the quantifier.

Finally, in connection with the last sentence of the passage quoted above, it is tempting to infer that Galen reserves the phrase γενικὸν ἀξίωμα for the fully general axiom which articulates all inferences of this kind, leaving "universal axiom" (καθόλον ἀξίωμα) to cover the particular version of it necessary for the argument as it refers, say, to Socrates and Lamprocles, but such precision is in general foreign to Galen's style, in spite of his contrary protestations. It is reasonably clear that in the opening sentence of the next chapter (quoted above, p. 68), καθολικὸν ἀξίωμα means the same as γενικὸν ἀξίωμα does in this sentence. (One might even so postulate separate technical senses for καθόλον and καθολικὸν: that would certainly be *ben trovato* for me, but I am disinclined to place much weight on the suggestion.)

What should we conclude from this? To begin with, Galen's account is confusing and confused, and it is difficult to believe that all the confusion can be ascribed to a corrupt manuscript tradition. In particular, the argument of chapter seventeen is marred by corruptions, incompletenesses, and infelicities of phrasing, and our appreciation of its force is not aided by the clumsy punctuation adopted by Kieffer.[36] In spite of that, a reasonably clear general line of argument emerges, one which is bolstered by Galen's treatment of the relations 'more' and 'less', even in cases where the actual words "more" and "less" do not occur, but their force is conveyed by alternative comparative forms (*Inst. Log.* 16.12).[37] The examples he gives are similar in form; I quote the second only:

36. Particularly in *Institutio Logica* 17.3, where his text suggests that the whole of the following argument "What a man who tells the truth says is so; someone, e.g., Theon, says 'it is day'; Theon always tells the truth; therefore it is day" is supposed to be the "universal axiom (καθολικὸν ἀξίωμα) rather than merely the first proposition. Here again one might hold that the "axiom" is not expressed with sufficient generality, or perhaps rather (following the geometrical examples of *de Methodo Medendi* 10:34 ff., Kühn) that this axiom derives its force from a higher order axiom, namely "truth is a statement expressing existing things" (*Inst. Log.* 17.8). Cf. the Aristotelian definition offered at *Inst. Log.* 17.6: "all the Greeks say that he tells the truth who reveals things that are or were as they are or were, just as he tells a lie who says that things that are not are, or that things that are are not"; cf. Aristotle, *Met.* 4.7.1011b26f. Galen in fact says that, in order to exhibit the validity of an informal argument like "You say 'it is day'; but you are also telling the truth; therefore it is day" (*Inst. Log.* 17.2), you need to pull apart the concept of truth, and to substitute the real definition in place of the simple occurrence of the term. This procedure, Galen thinks, applies quite generally to science (see *de Methodo Medendi* 10:50, Kühn). When you want to spell out the articulation of an argument, to show why it is necessarily true, you do so by replacing the purely referential occurrences of names with definitions that explicate the structure of their referents.

37. Galen is always at pains to emphasize that attention to the mere verbal form of argument (indeed of propositions in general) is radically misleading—what matters is the real significance, not the surface structure, of what is said (see my "Usage and

[E] The good of the better is worthier of choice; soul is better than body; therefore [the good] of the soul is worthier of choice than that of the body. (*Inst. Log.* 16.13)

Galen does not explicitly state which axiom he takes to be operative here, but it is formally analogous to the examples of proportionality which he treats in chapter eighteen. These he takes to turn on the logic of the terms "similarly" and "likewise" (or whichever equivalent crops up in the expression of the proportion, *Inst. Log.* 18.1; here again Galen is studiedly indifferent to the actual terms used), which is expressed by the following general axiom which everyone understands and believes:

(Ax7) things which are in general in the same ratio are also in the same particular ratio (ibid. 18.6)

Galen goes on to give an example of what he means: "so he who posits that [F] the first is in the same relation to the second as the third to the fourth, and that the ratio of the first to the second is double, will not deny that the ratio of the third to the fourth is double" (ibid. 18.6). And of course this goes for any multiple you care to substitute. In the case of the more and the less, the axiom would presumably have to look *something* like

(Ax8) If there is some property P such that P belongs to both A and B, and A is more F than B, then the P of A will be more G than the P of B

That "axiom" is of course capable of being formulated with greater mathematical precision as follows:

(Ax8*) If there is some property P such that P belongs to both A and B, and A is more F than B to degree D, then the P of A will be more G than the P of B to degree D

where D can (at least in principle) be given a precise numerical value. The trouble with accepting (Ax8) as an axiom, however, is that it does not look as though it should immediately commend itself as being obviously and necessarily true for all substitution-instances of its variables; indeed, in its full generality, it is quite evidently false (what is needed is some specification of particular values for F and G, plus some further axiom relating them). What does link arguments [E] and [F] is that in each case what is concluded is concluded as being a particular instance of some general theorem. Because the general

Abusage: Galen on Language" in S. Everson, ed., *Ancient Philosophy of Language: A Philosophical Introduction*, forthcoming from Cambridge University Press.

theorem is, like the others we have been examining, multiply general, it can't be squeezed into the framework of categorical syllogistic as it is strictly construed. What is perhaps needed, instead of (Ax8*), is something like

> (Ax8**) If there is some good G such that G belongs to both A and B, and A is better than B to degree D, then the G of A will be more choiceworthy than the G of B to degree D[38]

and that in its turn presumably rests on some generality such as

> (Ax9) whatever is good is choiceworthy[39]

given a suitable comparative relational expansion.[40] The structure begins to look somewhat unwieldy; and no doubt it is. Part of the problem is that Galen does not explicitly distinguish between the purely formal validity (as we should see it) of a syllogism in Barbara, which relies for its validity (as opposed to soundness) purely on the logical relations of its syncategorematic terms, on the one hand, and the semantic interpretations necessary to ground the axiomatic truth of propositions like (Ax8**) or the axiom of the parental relation, on the other. However, as we saw above (n. 31), Galen probably did not believe that Barbara was in need of any articulating axiom, and if he did not, perhaps he did indeed have some inkling of the important distinctions at issue here.

Even if he did believe this, he lacks the means to distinguish between issues of syntax and those of semantics. And because he does not, perhaps cannot, produce an analysis of purely formal validity that would distinguish between these concepts, his method cannot attain to the generality of Frege's system of translation into function and argument. In this regard, perhaps it is Alexander—who at least sees that the "axioms" (at least the nonlogical ones) must be made part of the argument—who has a clearer logical sense than Galen. For all that, Galen's achievement is considerable: he recognizes the formal

38. That formalization is a little misleading, suggesting as it does that the good of A must be the same type of good as that of B—this is of course unnecessary.

39. Which is of course an ancient commonplace: see *Stoicorum Veterum Fragmenta* (cited in n. 6 above) 3:87–94; and Sextus Empiricus, *Outlines of Pyrrhonism*, 3.183 ff., and *Adversus Mathematicos* 11.114 ff.

40. The relational expansion itself will no doubt have the form of a theorem:
(T) whatever is more good is more choiceworthy
or perhaps better
(T*) If A is more good than B, then A is more choiceworthy than B
and that in turn rests on
(Ax.9*) If F and G are covariant, then if A is more F than B, A is more G than B
and so on.

isomorphisms that hold between apparently very different types of inference, and if his claim that "nearly all the syllogisms derive their construction (σύστασις) through the validity of the universal axioms that are set over them" (*Inst. Log.* 17.1: see above; and cf. 17.7) is to be taken seriously, then what he has seen is that it is incumbent upon the logician to give an account of the highest-level true meta-proposition in virtue of which some particular inference holds. Failure to do that will result in the piecemeal treatment of similar cases in a manner which disguises the fact that they are related, and hence radically mistakes their logical form. For this insight, logic and its history owe him thanks.[41]

41. I should like to record my thanks to the audience at The Catholic University of America, where this paper was originally read, for their acute comments; my gratitude to my colleague Ignazio Angelelli for reading an earlier draft and my appreciation for several points raised by Jonathan Barnes.

4　　Alexander on Aristotle's Species and Genera as Principles

ARTHUR MADIGAN, S.J.

Down the street from the house where I grew up there was a shoe repair shop. It was dark and noisy with the whir of machines and the shoemaker's hammering. The shoemaker hardly spoke English, and he seemed to be hard of hearing, and in any case he was shouting over the noise of his machines. The whole place had a distinctive odor, compounded of leather scraps, sweat, and machine oil. The shop seemed to be in perpetual disarray. And yet shoes got fixed in it!

This shoemaker's shop may serve as an image of Alexander of Aphrodisias's lecture hall around the year A.D. 200, and my hope is to bring the reader in spirit into that lecture hall, and into the mind of Alexander, as he tries to make sense of his master, Aristotle, and in particular as he interprets a series of arguments that Aristotle deploys on either side of the question of whether genera and species are the first principles of things. I refer to the sixth, seventh, and eighth aporiae of book three of the *Metaphysics,* and to the twenty-five arguments they contain.[1]

Most of us, I suppose, have seen films in which the plot was somewhat artificial, even contrived, and the real point of the film was to display other things. In this essay the question, What did Alexander think of the claims of species and genera to be principles? is like the plot, and I will certainly try to tie it up in the end. But in some ways the real interest is in watching Alexander work his way through the twists and turns of the plot, and in trying to determine what kind of Aristotelian he is.

Immediately we face a difficulty. It is commonly held, and correctly held, that the arguments of *Metaphysics* 3 are in large part dialectical, that is, that they proceed from premises that are plausible or agreed

---

1. All references to Alexander are to his *In Aristotelis Metaphysica Commentaria,* ed. M. Hayduck, *Commentaria in Aristotelem Graeca* (Berlin: Reimer, 1891).

upon, but not known to be true. And it is notorious that the arguments of *Metaphysics* 3 come to contradictory conclusions. So one might say, Why look here for Alexander's views on the status of genera and species as principles? My answer is, I want to turn the difficulty into an opportunity. When Alexander handles dialectical material, he tries, at times, to sort out the wheat from the chaff, the sound from the unsound. He does not always limit himself to explaining the arguments on their own terms and within their dialectical assumptions. On the contrary, he often gives signs of which assumptions he regards as merely dialectical, and which he regards as more than merely dialectical. To observe Alexander's handling of these largely dialectical arguments will show us something about his philosophical gut instincts.

The problem of aporia 6 (*Met.* 3.3.998a20–998b14) is, whether the elements or principles of things are the kinds (genera, species) which are predicated of the things, or, on the contrary, the constituents out of which the things are composed. Aristotle begins with four arguments in favor of taking constituents as principles.

Argument 1 (*Met.* 3.3.998a23–25) is from the instance of syllables. The principles of a syllable seem to be its constituent letters, not common sound or sound in general. Alexander (202.10–12) paraphrases this argument but adds nothing of significance beyond the fairly obvious point that by "common sound" Aristotle means the genus of sound.

Argument 2 (*Met.* 3.3.998a25–27) is from the demonstration of theorems. The more basic points which appear as constituents in the demonstration of more advanced points are spoken of as the elements. All Alexander adds (202.12–19) is a a slight clarification on the use of the term "elements" (στοιχεῖα).[2]

I bypass argument 3 for the moment and turn to number 4 (*Met.* 3.3.998a32–998b4). In Aristotle's text this is an argument that in general we know things by knowing their constituent parts; Aristotle's illustration is a bed. Alexander (202.25–32) takes the argument as an argument from the case of artifacts. He gives a fuller and to my mind a fairer statement of the case: we know artifacts when we know their parts and the manner in which the parts are put together (τρόπος τῆς συνθέσεως). It is this little addition that gives away Alexander's own position. Arguments 1, 2, and 4 do something to suggest that constituents are principles, but they certainly cannot be the *only* principles.

2. One might perhaps think that *diagrammata* are diagrams, but Alexander (202.13–14) takes them to be theorems, as does W. D. Ross, *Aristotle's "Metaphysics": A Revised Text with Introduction and Commentary* (Oxford: Clarendon, 1924), 1:234.

Even in artifacts there has to be a way of putting the parts together. Somewhat as the oracle in Heraclitus which does not say but points, Alexander is pointing to the formal cause without quite saying so.

Argument 3 (*Met.* 3.3.998a28–32) is an argument *ab hominibus* or from authority, specifically from the Presocratic natural philosophers. The monists understood the constituent of a thing to be its principle, while the pluralists understood the several constituents of a thing to be its principles. Alexander (202.19–25) does not comment on the argument in any major way; but any student familiar with *Metaphysics* 1, or, more to the point, with Alexander's commentary on *Metaphysics* 1, would know that Alexander regards the Presocratic naturalist account of principles as inadequate. Alexander has, then, quietly pointed to the inadequacy of the case for constituents as the principles of things. That is not, however, to say that he regards the case for kinds or genera to be any more conclusive.

Argument 7 (*Met.* 3.3.998b9–17) is another argument *ab hominibus*. The Platonists, says Aristotle, *spoke* of one and being and great-and-small as elements (στοιχεῖα) of things, but in their actual practice they treated these (not as elements but) as kinds or genera. Their authority as philosophers is a reason in favor of taking the principles to be kinds or genera. Aristotle speaks of "certain people" (τινες) as taking this view; Alexander (203.27–204.7) pins the reference down to Plato, and explains that Plato was impressed by the way that one and being are predicated of all particulars, while great and small are predicated of all particulars because they are in flux. Whatever we may think of the relations between *Metaphysics* 1 and *Metaphysics* 3, or of how much weight *Aristotle* assigns to this sort of argument, I think it is fairly clear that Alexander, living five hundred years later, assigns it little or no weight. He says that Aristotle uses it πρὸς τὸ εὐλόγως ἂν δόξαι, "so that it could seem reasonable" (203.27).

Arguments 5 and 6 move on a different level. Argument 5 (*Met.* 3.3.998b4–6) is that if we know things by way of their definitions, and if genera are the principles of these definitions, then it follows that genera are the principles of the things defined. Alexander (203.3–11) clarifies the argument in three ways. He notes the unstated assumption, that the principle of the knowledge of a thing is also the principle of the thing known, the thing itself. He alters the statement that the principle of definition is the genus, to the more nuanced statement that the principle of the definition is the grasp (λῆψις) of the genus. These two points may be taken as criticisms of the argument. But Alexander then defends the argument against an obvious objection (what about difference?) by pointing out that the word γένη can be taken in an inclusive sense, including differences. Alexander offers no further evaluation of the argument from definition.

Argument 6 (*Met.* 3.3.998b6–8) is also an argument from knowledge: we know things by way of their species (εἴδη); but kinds (γένη) are the principles of species; hence (Aristotle leaves the conclusion to be supplied) kinds are the principles of things. Alexander (203.14–23) supports the first premise by reference to the standard Aristotelian doctrine that there is no scientific knowledge of particulars. He then distinguishes on the term εἶδος, which I have thus far translated as "species": there is εἶδος as derived from γένος, or species as derived from genus; but there is also εἶδος as opposed to ὕλη, species/form as opposed to matter. It is εἴδη in this latter sense that are principles of things, not the εἴδη that are derived from genera; given this understanding of εἴδη, the argument back to genera as principles cannot get off the ground. Alexander is making a good point. But note that instead of fairly and squarely facing the issue about the implications of the universal character of knowledge, he transmutes the argument from *knowledge* that appears in Aristotle's text into a rather different argument based on facts about the very *being* of things.

Now to aporia 7 (*Met.* 3.3.998b14–999a23), arguments 8 through 14. Whatever the real or perceived merits of arguments 1 through 7, Aristotle proceeds as though aporia 6 has been settled in favor of kinds or genera as principles. The issue in aporia 7 is, *which* kinds are the principles: the highest and most universal, or the lowest kinds, those closest to particulars? Arguments 8, 9, and 10 are against the highest kinds, and so by implication in favor of the lowest kinds. Arguments 11, 12, and 13 then argue the positive case for the lowest kinds. Argument 14 stands by itself as an argument against the claims of the lowest kinds to be principles, and in favor of the highest kinds.

Argument 8 (*Met.* 3.4.998b17–28) is perhaps the most difficult argument of the lot. It takes up a mere eleven lines in Aristotle's text, but Alexander's explication of it occupies over two full pages of the *Commentaria in Aristotelem Graeca* (204.29–207.6). Let me first say what I think is going on in this argument, in the hope that this will make it easier to appreciate what is distinctive about Alexander's interpretation. As I read it, argument 8 is a *reductio ad absurdum* that went off the tracks: If we accept that the more universally something is predicated the more of a principle it is, then it follows that the primary or most universally predicated genera are principles. If that is so, then one and being are principles, because they are predicated of everything. But it is absurd for one and being to be principles, hence. . . . That would have been a straightforward *reductio*. But Aristotle, instead of saying that it was absurd for one and being to be *principles*, and telling why, decided to argue, with considerable ingenuity, that one and being are not *genera*. They are predicated of everything, but they are not genera. In fact, it is *because* they are predicated of everything that they are not genera. How so? Because they are predicated of everything, they are predicated even of their own differences; every difference is one and a being. But—here is the ingenious part, backed up by Aristotle's doctrine in *Topics* 6.6.144a36–144b3—no genus is ever predicated of its own differences. So, if we find that something is predicated of its differences, the way being or unity is predicated of its differences, we know that it is not a genuine genus. The victory is Pyrrhic: if this part of the argument succeeds, and being and unity are *not* genera or kinds, then nothing Aristotle can show about being and unity will count against the claims of genuine genera or kinds to be principles, and so the overall argument against kinds or genera as principles will fail. As I suggested above, the *reductio* is derailed.

But what does Alexander say? First and perhaps foremost, he does his level best to explain Aristotle's argument, in particular the case against one and being as genera, and the key premise, that a genus is not predicated of its own differences. Alexander makes three points in defense of this premise. First (205.10–21), genera are not predicated of their differences because differences cut across genera; they serve to divide, to specify, in more than one genus; so they are predicated more widely than a given genus; but a term of lesser extension (here the genus) is not predicated of a term with greater extension (here the difference). Second (205.21–28), in face of the obvious objection that we do say things like "the rational is an animal" and "the rational is a substance," Alexander replies that in such cases we are not really predicating the genus or kind of the difference as such, but rather of the composite being of which the difference forms a part. Third (205.28–206.6), Alexander points out that differences, even the differences of substance, are not substances, οὐσίαι, but qualities, ποιότητες; they are differences *of* substance, but they are not substances; the genus substance is not predicated of them.

Alexander has bent over backwards; he has given this text the Roman imperial equivalent of the old college try. Then, at 206.12, without warning, Alexander begins a devastating critique, saying that the argument is rather verbal, like most of Aristotle's arguments (λογικωτέρα ... ὥσπερ ... αἱ πλεῖσται). Against the thesis that genera are not predicated of differences, Alexander insists that whatever genus a difference may be in, it has to have that genus predicated of it. He thinks that the differences of substances are in the genus of substance, and have it predicated of them. Even if we say that differences are qualities, not substances, they still have that genus, quality, predicated of them. The attempt to evade this obvious truth is, he says, artificial and absurd (πλασματῶδές τε καὶ ἄτοπον; 206.21–22). And against the claim that differences cut across different genera, and so are predicated more widely than genera, Alexander says (207.1–4) that this is a misleading impression due to homonymy; if we consider not the bare word but what is meant, we will not say that the same difference is found in different genera. This passage is typical of Alexander at his best: first strive to make sense of the Master's text; but if it does not make sense, say so.

Argument 9 (*Met.* 3.3.998b28–30) is a *reductio.* If we suppose that all kinds higher than the lowest kinds are principles, that means asserting that all intermediates are principles. But that is absurd on two counts: the outrageous multiplicity of principles that would result, and the recognized opinion that some intermediate kinds are principles, but others are not. Alexander's exposition occupies 207.9–29. He astutely points out that this aporia deals not only with the issue of higher or primary genera as principles but with the more basic issue of whether any genera are principles (207.9–10). An interesting point in Alexander's exposition is his reference (207.18–20) to Aristotle's book on animals—apparently the reference is to *Parts of Animals* 1.3, on the inadequacy of privative differences to determine species—to confirm Aristotle's position. My impression is that when Alexander cites other works of Aristotle, it is in confirmation of at least the directly relevant part of the argument.

Argument 10 (*Met.* 3.3.998b30–999a1) is a similar *reductio.* The position that intermediate kinds are principles means that differences have a stronger claim to be principles than do kinds. But for differences to be principles would make the number of principles practically infinite, which is absurd. Alexander (207.29–208.3) explains Aristotle's claim that differences would have a stronger claim to be principles than species would, on the ground that differences are predicated more widely than species. But this is close to the position that Alexander took in his explanation of argument 8, then rejected in his critique of argument 8; and in fact he argues against it, holding that difference is not predicated of species essentially (ἐν τῷ τί ἐστιν; 208.2), or in the way that genera *are* predicated of their species. It is pretty clear that Alexander regards argument 10 as inconclusive.

Now to the three positive arguments for taking lowest kinds as principles. Argument 11 (*Met.* 3.3.999a1–6) is that unity, in the sense of indivisibility, is characteristic of principles, and that lowest kinds possess this indivisibility in a way that higher kinds, divisible into species, do not. Alexander (208.5–25) does not add much to what Aristotle says, nor does he offer an overall evaluation of the argument. He does remark that Aristotle presents the argument as ἔξωθεν (208.18), which I take to mean, something from outside Aristotle's own position, based on assumptions different from his own.[3]

Argument 12 (*Met.* 3.3.999a6–13) is an argument *a fortiori* and *ad hominem*. It is really another argument against highest kinds, in this case, against their very existence. It is admitted (by whom is not said) that in cases of prior and posterior, e.g., 1, 2, 3, or triangle, square, pentagon, there is no higher kind: there is no number that is not one of the numbers, no figure that is not some figure or other. But if there is no higher kind in these cases, there can hardly be a higher kind in other cases. Alexander's exposition fills 208.28–209.34. He extends the argument from the cases of number and figure mentioned by Aristotle to the Platonic one and being and great-and-small, and says that the Platonists recognized these as cases of priority and posteriority, and did not posit any further Forms of them. He says, on the strength of *Nicomachean Ethics* 1.6.1094a17ff., that Platonists did not recognize Ideas of things which had prior and posterior. My impression is that a Platonist might well have said that there were no further Forms or Ideas of one and being, and great-and-small, because these were themselves ultimate principles, and that this would have been a natural part of a Platonist strategy to head off an infinite regress in principles. But Alexander does not seem to see any difficulty with the reasoning. When he cites the conclusion of *this* argument at 211.12–17, in his discussion of argument 16, he gives no sign that he finds it anything less than probative. Higher kinds do not really exist, so there is no question of their being principles; so if kinds are principles at all, it must be the lowest kinds.

Argument 13 (*Met.* 3.3.999a13–14) is just an extension of argument 12: wherever there is better and worse, there is prior and posterior, and so the impossibility of separate higher kinds applies, as claimed in argument 12. Alexander's interpretation (209.34–210.3) goes beyond Aristotle's text here, in claiming that all genera involve better and worse. Alexander cites *Categories* 12.14b4, to confirm the point that better/worse is a species of prior/posterior. Alexander then criti-

---

3. The whole argument, or just part of it? Alexander presents a rank ordering in terms of indivisibility: undivided in kind or form, undivided in quantity, divided in quantity. Perhaps it is just this rank ordering which is considered to come from outside Aristotle's position, not the more basic assumption that principles have to possess unity in the sense of indivisibility. But there is a textual problem in the statement of the rank ordering (208.17), and I hesitate to base anything on the passage.

cizes the argument for exploiting the homonymy of the term "prior" (πρῶτον): Aristotle has abused (συνεχρήσατο; 210.3) this homonymy. Alexander regards the argument as tainted and without probative value, even though he almost certainly agrees with the conclusion.

In argument 14 (*Met.* 3.3.999a17–23), at long last, the higher kinds have their day in court. A principle ought to be independent of that whose principle it is. But the fact that something is predicated of a plurality of particulars tends to show that it is independent of them; predicability argues independence. But the higher or more universal a kind, the more widely it is predicated. Alexander (210.12–20) takes this not only as an argument against particulars as principles, but also against lowest kinds as principles; that is hardly explicit in Aristotle. Of course a principle has to be capable of existing separately from that whose principle it is; but then separate existence is particular existence, being καθ᾽ ἕκαστον (that is not at all explicit in Aristotle's text). Having interpreted Aristotle along these lines, Alexander then stigmatizes the argument as relying on plausibility and verbal confusion (πάνυ κατὰ τὸ ἔνδοξον καὶ λογικῶς; 210.20–21). It is difficult to be sure how much of the argument Alexander is condemning, but the obvious target is the premise that predicability shows independence. Alexander interprets Aristotle's rhetorical question (on what other grounds would one suppose . . .?) as asserting that predicability is the only possible reason for positing non-particulars; if predicability is not a ground for positing non-particulars, then there is no ground for positing them.

Now to aporia 8 (*Met.* 3.4.999a24–999b24), arguments 15 through 25. The issue of aporia 8 is whether there exists anything besides particulars. Although Aristotle does not say so in so many words, he writes as though aporia 7 has led to the conclusion that kinds (kinds above the level of lowest species) not only are not principles but also do not even exist. In such a context the question, is there anything besides particulars? is a natural one. Aristotle first offers an argument for non-particulars, then two arguments against non-particulars, then five more arguments for non-particulars, then three more arguments against non-particulars, for a total of eleven arguments in all. I will depart somewhat from Aristotle's order so as to group similar arguments together.

Argument 15 (*Met.* 3.4.999a26–29), the first argument for non-particulars, is an argument from the requirements of knowledge, or more specifically, from the impossibility of knowing an indefinite number of particulars without a one that is distinct from them. Knowledge of a multiplicity requires a unity. It is a familiar Platonic move. Alexander (210.35–211.5) paraphrases the argument but does not evaluate it.

Akin to argument 15 is number 18 (*Met.* 3.4.999b1–4), the second argument for non-particulars. It is also an argument from knowledge, but in this case from the need of an intelligible, rather than a sensible, object. Particulars are sensible, not intelligible; if all that exists is sensible, then knowledge is reduced to sensation, which is absurd. Again Alexander's treatment is brief, and certainly not adverse.[4] Certainly he and Aristotle would agree that knowledge is not to be reduced to sensation.

Argument 16 (*Met.* 3.4.999a29–32), against non-particulars, is framed as a reply to the argument from the requirements of knowledge. The argument from knowledge would imply the independent existence of kinds, which has already been shown to be absurd. The reference appears to be to arguments 12 and 14 above. Alexander's commentary (211.5–17) consists mainly of references to these arguments, and this suggests that, whatever Aristotle may have thought, Alexander thinks that arguments 12 and 14 are conclusive against the separate existence of kinds. Aristotle says, "we have concluded from our aporia [διηπορήσαμεν]" (*Met.* 3.4.999a32). Alexander's δοκεῖ δεδεῖχθαι, "it appears to have been proven" (211.13) seems to me to upgrade the level of certainty. As with arguments 6, 15, and 18, Alexander's commentary never quite comes to terms with the argument from knowledge as such. Even if the conclusions of arguments 12 and 14 are certain, so that there is something wrong with the argument from knowledge to the existence of non-particulars, what precisely is wrong with argument 15 or with argument 18? Where is the flaw *in* these arguments?

Argument 17 (*Met.* 3.4.999a32–999b1) is not strictly an argument, but rather a rhetorical question meant to embarrass: suppose that there exist non-particulars, in which cases do they exist? The suggestion is that there is no acceptable answer to the question, and that hence the supposition of non-particulars should be rejected. To posit non-particulars corresponding to every particular seems extravagant; but to posit non-particulars for some particulars but not for others seems arbitrary. To denote particulars Aristotle uses the term σύνολον, "composite," and explains this as a case of something's being predicated of matter. Alexander (211.20–212.2) translates this talk of matter and predication into the more obviously physical language of matter-form composition. Alexander does not raise any objection to

---

4. Given that Alexander *is* critical of the next argument for non-particulars, 19, I take it that the absence of criticism of 18 indicates at least a measure of agreement.

this argument, or rhetorical question, but he does seem to me to leave a loose end, the looseness of which he surely recognized. I refer to the ambiguity of εἶδος: the εἶδος which combines with matter to form a composite is not the same as the εἶδος which is common (211.33) and universal (211.31). Alexander exposed that very ambiguity apropos of argument 6, but he does not comment on it here.

Argument 19 (*Met.* 3.4.999b4–5) is a *reductio*: if everything is particular, then there is no eternal unmoved object, which is absurd. The argument explicitly assumes that all sensibles are perishable. Implicitly, it assumes, as did 18, that all particulars are sensible. Thus the argument is a bit of a tease. Aristotle himself seems to have posited a number of eternal sensibles, the heavenly bodies, and at least one eternal and unmoved non-sensible entity; and Alexander was surely aware of this. Alexander (212.10–20) interprets the argument as Platonic, in the sense of identifying motion with total flux, and remarks that the argument assumes that all sensibles are generated and perishable. Alexander clearly regards the argument as dialectical in the sense of having a premise or assumption which was accepted by someone noteworthy, but this premise or assumption is now clearly recognized as mistaken. The passage illustrates a significant difference between Aristotle's conception of a dialectical argument and Alexander's. For Aristotle, if I understand correctly, the premises of a dialectical argument are regarded as at least plausible, even if only on the strength of authority. But when Alexander, five centuries later, comes to interpret Aristotelian dialectical arguments, he does so with the awareness, gained from the rest of Aristotle's work, that certain premises are false. Thus he can echo Aristotle and speak of a premise as ἔνδοξον while at the same time considering the falsity of the premise to be manifest. In Alexander, a dialectical argument is basically an argument with at least one false premise, and the Aristotelian distinction between dialectical argument and contentious argument seems to disappear.

Arguments 20, 21, and 22 form a set. They all argue for the existence of non-particulars (actually it is a bit more complicated than that: the general line of argument is that coming to be requires something eternal, and the assumption is, as in 18 and 19, that this must be non-particular, for all particulars are perishable), and they all argue from the conditions of possibility for things to come to be. They are all in that sense "physical" arguments.

Argument 20 (*Met.* 3.4.999b5–8) makes the case that something eternal is required as that-from-which coming to be occurs; otherwise, there would be an infinite regress. Alexander's exposition occupies a full page of the *Commentaria in Aristotelem Graeca* (212.20–213.23). Without something that does *not* come to be, nothing would come to be. Alexander interprets the text as an argument for the eternal reality of primary matter: without it we have either an unacceptable infinite regress in matters or else an unacceptable coming to be out of nothing. The way in which Alexander guides the argument, by way of the universal agreement of the natural philosophers and the unacceptability of an infinite regress (cf. *Met.* 2.2), to a manifestly Aristotelian conclusion, suggests to me that he endorses it without reserve.

Argument 21 (*Met.* 3.4.999b8–12) makes the case that something eternal is required as the limit or *terminus ad quem* of coming to be and motion. Alexander (213.26–214.18) seems to accept this argument without reserve. He explains it in terms of the very notion of a motion, κίνησις, then illustrates this by way of the types of motion, increase and alteration, and finally extends the analysis to becoming in the strict sense, γένεσις. Alexander reads the argument as one based on Aristotelian physics, and as such conclusive. (Note his vocabulary: ἐν ἄλλοις δέδεικται, 213.33; and καὶ τοῦτα δέδεικται, 214.1.)

Argument 22 (*Met.* 3.4.999b12–16) is an argument *a fortiori* based on the conclusion of 20. If matter exists, as 20 appears to have shown, then it is all the more reasonable for something else to exist. This something else is characterized in four different ways in Aristotle's text: οὐσία ("substance" or "essence"), something besides the composite or particular, μορφή ("shape"), and εἶδος ("form" or "species"). Alexander corrects Aristotle's imprecise expression ("if neither matter nor form is eternal, then there will be nothing at all"; *Met.* 3.4.999b14–15) to "if they, matter and form, are not both eternal, then nothing at all could come to be" (215.6–7). As Alexander reads it, this is an argument to show that the εἶδος which comes to be in matter must itself be eternal, an eternal unitary substance (μοναδική, "unitary," is Alexander's term, not Aristotle's; 214.29). Alexander reads the argument in terms of the hylomorphic framework, and one might expect him to endorse it without qualification. Instead, he makes a point of adding a significant qualification: Aristotle is right to hold that there must be an eternal εἶδος, eternal as matter is, but this does not have to be the εἶδος that comes to be in matter. On the contrary, the εἶδος that preexists is productive εἶδος (the εἶδος of the parent or agent or efficient cause), and this is like (ὅμοιον; 215.18) the εἶδος which is produced. Thus, in four lines (215.15–18) Alexander undercuts the whole of argument 22—not because he disagrees with any of its premises, but because the argument does not conclude to *non-particular* form. There is always form, yes; but this form is particular. If I get it right, Alexander affirms the eternity of εἶδος in the sense of an eternal succession of particular εἶδος, *not* in the sense of a single eternal unitary non-particular substance.

Argument 23 (*Met.* 3.4.999b17–20) is an embarrassing question, very much like 17. Suppose that there are some non-particulars (suppose that arguments 20, 21, 22 have established that there are some non-particulars); in which cases are there such non-particulars? This is, as Alexander (215.18–29) sees, very close to the move in 17. Alexander specifies the issue as the *pre*existence (προϋπάρχειν; 215.23 and 24) of μορφή or εἶδος. He notes that the argument can be taken as directed against the Platonic Ideas. If I get it right, Alexander thinks that the embarrassing question is a perfectly fair question if directed against the Platonic doctrine of Ideas, but that one can (and should) be committed to Aristotelian enmattered form (ἔνυλον εἶδος), without any commitment to Platonic Ideas or (I take it) to non-particulars.

Argument 24 (*Met.* 3.4.999b20–23) is a dilemma directed against non-particulars. Suppose that there is some non-particular οὐσία corresponding to particular human beings. Then either (*a*) it is one and the same οὐσία for all human beings, so that all are reduced to one human bieng, or (*b*) there are many different οὐσίαι for human beings. The tricky point here is to say why (*b*), the second horn of the dilemma, is unacceptable.[5] Alexander's move (215.32–216.3) is to say that the whole argument assumes a *pre*existent form or οὐσία. In the light of that assumption, the absurdity of (*b*) is easy to understand. Given the doctrine that matter is the ground of differentiation, a plurality of preexistent forms is unintelligible because preexistent forms are without matter.[6] By focusing the argument on preexistent form Alexander has in effect defused 24 as an argument against Aristotelian enmattered form, for that is not preexistent.

Argument 25 (*Met.* 3.4.999b23–24) is another embarrassing question, really two questions, directed at arguments 20, 21, 22: how does matter *become* each of these substances? and how *is* the composite both substance and matter? Some teachers might have replied "Read the *Physics!*" and "Read the *Metaphysics!*" Alexander's answer is more subtle, and it reads as a complement to his remarks on 22 and 23. The problems are only acute, the questions are only embarrassing, on the false assumption that the form which joins with matter exists prior to

---

5. This is especially tricky for Alexander, if I am correct in thinking that (*b*), in its straightforward sense, is a claim he accepts.

6. I hope some day to test the hypothesis that reflection on Alexander's treatment of this Aristotelian argument was one of the things that led Plotinus to his own rather different view of individuation.

the matter (προϋπάρχοντα εἴδη; 216.4); that is what makes the problem difficult or insoluble, and talk about σύνθεσις, κρᾶσις, μῖξις does not get you anywhere. There is no problem about the composition of matter and form as such, only about the composition of matter and preexistent form.

How has the story come out? What did Alexander think about the claims of species and genera, or anything else, to be the principle or principles of things? First, Alexander gives no sign of believing that the material parts of a thing are its principles. He gives signs that these are certainly not all the principles of a thing. And he indicates that the ultimate underlying matter of a thing is one of its principles. Second, Alexander gives no sign of believing that genera are principles. He appears to reject every argument advanced to show that genera are principles. But he gives clear signs of believing that species, that is, *infima species*, is in some sense a principle. Third, in what sense is *infima species* a principle? Certainly not as a predicate or a universal, even a universal of lowest degree. The species that is a principle is rather the species that goes together with matter to account for the being of the thing whose species it is. But it is also the species of the parent or agent responsible for the coming to be of the composite thing. Thus species as principle is twofold: species as antecedent to a given thing, but present in the parent; species as present in the thing itself, organizing its matter. Finally, Alexander believes that in both these senses the species which is a principle is individual. In terms of the contemporary debate, Alexander holds for individual form as opposed to universal form.

If that is how the story has come out, what else have we learned along the way? At least this, that Alexander tries to make Aristotle's arguments work out right, but that when he cannot do so, he lets us know. We have learned that he regards a number of the arguments that we have seen as dialectical arguments, in a pejorative sense of "dialectical." Further, we have learned that he treats different types of arguments in different ways. It will be easier to see this if we review the arguments in terms of seven rough and ready categories.

1. Arguments based on commonsense beliefs (arguments 1, 2, 4). Alexander regards these as indecisive, and indeed as light-weight.

2. *Ab homine* and *ad hominem* arguments (3, 7, 12, 13). This category is a mixed bag. Alexander does not regard any and every appeal to Presocratic natural philosophy as probative—the Presocratics may have thought that the principles of things were their constituent parts, but that is not enough—but he does regard the common affirmation

of Presocratic naturalism that nothing comes from nothing as assured. Perhaps here an appeal to basic self-evidence is presented as an appeal to the naturalists. I am not entirely certain how Alexander takes the *ad hominem* arguments against the Platonists. He sometimes notes that a given argument can be taken *ad hominem,* even if it is intelligible without the *ad hominem* aspect.

3. Arguments based on philosophical theses which Alexander takes to be Aristotelian and true (9, 10, 11, 16, 19, 24). This somewhat elastic category is also a mixed bag, as the theses in question are rather diverse, and Alexander's handling of them is correspondingly mixed.

4. "Unresolved question" or "embarrassing question" arguments (17, 23, 25). These questions are used in response to arguments *for* a given position. The suggestion is that the position raises a question, and that the position is not securely established until the question is answered satisfactorily, and not arbitrarily. I take it that Alexander already has, and his students already have, a fairly clear idea of which questions can be answered satisfactorily and which cannot.

5. "Logical" arguments, that is, arguments based on facts about predication, about what is predicated of what (8, 14). These arguments tend to count in favor of genera and species as principles, but Alexander views them as lacking in probative value.

6. "Physical" arguments, that is, arguments based on the necessary conditions of coming-to-be (20, 21, 22). These arguments tend to count in favor of the reality of species (but not of genera), and in favor of species as principles of the things whose species they are. But Alexander insists that the species in question is a productive cause rather than a universal predicate.

7. "Epistemic" arguments, that is, arguments based on the necessary conditions of knowledge and of definition (5, 6, 15, 18). These arguments tend to count in favor of species and genera as principles, and precisely in favor of species and genera understood as universal— in contrast to the unintelligibility of the particular as such—and as providing the ground for the definability and knowability of a plurality of particulars. In Platonic terms, these are one-over-many arguments. The most distinctive feature of Alexander's treatment is that he neither accepts the epistemic arguments as conclusive nor identifies the false premises or fallacies which mgiht render them inconclusive. Thus, while Alexander regards species—the species form in the parent and the species form that combines with matter to make up a thing—as the principle of the being, or more strictly, of the becoming, of things, he is not at all clear about the principle of things' definability

and knowability. This is the great unresolved question in the commentary on aporiae 6 through 8.[7]

Students of *Metaphysics* 7 are familiar with the representation of Aristotle's problem in terms of an inconsistent triad of propositions: (a) What is real is individual, (b) What is knowable is universal, and (c) The knowable is the real. If we ask how Alexander would resolve this triad, indications are that he would be strongly attached to proposition (a). But it is not clear from his commentary on aporiae 6–8 how he would choose between (b) and (c), or how he would avoid such a choice. He seems not to have faced the problem.

Suppose, then, that Alexander fails to integrate considerations of definability and knowability into his view of the principles.[8] Is it possible to say why? I offer a speculation. There is an old problem about how to reconcile the affirmation in the *Categories* that the concrete individual is primary substance, the species and genera secondary substances, with the affirmation in the *Metaphysics* that form is substance while the composite is something posterior. Some admit a contradiction between these two positions and postulate a development from one to the other. We are familiar with attempts to reconcile the two, such as the position of Joseph Owens that both theses are true: the thesis of the *Categories* is true in the realm of logic, and the thesis of the *Metaphysics* is true in the realm of being.[9] Alexander exemplifies a different approach. For him the *Categories* and the *Metaphysics* are saying the same thing, but it is the position of the *Categories*—I would call it the individualism of the *Categories*—that controls the reading of the *Metaphysics*. Starting from the individualism of the *Categories*, Alexander is not impressed by the arguments from predication. He has no great difficulty fitting the "physical" arguments into the individu-

---

7. That it remains unresolved in the rest of the commentary on *Metaphysics* 3 is suggested by Alexander's handling of the final *aporia* in the book. That *aporia* (*Met.* 3.6.1003a5–17) presents an antithesis between the requirements of being, which favor the particular over the universal, and the requirements of knowledge, which favor the universal over the particular. Alexander (235.32–236.25) does not settle the *aporia*, and if the concluding remarks of the commentary (236.26–29) apply to this aporia, he dismisses it as dialectical, resting on merely plausible premises, employing merely verbal arguments. I myself regard this *aporia*, or perhaps better, antinomy, as summarizing the key issues of *aporiae* 6–8, and as setting out the fundamental problem of *Metaphysics* 7.

8. This judgment might well be different if we had at our disposal Alexander's commentary on *Metaphysics* 7, or if we could be sure of disengaging the genuine Alexander from the commentary on *Metaphysics* 7 circulated under his name but now widely regarded as the work of someone else.

9. Joseph Owens, "Aristotle on Categories," *Review of Metaphysics* 14 (1960–61): 73–90.

alist framework. But he does not manage to fit the "epistemic" arguments into the individualist framework, and the reason is that they do not fit.[10] If I read Alexander correctly, the fact that the "epistemic" arguments do not fit into the individualism of the *Categories* leads Alexander to neglect those arguments rather than to reconsider his individualism.

Pierre Aubenque, in his discussion of different types of aporiae that occur in Aristotle, distinguishes between aporiae that are solved with relative ease and aporiae that give rise to further aporiae, and between these and aporiae that seem insoluble, that stem from something fundamentally mysterious in the nature of being.[11] Perhaps the aporia about how to reconcile the individuality that seems to be the mark of genuine being with the universality that seems required for knowledge and definition is of this latter type. If it is, Alexander seems, for all his subtlety, to have missed the mystery. But if this is a demerit, he still has many merits. And the present survey has at least opened another window on one Aristotelian of late antiquity and how he read his master.[12]

10. As I see it, a heightened sensitivity to the requirements of knowledge and definition was a major factor in Aristotle's shift away from the individualist metaphysics of the *Categories*; but this is not the place to argue that claim.

11. Pierre Aubenque, "Sur la notion aristotélicienne d'aporie," in *Aristote et les problèmes de méthode* (Louvain: Publications Universitaires; Paris: Béatrice Nauwelaerts, 1961), 14–19, especially 16–17.

12. It is a pleasure to thank Dean Jude P. Dougherty of the School of Philosophy of the Catholic University of America, whose kind invitation to speak in the series on Aristotle in Late Antiquity occasioned the writing of this paper, and Professor Lawrence P. Schrenk, gracious host, meticulous and understanding editor.

5   Proof and Discovery in Aristotle and the Later Greek Tradition: A Prolegomenon to a Study of Analysis and Synthesis

LAWRENCE P. SCHRENK

I. INTRODUCTION

In discussing the notions of discovery and proof, we shall explore the relationship in ancient philosophical and scientific thought between the process by which one comes to discover a scientific or philosophical theory and the process by which one subsequently demonstrates the same. Our journey shall be chronological, commencing with the classical precedences and concluding with select late Greek discussions of discovery and proof. Since the entirety of such a topic is certainly too vast for the narrow constraints of this study, we shall elucidate this relationship by focusing on the history and development of the techniques of analysis and synthesis as they are developed in the ancient, and especially the Aristotelian, tradition.[1] This is, one might say, a *prolegomenon* to the study of proof and discovery in later antiquity.

But such a study must also be placed within the wider context of what are termed the four "dialectical methods: division (διαίρεσις), definition (ὁρισμός), demonstration (ἀπόδειξις), and analysis (ἀνάλυσις). Such dialectical methods permeate the methodology of many of the late Greek philosophical sects, yet are neglected in modern studies of that period. After considering the specific nature of analysis (and the corresponding synthesis), we shall in a somewhat more general way look at the systematic account of all four dialectic methods. That is to say we shall examine the philosophy of science espoused by

---

1. While there are numerous modern analyses of mathematical analysis and synthesis, only two studies have significantly addressed the development of these techniques in later antiquity, and to both my research is greatly indebted: Norman Gulley, "Greek Geometrical Analysis," *Phronesis* 33 (1958): 1–14 and Jaakko Hintikka and Unto Remes, *The Method of Analysis: Its Geometrical Origin and Its General Significance,* Boston Studies in the Philosophy of Science, vol. 25 (Dordrecht: Reidel 1974).

the commentators and place it within the development of the Aristotelian (and also Platonic) tradition.

Finally, one must note that interest in analysis and synthesis is by
no means restricted to the ancient period. Al-Farabi, Galileo, Hobbes,
Newton are just some of the later philosophers who use or comment
on these two methods. In part, this research will lay the necessary
groundwork for others to continue the study of these techniques into
later philosophical periods.

II. THE NATURE OF ANCIENT DISCOVERY AND PROOF

The distinction between the research or discovery and the proof or
exposition of knowledge is clearly manifest in ancient thought. Cicero,
Quintilian, and Boethius all call for a rational method of discovery,
an *ars inveniendi*.[2] In the later Aristotelian tradition such an explicit
and conscious method is even attributed to Aristotle.[3] While several
ancient authors remark on this distinction, the most startling occurrence is found in Greek mathematics.

A. Discovery in Ancient Mathematics

For many centuries the modern world, in spite of hundreds of extant proofs, knew little of Greek methods of discovery in mathematics,
but in 1906 a remarkable treatise came to light: Archimedes' *The
Method of Treating Mechanical Problems*, addressed to a certain Eratosthenes.[4] While we possess, of course, numerous texts by this ancient
master each containing a wide variety of mathematical proofs, this
new work was remarkable for describing not additional proofs, but
rather his method of discovering such proofs. The distinction between
these two processes is quite clear, for in *The Method* Archimedes not
only differentiates discovery and proof in general, but he also sharply
distinguishes those mathematical tools which are valid for proof or
demonstration from those which are only legitimate (or useful) for

---

2. Cicero, *Topica* 6, *De oratore* 2.157–59; *De finibus* 4.10; Boethius, *In Cic. top.* 1045A.
I take these references as well as those in the next note from Frede's introduction to
Richard Walzer and Michael Frede, trans., *Galen: Three Treatises on the Nature of Science*
(Indianapolis: Hackett 1985), xxxiii–xxxiv.

3. Diogenes Laertius, 5.28–29. Cf. also Alexander of Aphrodisias, *In An. Pr.* 1.7–8.

4. On the *Method*, see Eduard Jan Dijksterhuis, *Archimedes,* trans. C. Dikshoorn (Co-
penhagen: Meelesgaard 1956); G. Giorello, "Archimede e la metodologia dei pro-
grammi di ricerca," *Scientia* 110 (1975): 111–35; and E. Ruffini, *Il "Method" di Archimede
e le origini del calcolo infintesimale nel' antichita,* 2nd ed. (Milan: 1961). The text (with
French translation) can be found in Charles Mugler, ed., *Archimède,* vol. 3 (Paris: Bude
1971), 82–127.

the discovery of a theorem. In his opening address to Eratosthenes, Archimedes states:

> The proofs then of these theorems I have written in this book and now send to you. Seeing moreover in you, as I say, an earnest student, a man of considerable eminence in philosophy, and an admirer [of mathematical inquiry], I thought fit to write out for you and explain in detail in the same book the peculiarity of a certain method, by which it will be possible for you to get a start to enable you to investigate some of the problems in mathematics by means of mechanics. *This procedure is, I am persuaded, no less useful even for the proof of the theorems themselves; for certain things first become clear to me by a mechanical method, although they had to be demonstrated [ἀπεδείχϑη] by geometry afterwards because their investigation by the said method did not furnish an actual demonstration.*[5]

For Archimedes, certain techniques were useful for the rational discovery of theorems, but were not sanctioned for use in strict demonstrations. We might as a simple example apply the technique of *The Method* to the question of the area of a circle. What *The Method* proposes is an ancient thought experiment. We might imagine the circle to be made up of many narrow rectangles—but this, of course, would only yield varying approximations of the area of the circle. Suppose that we imagined that the circle was not made of merely *many* narrow rectangles, but rather of an *infinite* number of them—this would appear to yield the correct formula for the area of the circle. Indeed, in modern calculus such a proof is common. Such a method could not be made rigorous within the confines of ancient mathematics, for it required that we postulate infinitesimals, that is lines that are not infinitely long but rather infinitely short. What *The Method* proposed is that the end of each rectangle was conceived of as an infinitesimal in length. This was not rigorous by the lights of ancient mathematicians, for the infinitesimal was not valid for actual demonstration. The restriction did not, however, bar the use of this "mechanical" method in discovery. The first formula which is *discovered* in *The Method* is in turn *demonstrated* through legitimate means in the *Quadrature of the Parabola*. Archimedes gives us not only a precedent for distinguishing discovery and proof, but also a precedent for invoking quite different methodologies to be used in each process.

B. Analysis and Synthesis

Now let us turn to the question of analysis and synthesis. "Analysis" (ἀνάλυσις) is a "taking apart" or better in our context a "resolution"

---

5. *Method* 569–70 (emphasis mine), T. L. Heath, trans., *The Works of Archimedes*, vol. 2 (New York: Dover 1950).

or "reduction." "Synthesis" (σύνθεσις) is a "putting together," a "combination" or a "composition." Both of these procedures originate in the mathematical tradition. Here analysis involved taking an assumption and following its implications until one reached something either known to be true or known to be false. Though it was not in itself a proof, analysis showed how a proof might be constructed. When this had been accomplished, the line of implication was reversed (or, more technically, "converted") so that we might now show our original assumption to be either true or false depending on whether we had reached a true or false conclusion in our analysis. While these techniques are (relatively) clear in their mathematical context, the difficulty is to determine how these fundamentally mathematical procedures are to be understood in their philosophical application.

The most detailed classification of analysis is found in the Middle Platonic text, the *Didaskilikos,* which distinguishes three types of analysis: (1) that which is an ascent to the first intelligibles [ἐπὶ τὰ πρῶτα νοητά] from perceptibles [τῶν αἰσθητῶν], (2) that which is an ascent through proofs and demonstrations to those premises which are indemonstrable and immediate [ἐπὶ τὰς ἀναποδείκτους καὶ ἀμέσους προτάσεις], and (3) that which is an ascent proceeding from hypothesis [ἐξ ὑποθέσεως] to unhypothetical principles [ἐπὶ τὰς ἀνυποθέτους ἀρχάς]."[6] In spite of the differentiation of analysis into three types, its common character is visible. It is described in each instance as an ascent (ἄνοδος).[7] Further, the application of each method results in a proposition which is not within the scope of that method itself. Perceptual analysis yields a nonperceptual result; demonstrative analysis a nondemonstrable result; hypothetical analysis a nonhypothetical result.[8]

As an example let us look at an application of perceptual analysis deriving ultimately from the *Symposium* where we find the repeated application of abstraction to our perceptions: "from the beauty of bodies we could proceed to the beauty in souls, and from this to that in ways of living, then from this to that in laws, then to the great sea of beauty, so that proceeding in this way we might find in the end beauty itself."[9] In this method we begin with the beauty which is in bodies and, after several steps, approach beauty itself, i.e., the Idea of beauty.[10] In summary, each type of analysis is process of ascent

6. *Did.* 5.4. Unless otherwise noted, all translations are my own.
7. Cf. also *Did.* 5.1.4.
8. The adjective "nonhypothetical" must here be understood as meaning "not subject to hypothetical analysis," not as "real."
9. *Did.* 5.5.1–5.
10. *Did.* 5.5.1–5.

from facts about the world to a higher principle which is in the relevant way beyond those facts, and each type of analysis is opposed to a later and corresponding descent through synthesis or demonstration.[11]

With this overview in mind let us examine both the background to and the development of analysis and synthesis in later Greek thought. Three sources were available to the late Greek philosopher in his attempt to develop a theory of analysis and synthesis: Plato, Aristotle, and the mathematical tradition. While our primary task shall be to understand analysis as the development of an Aristotelian motif, we shall first consider (rather too briefly) the influence of both Plato and Greek mathematics.

III. THE PLATONIC BACKGROUND

Of the Platonic background I shall say little, not because of its lack of influence, but rather because such an important source cannot be adequately explored in a brief compass. Several later authors would even credit Plato with the introduction of analysis. Diogenes Laertius, for instance, says that it was Plato who taught the method to the mathematicians, in particular to one Leodamas of Thasos.[12] This story was later repeated and elaborated by Proclus.[13] While there is little reason to take this claim seriously, it does emphasize that later philosophers regarded analysis as a fundamentally Platonic technique. Actually, the method was probably developed by mathematicians contemporary with Plato.[14] While Plato cannot be credited with the discovery (or perhaps even significant influence on) *mathematical* analysis, many of his dialogues later came to be interpreted as exemplifying this particular *philosophical* method. Damascius, for instance, claims that Socrates uses analysis as well as division at *Philebus* 16c5–17d5.[15] Ammonius speaks of analysis in the *Philebus*.[16] And Proclus attributes analysis to Socrates in the *Alcibiades*.[17]

---

11. One might be puzzled that the *Didaskalikos* never actually develops an explicit philosophy of synthesis. Why does a text that is such a rich source for our knowledge of analysis not consider it parallel procedure? As we shall see below, in its philosophical application synthesis becomes assimilated to demonstration. Thus, while mathematics needed an explicit procedure to accompany analysis, philosophy, in bringing analysis within the hierarchy of dialectic, naturally paired it with demonstration.

12. Diogenes Laertius, 3.24.

13. *In Euc.* 211.12–23.

14. Charles Mugler (*Platon et la recherche mathématique de son époque*, Strasbourg-Zurich: 1948) has argued for this thesis on philosophical grounds, but his arguments have been (correctly) rejected by Harold Cherniss, "Plato as Mathematician," *Review of Metaphysics* 4 (1951): 395–425.

15. *In Phib.* 52–56.   16. *In An. Pr.* 78.9–12.

17. *In Alc.* 238.6–8, Segonds.

In addition to these somewhat anachronistic claims, a variety of Platonic modes of argumentation may be seen to have influenced the later development of analysis, for example, the use of *hypothesis*, the divided line of the *Republic* and the "exercise" in the second half of the *Parmenides*. Since our theme is Aristotelian, we shall not be able to explore these tempting suggestions, though one must note that a complete understanding of analysis would need to include its Platonic sources.

IV. THE MATHEMATICAL BACKGROUND

Both analysis and synthesis are, in origin, mathematical procedures, and analysis is closely associated with discovery.[18] Geminus, a famous mathematician of the first century B.C., defined analysis as "the discovery of demonstration" (ἀνάλυσίς ἐστιν ἀποδείξεως εὕρεσις).[19] The fullest account of these methods comes from the writings of the fourth century A.D. mathematician, Pappus of Alexandria:

Now, analysis is the path from what one is seeking, as if it were established, by way of its consequences, to something that is established by synthesis. That is to say, in analysis we assume what is sought as if it has been achieved, and look for the thing from it which follows, and again what comes before that, until by regressing in this way we come upon some one principle. We call this method 'analysis,' as if to say *anapalinlysis* (reduction backwards). In synthesis, by reversal, we assume what was obtained last in the analysis to have been achieved already, and, setting now in natural order, as precedents, what before were following, and fitting them to each other, we attain the end of the construction of what was sought. This is what we call 'synthesis.'[20]

We must note that analysis and synthesis are described as a unified process. We are to apply analysis, then synthesis to a given problem. In more simple terms, analysis assumes as true the proposition in

18. The mathematical procedures of analysis (and synthesis) are explored in Cherniss, "Plato as Mathematician"; Gulley, "Greek Geometrical Analysis"; T. L. Heath, *The Thirteen Books of Euclid's Elements* (Cambridge: 1926), 1:137–42; Hintikka and Remes, *Method of Analysis*; H. P. D. Lee, "Geometrical Method and Aristotle's Account of First Principles," *Classical Quarterly* 29 (1935): 113–24; M. S. Mahoney, "Another Look at Greek Geometrical Analysis," *Archive for History of Exact Sciences* 5 (1968/69): 319–48; Mugler, *Platon et la recherche mathématique*; W. Rehder, "Die Analysis und Synthesis bei Pappus," *Philosophia Naturalis* 19 (1982): 350–70; and Richard Robinson, "Analysis in Greek Geometry," in *Essays in Greek Philosophy* (Oxford: Oxford Univ. Press 1969), 1–15. One might also consult Wilber R. Knorr, "Construction and Proof in Ancient Geometry," *Ancient Philosophy* 3 (1983): 125–48.

19. *Apud* Ammonius, In An. Pr. 5, 27–31.

20. Pappus 7.1. The translation is from A. Jones, trans., *Pappus of Alexandria: Book 7 of the Collection*, Sources in the History of Mathematics and Physical Sciences, no. 8 (New York: 1986), part 1, p. 83.

question and then seeks what consequences follow from it until it reaches something known to be true or known to be false. Synthesis, in turn, starts from that which is known and shows that this implies the proposition in question. Only after analysis has assumed the unknown, or at least unproven, is synthesis able to start from the known.

But the interpretation of mathematical analysis has proven quite difficult, for there is a central and crucial question concerning the "direction" of analysis. Our texts seem to be unclear as to whether the process of analysis involves an upward movement to prior assumptions from which an initial assumption follows, or a downward movement of deduction from the initial assumption. While we may leave this particular debate to students of the history of mathematics, we might note that no such ambiguity exists in the case of philosophical analysis; as we have seen in the *Didaskalikos*, there is agreement that philosophical analysis is directed upward to principles.

V. THE ARISTOTELIAN BACKGROUND

The Aristotelian background to the issues of discovery and proof in philosophy has recently become quite controversial. While I do not here wish to enter into the center of this controversy, some summary and remarks are appropriate. The origins of the contemporary debate may be traced to a proposal by Jonathan Barnes that relegated the method of demonstration described in the *Posterior Analytics* to a theory of pedagogy.[21] This suggestion was an attempt to confront an obvious problem in the interpretation of Aristotle: how do we reconcile the theory of the *Posterior Analytics* with the actual scientific investigations of Aristotle? Why does the theory of demonstration not appear to guide Aristotle's own scientific investigations? One must indeed look hard to find strictly syllogistic reasoning in many of his writings. In summarizing his theory, Barnes claims that in the *Posterior Analytics*, "Aristotle was not telling the scientist how to conduct his research; he was giving the pedagogue advice on the most efficient and economic

21. Jonathan Barnes, "Aristotle's Theory of Demonstration," *Phronesis* 14 (1969): 123–52, revised version in *Articles on Aristotle*, vol. 1, ed. Jonathan Barnes, Malcolm Schofield, and Richard Sorabji (London: Duckworth, 1975), 65–87. In "Proof and the Syllogism," in E. Berti, ed., *Aristotle on Science: The Posterior Analytics* (Padua: 1981) 17–59, Barnes develops his view by distinguishing a "pre-syllogistic" theory of demonstration. Finally, in *Aristotle* (Oxford: Oxford University Press 1982), Barnes suggests that we should not expect to find the theory of demonstration in such works since these are not the "final presentation of an achieved science" (pp. 38–39).

method of bettering his charges."[22] The effect of Barnes's theory was to divorce utterly the logic of scientific discovery from Aristotle's theory of demonstration. Hence, we should not expect, on his view, to see syllogisms or other features of the theory of demonstration in works which are notebooks of discovery.

Such an understanding of Aristotle has recently been called into question. Several authors have argued (quite rightly, I would say) that the biological works in particular are very much directed by the guidelines of the *Posterior Analytics*.[23] While they do not contain formal syllogisms, their scientific program is indeed that of the *Posterior Analytics*. There seems little question that Aristotelian research was implicitly guided by the canons of the *Posterior Analytics*. But what then of the distinction between discovery and proof? I wish to argue here for an important distinction between the two, in a certain sense, for I do not wish to make discovery and proof utterly unconnected. They must remain independent though related processes. The logic of discovery is neither theoretically nor practically identifiable with the logic of proof.

Since my object here is not to consider in greater depth the wider issue of discovery versus demonstration in Aristotle, I should now like to move to the related issue of analysis and to examine a series of texts in which Aristotle discusses the use of analysis that will come to fruition in later Greek thought.

The *Posterior Analytics* makes clear that Aristotle is quite aware of the mathematical procedure and its possible, though more complicated use, in philosophy:

If it were impossible to prove truth from falsehood, it would be easy to make an analysis; for they would convert from necessity. For let A be something that is the case; and if this is the case, then *these* are the case (things which I know to be the case, call them B). From these, therefore, I shall prove that the former is the case. (In mathematics things convert more because they assume nothing accidental—and in this too they differ from argumentations—but only definitions.)[24]

22. Barnes, "Aristotle's Theory of Demonstration."

23. See, for example, James G. Lennox, "Divide and Explain: The *Posterior Analytics* in Practice," in *Philosophical Issues in Aristotle's Biology*, ed. A. Gotthelf and J. G. Lennox (Cambridge: Cambridge University Press 1987), 90–119; Robert Bolton, "Definition and Scientific Method in Aristotle's *Posterior Analytics* and the *Generation of Animals*," in ibid., 120–66; and Allen Gotthelf, "First Principles in Aristotle's *Parts of Animals*," in ibid., 167–98.

24. *Posterior Analytics* 78a6–13. All translations of Aristotle are from Jonathan Barnes, ed., *The Complete Works of Aristotle: The Revised Oxford Translation*, 2 vols. (Princeton: Princeton University Press 1984).

In this passage Aristotle recognizes the heuristic possibilities of this means of inquiry, and we can find several other texts which present a similar means of argumentation.

In book three of the *Nicomachean Ethics,* when he is considering the determination of ends, Aristotle makes an interesting allusion to the nature of discovery and its connection with analysis.

Having set the end they consider how and by what means it is to be attained; and if it seems to be produced by several means they consider by which it is most easily and best produced, while if it is achieved by one only they consider how it will be achieved by this and by what means *this* will be achieved, till they come to the first cause, which in the order of discovery [ἐν τῇ εὑρέσει] is last. For the person who deliberates seems to inquire and analyze in the way described as though he were analyzing a geometrical construction . . . and what is last in the order of analysis seems to be first in the order of becoming.[25]

This method is further elaborated, when Aristotle discusses the proper aim for man in the *Eudemian Ethics.*

We say the aim, because this is not attained by inference or reasoning. Let us assume this as starting-point. For the doctor does not ask whether one ought to be in health or not, but whether one ought to walk or not; nor does the trainer ask whether one ought to be in good condition or not, but whether one should wrestle or not. And similarly no art asks questions about the end; for as in theoretical sciences the assumptions are our starting points, so in the productive the end is starting point and assumed. E.g., we reason that since the body is to be made healthy, therefore so and so must be found in it if health is to be had—just as in geometry, if the angles of the triangle are equal to two right angles, then so and so must be the case. The end aimed at is, then, the starting-point of our thought, the end of our thought the starting-point of action.[26]

The language of these passages makes it clear the analysis has not yet been explicitly adopted as a philosophical procedure. It is nonetheless akin to an Aristotelian process, namely, the movement of the human mind from that which is better known by us to that which is better known in itself. This method is also implicit in the *Metaphysics* where Aristotle says that: "The healthy subject then is produced as the result of the following train of thought: since *this* is health, if the subject is to be healthy *this* must first be present, e.g. a uniform state of body, and if this is to be present, there must be heat; and the physician goes on thinking thus until he brings the matter to a final step which he himself can take. The process from this point onward, i.e. the process toward health, is called a 'making' [ποίησις]."[27]

25. *NE* 1112b15–24.
26. *EE* 1227b28–33.
27. *Met.* 1032b6–10.

I do not wish to claim that in any explicit way Aristotle saw himself using the method of analysis, but an implicit use of hypothetical argument, a forerunner of analysis proper, can be found in a variety of Aristotelian texts and form an important part of Aristotelian discovery.

VI. THE ARISTOTELIAN COMMENTATORS

With that survey of Aristotle completed, we must look to the later Greek tradition. We have already explored the views of the Middle Platonic *Didaskalikos* when considering the general nature of analysis. An even more sophisticated and more systematic exposition of analysis can be found in the later commentaries on Aristotle. While it is not here possible to consider every relevant passage in the extensive remains of the Greek commentaries on Aristotle, we shall attempt to piece together a coherent view.

One difficulty in our study is that the terms "analysis" and "synthesis" are used in a variety of ways, some relevant, some not so relevant to the philosopher. It became a *topos* in Greek commentaries to discuss the various meanings of, or we might want to say applications of, "analysis." In addition to the philosophical use, Alexander of Aphrodisias notes the geometrical analysis of Pappus; a use in natural philosophy whereby objects are analyzed into their elements, and these in turn into matter and form; the analysis of syllogisms into their simple parts; the analysis of imperfect syllogisms into perfect ones; and the analysis of syllogisms into the appropriate figure (it is from this final use that Alexander takes the title *Analytics* to derive).[28] To this list Ammonius adds the grammatical analysis of words into syllables and then individual letters.[29] In spite of the great variety of applications of this technique, every important commentator on the logical works is aware of a distinctive use of analysis, one whose goal is the discovery of new knowledge, specifically knowledge of principles.

We might best begin with Alexander, who is often and correctly reckoned the most perceptive and sober of Aristotle's later Greek interpreters. He describes our two methods as follows: "For analysis is the conversion of synthesis—for synthesis is the route from principles to those things which are from principles, but analysis is a return route from the ends to the principles."[30] Analysis is the process of discovery that begins with facts in the world and leads us to first

28. In. An. Pr. 7.11–33.
29. *In. An. Pr.* 5.10–6.33.
30. *In. An. Pr.* 7.13–15.

principles; synthesis begins with those principles and leads back down to conclusions.

Ammonius gives a similar rendition, though he adds an example quite reminiscent of the *Didaskalikos*: "But 'synthesis' and 'analysis' are also [used] among the philosophers—'synthesis' whenever from simple forms things come to be combinations [τὰ σύνθετα], for example, from the beautiful itself comes to be the beautiful in the intellect, and in the soul, and in bodies. And 'analysis' is whenever from the forms in perceptible objects they go up to those in the intelligibles."[31] The commentators are in agreement that analysis is both a discovery and an ascent to principles.[32]

Unfortunately, these brief theoretical discussions do not give us an adequate understanding of the method itself, and we must turn to some of the many uses of analysis found in the commentaries themselves. A detailed examination of what Alexander calls an "exhibition from analysis" (ἡ δεῖξις κατὰ ἀνάλυσιν)[33] might help to clarify the use of this method.[34] This "exhibition" occurs in the first section in his *Quaestiones*, where Alexander considers the query, "Through what might someone establish the first cause according to Aristotle?" His reply is that "The 'exhibition' is according to analysis. For it is not possible for there to be a demonstration [ἀπόδειξιν] of a first principle; rather, it is necessary—beginning from what is both later and apparent, and making use of analysis in accord with what is agreed concerning these—to establish [συστῆσαι] the nature of this [first principle]."[35]

---

31. *In. An. Pr.* 5.19–25.

32. Alexander, *In Met.* 55.7.

33. I should note that here I use the somewhat clumsy translation "exhibition" for the Greek δεῖξις; in other contexts it may well be translated "demonstration" but here we must reserve that English word for the technical term ἀπόδειξις. The point is that analysis, though a type of "exhibition" (δεῖξις), is not in the strict sense a "demonstration" (ἀπόδειξις).

34. The authorship of this passage is in some doubt. Robert Sharples ("Alexander of Aphrodisias: Scholasticism and Innovation" in *Aufstieg und Niedergang der Römischen Welt* II.36.2, ed. W. Haase [Berlin: De Gruyter 1987], 1176–1243) suggests that the minor works are "probably not all by Alexander himself, but nevertheless reflect the activity of his school" (p. 1189). The issue is complicated by the inclusion of our "proof from analysis" in the commentary on book twelve of the *Metaphysics* attributed to Alexander, for the commentaries on books six through fourteen are generally regarded as spurious (at least in their present form); see Sharples, p. 1182, for the relevant literature. Yet the repetition of our proof suggests that at least this section might in fact go back to Alexander, and Sharples (p. 1190) further notes the close connection between this section of the *Quaestiones* and the following discussion of the commentary on book twelve attributed to Alexander (687, 23–24). There is clearly a need for further study of the relationship between these two texts.

35. *Quaest.* 3.25–4.9.

The passage is clear concerning the need for analysis—there can be no demonstration of a first principle. But analysis does allow us, in Alexander's words, to "establish (συστῆσαι) the nature" of the first principle.

A more detailed application comes in a text from John Philoponus:

> by analysis the principles of this are discovered by us going up from the effects prior to us to that prior in nature, i.e., causes. For we know first in perception that the moon is eclipsed. And discursive reasoning [διάνοια] examining again [ἀναψηλαφήσασα] later discovers the cause; for it says "the moon is eclipsed, the eclipsed is blocked, therefore the moon is blocked." This is analysis going from the effects to the cause. Then demonstration goes down from causes to the effects: "the moon is blocked, that which is blocked is eclipsed, therefore the moon is eclipsed." Again, we see the earth quaking, and we say "the earth quakes, when something quakes the wind in its cavities and caves is shut out, in the earth the wind is shut out"—this is analysis. Then the demonstration: "in the earth the wind is shut out, when wind is shut out, then there is a quaking, thus a quaking occurs in the earth."[36]

In each case of analysis there is no claim that we are demonstrating anything, only that we know the one thing to be the cause of another.

Thus far our investigation of analysis has concerned itself with that method in isolation. I would now like to place it in the context of the other dialectical methods. In spite of their concern with the writings of Aristotle, we must not underestimate the Platonic influence on the commentators. The issue of dialectical method is a case in point. The commentators take the proper account of dialectic to be not the "five" methods offered by Aristotle in the *Topics*,[37] but rather what they hold to be the Platonic account: division, definition, demonstration, and analysis.[38] We shall discuss this wider account for the implicit claim is that dialectical methodology presents a systematic attempt to grant intelligibility to the object of our consideration. The commentators are at pains to show the distinctions among the four Platonic methods (no method can be reduced to another) and to show more precisely that there was a specific task (ἔργον) assigned to each.

The classification presented by Ammonius in his commentaries on Aristotle's *Prior Analytics* and Porphyry's *Isagoge* is typical.[39] First, division, most abstractly considered, separates the one into many; it cuts genera into species, for example, animal into rational and irrational

---

36. *In. An. Post.* 335.9–21.
37. By the "five" methods in the *Topics*, I take it that they mean the four predicables (definition, property, genus and accident) to which Porphyry would, in the *Isagoge*, add species.
38. Ammonius, *In Isag.* 34.17–20.
39. More spcifically I follow *In Isag.* I.34.17–38, 4 and *In An. Pr.* 7.26–8.14.

animal, mortal and immortal animal. Second, definition makes some whole from parts and distinguishes one thing from all others; that is, one constructs a unique definition from that which has been previously divided, e.g., ensouled is divided into animal and plant, and then animal into rational and irrational, mortal and immortal. Using this division we can then give the definition of man as "rational and mortal animal." Third, demonstration proves one existent by another; it proves effects from causes. The task of demonstration is to show what follows from a definition. Ammonius gives a Platonic example: Plato wishing to demonstrate his definition (λόγος) concerning the immortal soul uses the definition of the substance itself, saying that the soul is a self-mover, that a self-mover is always moving, that what is always moving is immortal; therefore, the soul is immortal.

There is a clear logical relationship among these dialectical methods: demonstration relies on definition, for definitions explicate the nature of a thing, and it is necessary that demonstrations come from the nature itself of things and not from accidental properties (you might note that Ammonius heeds Aristotle's implied warning in the *Posterior Analytics* that philosophical analysis is liable to go askew if it assumes anything accidental); definition in turn requires division to furnish the predicates that it combines into a definition. Finally, we may add analysis and its movement from effects to causes.

While many of the commentators stress the importance of distinguishing these methods, only one presents a systematic analysis of their goals. Elias recognizes the four methods and then pairs them with what he calls the four dialectical problems: (1) if it is (εἰ ἔστι), (2) what it is (τί ἐστι), (3) what sort of thing it is (ὁποῖόν τί ἐστι), and (4) through what it is (διὰ τί ἐστι).[40] While the first and fourth questions, "if it is" and "through what it is," are clear, a quick glance at the *Isagoge* will distinguish questions (2) and (3). There Porphyry makes clear that the second question, "what it is," seeks the genus of a thing, while question (3), "what sort of thing it is" seeks a property, either its differentia or an accident; when we ask What is man? the proper answer is "animal" but when we ask What sort of thing is man? the proper answer is "rational."[41] In sum, the four dialectical questions seek the existence, essence, properties and causes of things.

Elias, after introducing the four dialectical problems, then associates each of them with one of the four methods (the implicit claim is that we will only be able to make something fully intelligible if we are able, through the four methods, to answer each of these four questions):

40. *In Isag.* 37.10–11.
41. *Isag.* 3.8–14.

there are four dialectical problems: if it is [εἰ ἔστι], what it is [τί ἐστιν], what sort of thing it is [ὁποῖόν τί ἐστι] and through what it is [διὰ τί ἐστι]. And the one "if it is" is analogous to division (for "if it is" completely falls under division), and "what it is" [belongs] to definition [lacuna] (for all demonstrations are of "what sort of thing it is," for seldom is the [question] "if it is" disputed and there is no demonstration of a definition) and the "through what it is" is analogous to analysis—each of these is a discovery of causes.[42]

"If it is" is the purview of division, and as we have seen division is a classification of attributes. Definition determines what something is, that is, it produces the definition of that object by combining attributes achieved through division. Demonstration shows what follows from the definition or, as our commentator puts it, "what sort of thing it is." and finally, analysis displays its causes, it makes connections with the principles which are its cause.

The reader familiar with Aristotle will perhaps notice something quite familiar about these questions: They are quite similar, though not identical, to the four questions Aristotle addresses in the beginning of the second book of the *Posterior Analytics*. Elias has returned to Aristotle for the organization of the Platonic dialectical methods by means of the fundamentally Aristotelian dialectical problems. In *Posterior Analytics* 2.1 Aristotle undertakes his search for definitions with the following program: "The things we seek are equal in number to those we understand. We seek four things: the fact [τὸ ὅτι], the reason why [τὸ διότι], if it is [εἰ ἔστι], what it is [τί ἐστιν]."[43]

As I suggested above, these four programmatic questions set the structure for Aristotle's own research (at least his biological research). Let us begin with a brief description of Aristotle's rationale.[44] We sometimes begin with the fact, e.g., whether or not the sun is eclipsed. When this is known we seek the reason why, e.g., why the sun is eclipsed. In other cases we ask whether a thing is, e.g., a centaur or a god, and then ask what it is. In the first pair of Aristotelian questions we are interested in whether and why something has a certain property; in the latter pair, in whether a certain subject exists and what it is. Book one of the *Posterior Analytics* has already considered the first pair of questions; book two will go on to consider the second pair.[45]

It should be clear that the commentators, in spite of their avowed allegiance to "Platonic" dialectic, are very much in this tradition of the *Posterior Analytics*. A more detailed study of say, definition, would

42. *In Isag.* 37.9–16.
43. *An. Post.* 89b23–25.
44. This is a summary of *An. Post.* 1.1–2.
45. Here I follow W. D. Ross, ed., *Aristotle's Prior and Posterior Analytics* (Oxford: Clarendon 1949), *ad loc.*

show that this dialectical method is largely a development of the second book of that treatise. A closer study of division, however, would show its reliance on Platonic texts. It is essential that the student of late Greek philosophy recognize the complex and sophisticated use made by the philosophers of their earlier sources. As I noted above, this philosophical outlook can only be understood as a conscious integration of Platonic and Aristotelian thought.

VII. THE MEDICAL TRADITION

Finally as a coda to my discussion of discovery and proof, one might briefly consider another tradition in which the issue of the nature of discovery was explicitly (and indeed vigorously) discussed. For much of the history of ancient medicine the nature of discovery was one of the central points of contention between the various schools of medical thought.[46] In late antiquity there was a continuous connection between philosophy and medicine. While philosophy was only a modest expectation for the educated Roman, for the doctor it was considered essential. Unlike some modern medical education, it was not ethics that was paramount in the philosophical training of a physician; rather, the ancient medical student was trained in systematic philosophy. Thus, it was quite natural that when ancient doctors put philosophical questions in their own work, they questioned the nature of medical knowledge. More specifically, they asked whether there was any justification for a theoretical program of discovery or whether such an effort was misguided and only random experience would provide knowledge through chance trial and error.

The Empirical doctors (under the influence of the Sceptics) argued that medical knowledge was largely a matter of experience.[47] Sextus Empiricus claims that such Empiricists were closest to his own Pyrrhonian scepticism for this school "affirms the inapprehensibility of what is non-evident," and they conduct daily affairs by the four-fold sceptical "guide" to the common life: the compelling force of nature, the compulsion of affections, the tradition of laws and customs, and the tradition of the arts.[48] One example might illustrate this random

46. For a general overview of this debate, see Frede's introduction to *Galen* (cited in n. 2 above).

47. On this school see Ludwig Edelstein, "Empirie und Skepsis in der Lehre der grieschen Empirikerschule," *Quellen und Studiesn zur Geschichte der Naturwissenschaften und der Medizin*, vol. 3 (Berlin: 1933), 45–53. The texts are collected in Karl Deichgräber, *Die griesche Empirikerschule* (Berlin, 1930).

48. *Outlines of Pyrrhonism* 1.236–37.

"method." In his treatise *An Outline of Empiricism,* Galen discusses the way in which Empiricists come to a cure for a particular disease. After reciting several stories about how wholly chance incidents effected a cure for elephantiasis, he summarizes their position: "I have talked about these cases at length, since there are many things which are discovered by accident and by its imitation. For, just as good fortune here gave me the opportunity to make several observations by encountering by chance one case in which somebody was helped, in another case something else which belongs to the art is found out."[49]

Various other medical schools, loosely called the Rationalists, on the other hand, held that experience alone was inadequate. They held that theories were a necessary part of medical knowledge and in particular theoretical knowledge was an important guide in discovery. Asclepiades of Bithynia, for instance, whose thought Galen transmits in *On Medical Experience* was one of the more extreme Rationalists. In the beginning of that work Galen chides him for going so far as to disparage experience. Elsewhere, Galen reports of him that "Some of these criticisms of empiricism have been raised by Asclepiades. He thought he was able to show that nothing can be seen often to happen in the same way. *Hence he thought that this kind of experience was utterly unreliable and would not be in a position to make possible even the most modest discovery.*"[50] While we cannot pursue this intriguing discussion of discovery and proof, I do mention it, so that you might be aware of how these are not merely the academic concerns of the philosophers of antiquity; rather, the question of the proper method of discovery and the subsequent proof reverberated throughout ancient philosophy and science. The way in which ancient physicians treated their patients very much depended upon their philosophy of science and discovery.

VIII. CONCLUSION

In conclusion, I must consider what this study has accomplished. First, I have examined the workings of analysis as a method of discovery. Second, I hope to have at least sketched out a late Greek philosophy of science, and the way that such pursuit of knowledge focuses on the four dialectical questions. Third, I have tried to show

49. Frede, *Galen,* 41.
50. *On the Sects for Beginners* §5 (p. 9); translation from Frede, *Galen,* 8 (emphasis mine).

some of the dynamics of the development of the late Aristotelian (and indeed Platonic) tradition. While such thinkers as Alexander, Ammonius, Elias, and John Philoponus were in some sense "bound" by both the genre of the commentary and their allegiance to Platonic and Aristotelian texts, there was nonetheless sufficient flexibility and opportunity for them to develop a number of interesting and sophisticated positions within those constraints.

PART III

ARISTOTLE IN BYZANTIUM AND ISLAM

6 The Greek Christian Authors and Aristotle

LEO J. ELDERS, S.V.D.

More research has been done on the relationship between the Church Fathers and Platonism than on the influence of Aristotle on the Christian authors of the first four centuries. The reasons for this difference will become clear in the course of this discussion. There exist, nevertheless, a good number of studies on this theme. Petavius, in the prolegomena to his *Dogmata Theologica,* presented a choice of relevant quotations, and J. Launoi lists some thirty statements unfavorable to Aristotle, dating to the period running from Justin to 500 A.D.[1] In 1696, Faydit published his *Altération du dogme théologique par la philosophie d'Aristote.* Closer to us are studies by Adolf Harnack, J. Waszink, J. de Ghellinck, A.-J. Festugière, G. Lazzati, J. Daniélou, H. A. Wolfson, and others which we shall have an opportunity to quote in this paper.

I propose to study the subject in this order: the state of Aristotelian studies in the first four centuries of our era; the Christian authors and philosophy; the Apologists and Aristotle; the third-century Christian authors, Eusebius of Caesarea, and Aristotle; the great Doctors of the fourth century, the heretics, and Aristotle; the historians, Theodoretus and Nemesius; and finally, some conclusions, and a comparison with today's situation.

I. ARISTOTLE AND THE PERIPATETICS FROM A.D. 1 TO 500

At the beginning of the Christian era, the state of philosophical studies was at its best mediocre and often bad. Philosophy was taught mainly in combination with rhetoric, the knowledge of the teachings of the great philosophers being based mostly on summaries or popular texts. There was much syncretism of the teachings of the various schools, in particular of Platonism, Aristotelianism and Stoicism. On

1. J. Launoi, *De variis Aristotelis in Academia Parisiensi fortuna,* in *Opera omnia* (Grenoble: 1732), 175–89.

the other hand, the edition of Aristotle's school writings by Andronicus of Rhodes (about 60 B.C.) gave a new impulse to the study of Aristotle's thought. During the first two centuries of the Christian era a number of Platonists adopted certain tenets of Peripatetic theology.[2] Philo of Alexandria as well as Plutarch are familiar with both the esoterical and exoterical writings. Plutarch uses several of Aristotle's insights, but he makes no attempt to establish a perfect harmony between the latter's doctrine and that of Plato. He does not accept the self-centered thinker of *Metaphysics* 12.9 as the supreme God. Although in the second century more serious study of the main texts of Aristotle was slowly getting underway, the prevalent view of Aristotle's philosophy remained dependent on its presentation by Platonists, Stoics, and Epicureans. In their controversy with the Peripatetics, Platonists accused Aristotle of materialism because he attributed divine properties to the fifth element (the ether replaced Plato's astral soul). Their second main criticism: if the human soul is the ἐντελέχεια of the body, it becomes material itself like the body.

Knowledgeable philosophers, however, noticed that the Stagirite's theory of the νοῦς is all but materialistic: it asserts the transcendence of the divine mind as well as the immateriality of the human intellect. In the ancient tradition, the Aristotelian expression "being inasmuch as being" was thought to signify God. Aristotle's impressive arguments against the theory of self-subsisting Ideas appear to have convinced quite a number of Platonists. For this reason the doctrine of the Ideas as the thoughts of God could develop at the beginning of the Christian era. Aristotle's theory of the agent intellect also drew the attention of Plotinus, who identified the supreme νοῦς of Aristotle with the second ὑπόστασις of his own system. The Stagirite's identification of the objects of thought with the act of thinking likewise profoundly impressed him. Plotinus accepts the principle that act is prior to potency, although the concepts of act and potency are not nearly so important in the *Enneads* as they are in Aristotelian philosophy. However, Aristotle's concept of primary matter was not understood correctly by Plotinus nor by many others.

It is a central tenet of Aristotelian cosmology that the cosmos does not have a beginning in time. The arguments to this effect in *On the Heavens* 1.10, the *Physics*, and the *Metaphysics* are so convincing that many a Platonist preferred to understand the description of the making of the world in the *Timaeus* in a figurative sense. Certain teachings of the *Nicomachean Ethics* also gained wide acceptance: the definition

2. See R. E. Witt, *Albinus and the History of Middle Platonism*, 126.

of virtue; the theory of the mean; the account of free choice and, to a certain extent, the description of happiness.

While Plotinus and the professional schools of philosophy did use the text of Aristotle's esoterical writings, a more popular learning was spreading based on secondary sources. Arius Didymus, who flourished during the reign of the emperor Augustus, composed an epitome of this nature. Arius directs his attention to certain doctrines and omits others; his terminology is influenced by Stoicism. In the first centuries of the Christian era the pseudo-Aristotelian treatise *De mundo* which shows Stoic and other influences became rather influential in propagating a particular view of Aristotle's philosophy with regard to the doctrine of Divine Providence.[3] Aëtius (between 50 and 150 A.D.) reproduced this presentation in his *Placita* (2.3.4). Most of the Christian authors were convinced that this was the authentic doctrine of Aristotle.

The Jewish philosopher Philo has a good knowledge of Aristotle and is not without admiration for him. In his *Questions and Answers on Genesis* (3.16), Philo writes that the doctrine of perfection as arising from three goods, namely, spiritual, bodily, and external goods, "was praised by some of the philosophers who came afterwards [that is, after Moses]. It is also said to have been the legislation of Pythagoras." It is quite an honor for Aristotle to be linked with Pythagoras and Moses.

Although Philo is an eclectic, Platonism set its mark on his thought. The Jewish philosopher takes for granted Posidonius's idea that general education is a stepping stone to philosophy, and philosophy to theology (*De Somniis* 1.205). In his cosmology Philo shows a tendency toward the Stoic view of a basic sympathy between the different parts of the world, but he integrates into this theory all the Platonic and Aristotelian concepts that fit in.[4] Philo is quite positive with regard to body and the material world, although he also writes that on earth the soul is a pilgrim and must seek liberation from the bondage of the flesh.

Philo develops Greek cosmology in the sense that he makes the world dependent on God. There exists a great gulf between God and his creatures: being created presupposes an ontological fall. Philo is the earliest witness to the view that the Ideas are the thoughts of God. God is free to intervene in the world, and Philo sees no conflict between the immanence and the transcendence of God. In the field of ethics he argues over and against the Stoics that not self possession

3. God works through intermediaries; he himself is not directly concerned with the sublunar world (*De mundo* 391a9ff.).

4. See E. Bréhier, *Les Idées philosophiques et religieuses de Philon d'Alexandrie* (Paris: 1925), 161.

but love of God is man's highest attainment. He rejects the Stoic view that happiness consists simply in the presence of virtue in the soul: This sort of perfection is proper of pure spirits only. Man can attain only imperfect happiness.[5] This latter, Peripatetic theory is superior, "this sweet and sociable philosophy."[6] Nevertheless, Philo often views Aristotle's doctrine through the spectacles of the Stoa, in particular with regard to the definitions of the various virtues.

In writings of the first five centuries, one frequently encounters an Aristotelianism contaminated by Stoicism. Even such Peripatetics as Boethus of Sidon and Xenarchus of Seleucia show Stoic influences. Platonism was also exposed to such tendencies, and different expressions of it circulated. Plutarch and Atticus advocated a pure and undiluted Platonism, while Albinus taught a more syncretistic system. His *Didaskalikos* contains some Aristotelian doctrines. Apparently the author did not see anything un-Platonic about certain tenets of Aristotle.[7] Albinus presents a summary of Aristotle's syllogistic, accepts the theory of virtue as a mean between extremes, and his view of friendship is also Aristotelian.

While Albinus did not hesitate to use Aristotelian doctrines which he considered reconcilable with Platonism, with Atticus a vehement opponent of Aristotle occupied the chair of Platonic philosophy established in Athens by Marcus Aurelius. In his *Praeparatio evangelica*, books twelve and fifteen, Eusebius preserved a polemical tract of Atticus against the Peripatetics.[8] Atticus's critique is directed against the following Aristotelian doctrines: providence is concerned with the celestial bodies only; God is not even interested in the moral well-being of man; the sublunar world is governed by nature; and the human soul, as the form of the body, loses its spirituality and is not immortal. As Paul Moraux has pointed out, none of these theses is found in so many words in Aristotle; they go back to Peripatetic theories which are a further elaboration of Aristotle's own doctrine. The great commentator Alexander of Aphrodisias has a more differentiated view.[9] However, the doxographical tradition where Atticus found this material, was to survive for several centuries; it had a decisive influence on the Christian authors who, like Atticus, did not carefully study Aristotle's own position.

5. Bréhier, *Les Idées philosophiques*, 276–77.

6. *Migr. Abr.* 1147; *Quaest. in Gen.* 121 and 339.

7. P. Moraux, *Der Aristotelismus bei den Griechen*, vol. 2 (Berlin: 1984), 445.

8. John Dillon, *The Middle Platonists* (London: 1977), 250, assumes that this tract was meant as a defence against the Peripatetic Aristocles, who presented Aristotelianism as the perfection of Platonism.

9. *De quaestionibus* 2.2.70, 24–71.3 Bruns.

Led by Porphyry most third-century Platonists accepted Aristotle's doctrine of the categories of being. Porphyry even used the writings of Alexander of Aphrodisias.[10] Later Platonists show a surprising interest in Aristotle's thought. As A. C. Lloyd writes, the greater part of the surviving Neoplatonic literature consists of commentaries on the *Corpus Aristotelicum*.[11] As a matter of fact the teaching of philosophy at the schools in Athens, Alexandria, and Constantinople demanded a program of studies and a clear distinction between disciplines: in logic, natural philosophy, and ethics Aristotle's texts were used, while theology was reserved to Plato.

Porphyry and other Neoplatonists attempted to make philosophy into a religion that would be a rival to Christianity, while such Stoics as Epictetus proclaimed themselves spiritual directors called by God to be the heralds of truth.[12] Concern about this ideological rivalry is likely to have influenced Christian authors in their attitude toward philosophy.

II. THE CHRISTIANS AND PHILOSOPHY

In the Roman Empire philosophy was considered the queen of all sciences. But the predominant climate of the second and third century was syncretistic. In the wide-spread haze of more or less commonly held philosophical views certain compact masses stood out, such as the philosophies of Plato, the Peripatetics, the Stoa, and Epicurus. On the other hand, the Christian doctrine of the Faith had not yet been fully developed with regard to the mystery of Holy Trinity, the Person of Christ, Grace, the Sacraments, and the structure of the Church. Christians adhered to the rule of the Faith transmitted from generation to generation. Their attitude toward philosophy was wavering and depended on what sort of contact they had with philosophical ideas, their own intellectual background, and the presence of heretics using philosophical theories to corroborate their views.

Athenagoras of Athens attempts a rational justification of the Faith. His attitude toward philosophy is positive; he has words of praise for Plato's theory of immaterial being lying outside becoming.[13] However, he is sharply critical of the identification of the gods with the elements. He also rejects the theory of the atomists according to which the world

10. See P. Henry, in *Les Sources de Plotin*, vol. 5 of *Entretiens Hardt*, 429–49.
11. A. C. Lloyd, *The Cambridge History of Later Greek and Early Medieval Philosophy*, 273.
12. Epictetus, *Dissertationes* 3.1.36; 3.26.28.
13. *Oratio pro christianis*, 19.

is the playground of chance.[14] Athenagoras avails himself of doxographies for his information on Plato and Aristotle.[15] He uses Albinus insofar as it suits his purpose. His idea of God is biblical: God is a personal being. God has goodness, rather than being the good itself as Plato said.[16] Athenagoras probably believed in the creation of each individual soul by God. His overall attitude toward philosophy is admirable: he shuns the extremes of total rejection and indiscriminate assimilation.[17]

Tatianus, on the other hand, has a very negative view of philosophy: he draws attention to allegations of unusual or immoral conduct by certain philosophers, the rivalry of schools,and the variety of opinions. But he himself does use philosophical arguments. His pessimistic view of matter is Platonic, and he blames Aristotle for rejecting the immortality of the soul.[18] It is possible that to a large extent his attitude was determined by a controversy with Cynic philosophers who proclaimed themselves heralds of the truth.

Aristides of Athens voices his surprise that the philosophers consider the elements divine and accept strife as one of the gods.[19] An important witness to the attitude of Christians toward philosophy is Justin. Justin considers philosophy to possess part of the truth because sparks of the *Logos* are present in it.[20] Philosophy is the knowledge of that which is and of truth.[21] Whatever the philosophers said that is true belongs to the Christians. Socrates, Heraclitus, and Plato must be praised.[22] Those who live according to reason are Christians.[23] However, the knowledge reached by the philosophers is only vague. Justin regrets the plurality of philosophical opinions, which came about, he says, because of the stubbornness and shortsightedness of the disciples of the great founders. Justin's interest is not historical; what matters is truth alone.[24] Thus, he rejects the Stoic view of the immanence of God which made God subject to change.[25] Many of Justin's philosophical ideas originated in Middle Platonism.

14. Ibid., 25.
15. L. W. Barnard, *A Study in Second Century Christian Apologetic* (Paris: 1972), 40ff.
16. Athenagoras, *Leg.* 24.
17. Barnard, *A Study,* 178.
18. *Ad graecos,* 25.
19. *Apologia* 3.3–4; 13.5–7.
20. *2 Apol.* 10.1–3; 13.2–3.
21. *Dialogue with Trypho* 2.2.
22. *Dialogue with Trypho* 1.1–2.
23. 1 Apol. 46.
24. See J. C. Van Winden, *An Early Christian Philosopher* (Leiden: 1971), 100–106; 126f.
25. *2 Apol.* 7.

Another Christian apologist, Hermias, who probably lived at the end of the second and the beginning of the third century, wrote a sharply sarcastic treatise against the philosophers, the *Irrisio*. Not without talent, Hermias ridicules the many contradictions between the various philosophical views. His pungent criticism, as well as that of Theophilus of Alexandria, must be explained as a reaction against the attacks by some of the philosophers on the Christians. Because of the authority philosophy possessed in those days, these attacks were harmful and had to be countered. Hermias apparently felt that the best way to do so was by pointing out the contrast between the teaching of the philosophers and their personal behavior and to expose the enormous variety in philosophical opinion.

Hippolytus of Rome writes that the Christians should not disregard philosophical views. These views are important.[26] For instance, the Gnostic Valentinus found his inspiration in the mystic of numbers of Pythagoras and also, to a certain extent, in Plato; Basilides, on the other hand, took over certain doctrines of Aristotle. Marcion borrowed from Empedocles. But the heretics made worse what they used. Indeed, Hippolytus's general theme is that philosophy provided the materials for heresy.

The rift between philosophy and the doctrine of the Faith was sharply formulated by Tertullian: "What does a Christian have in common with philosophy, a disciple of Greece with a disciple of heaven, one who preaches only words, the other who sets deeds?".[27] Plato's works are the market where all the heretics found their ideas.[28] The pure blue sky is darkened by the mist of philosophy.[29] However, Tertullian does not mean to condemn all of philosophy. He himself uses philosophical ideas, arguments and examples, and his own ontology is close to Stoicism.

While Tertullian wrote that now that the Gospel is preached, there no longer is any need of scientific research,[30] Clement of Alexandria insisted on the importance of pagan philosophy for, and its use by, Christians. Clement followed Philo in assuming that that Greek philosophical wisdom is a certain preparation for faith in God and Revelation; it is the work of Divine Providence. He reports that some say that it owes its existence to the devil, others that it is a product of chance or that it has been inspired by subordinate powers. Neverthe-

26. *Refutatio* 1, intr., *Patrologia graeca* 16:3017. The *Patrologia graeca* will be cited hereafter as *PG*.
27. *Apol.* 46.
28. *De anima* 23.
29. *De anima* 3.
30. *De prescriptione* 7.

less, philosophy has grasped part of the truth; it makes people reflect, prepares them for accepting the truth,[31] and leads them to virtue.[32] It is a protecting fence around the vineyard of the Lord.[33] However, some Christians fear philosophy, as children spectres.[34] He himself borrows philosophical concepts and principles to elaborate the Christian doctrine. His outlook is predominantly Platonic. He distinguishes, however, between philosophy and sophistry, saying that the latter is to be rejected. Indeed, for Clement philosophy is not so much one particular view or another, but sure and unshakeable wisdom about human and divine things.

Because he did not draw a sharp distinction between the order of faith and that of reason, Clement even considered philosophy a sort of parallel economy of salvation, which could bring justification.[35] It is a sort of alliance offered by God to the Greeks and a first step toward the philosophy of Christ.[36] Moreover, he observes, the ancient philosophers borrowed extensively from the Hebrew prophets. Clement hardly speaks of contemporary philosophers and does not frequently mention even Plato, Aristotle and the Stoics. In his view philosophy reached its zenith with the Presocratics, for what is oldest is closest to the source.[37]

Clement convinced Origen of the importance of philosophy. So Origen studied at the school of Ammonius Saccas. In this way he became a Platonist, though he borrowed terms and distinctions wherever he found them—hence his use of ἡγεμονικόν, ἀσώματον, etc. Throughout his works, Origen insists on the reality of the transcendental world, the immateriality and preexistence of the soul, and the presence of Divine Providence, goodness, and finality in the world. His works attempt to show the compatibility of Christianity with Platonism. He was criticized, however, by some Christians because of his use of philosophy. His answer is the De principiis. With an apparent allusion to the opening sentence of the Metaphysics, he writes that the soul is aflame with an ineffable desire to know the truth. Since God himself gave it this desire, fulfillment of it must be possible.[38] Plato's influence on Origen was so strong that he began to interpret the doctrine of God

31. *Stromata* 1.16.80.
32. *Stromata* 6.17.
33. *Stromata* 1.15.2–18.4.
34. *Stromata* 6.10.
35. *Stromata* 1.20.99.
36. *Stromata* 6.8.67.
37. See Salvatore R. C. Lilla, *Clement of Alexandria: A Study in Christian Platonism and Gnosticism* (Oxford: 1971).
38. *De principiis* 2.11.4.

in Platonic schemes of thought, in particular with regard to the *Logos* and the preexistence of the individual soul—the life of which in the body is considered a punishment.[39] Although he holds that the union between soul and body is fortuitous and that terrestrial things are indifferent, Origen denies that the body would carry an innate evil within itself: it was made by God and, moreover, the *Logos* has taken up a body to redeem mankind. The body is an instrument of the soul; its value lies in its being subservient to the mind.[40]

Origen urges the study of philosophy as a preparation to theology, for it is helpful in the explanation of the Sacred Scriptures,[41] and some of the philosophers have taught excellent things.[42] The very learned Numenius, for instance, affirms the immateriality of God.[43] But many philosophers made serious mistakes. Even an author such as Plato did not keep himself free from idolatrous practice.[44] Students must stay away from those teachers who do not instruct them in the truth, such as those who say that pleasure is the highest value or deny a relation between God and the world.[45] Sophists and dialecticians, with their deceitful astuteness and tricky arguments, bring darkness.[46]

In his learned and courageous *Contra Celsum*, Origen fought against the materialism of the Epicureans as well as against the anti-Christian critique of some intellectuals and Platonists. In the third century, the Christian authors repeatedly criticized the Epicureans and, to a lesser extent, the Stoics because of their materialistic views.[47]

Pagan authors, on the other hand, frequently charged Christians with betraying their ancestors by turning to a new religion. Countering this criticism, Eusebius of Caesarea attempts to show that Greek culture and philosophy are a natural preparation for the Gospel. He first points out that faith is needed in human life in general as Plato had acknowledged in his discussion of constitutional law.[48] In Plato's dialogues many Christian doctrines are foreshadowed: the judgment after

39. See J. W. Trigg, *Origen, the Bible and Philosophy in the Third-Century Church* (London: 1985); E. von Ivanka, *Plato Christianus* (Einsiedeln: 1964), 142–44.

40. See J. Dupuis, *L'Esprit de l'homme: Etude sur l'anthropologie religieuse d'Origène* (Tournai: 1967), 54ff.

41. *Epist. ad Gregorium thaum.*, 1.

42. *Contra Celsum* 7.49.

43. Ibid. 1.15.

44. Ibid. 6.3–4.

45. Ibid. 3.75.

46. *In Exod. hom.* 4.6, *PG* 12.322.

47. One finds such criticism in Dionysius the Great, a disciple of Origen and later bishop of Alexandria who argues against the atomists and their theory that the world was formed by chance (see Eusebius, *Praeparatio evangelica* 24.25; cited hereafter as *PE*). Lactantius, *Div. instit.* 3.17 also launches an attack against the atomists.

48. *PE* 21.1.

death; paradise; the deluge; the fact that human laws are based on divine law; the likeness of the world to God; the necessity of the struggle against concupiscence. Eusebius draws also attention to Plato's rejection of atheism and his defence of the presence of a design in the world. Motion and order require a cause; hence, God exists.[49]

In other books of his *Praeparatio evangelica*, Eusebius argues that the Greeks borrowed their wisdom from the Hebrews: the basic tenets of Greek philosophy agree with the teachings of the Bible. Those philosophers who disagree with the Scriptures, disagree also with their fellow Greeks.[50]

Saint Athanasius is a theologian and a man of action. In his *Contra Arianos* he does not take a position with regard to philosophy, although he does use certain philosophical terms. His earlier works *Contra Gentiles* and *De incarnatione Verbi* do have some references to philosophers. In the latter he criticizes the Epicureans for teaching that the world came about by itself: nothing valuable comes about by itself. In *Contra Gentiles* 6–7, he attacks with vigor the view that evil is a being. To denote God, Athanasius uses the Platonic metaphysics of the ὄντος ὄν.

Saint Basil is quite positive with regard to pagan culture and education. In his letter to Libanius he praises Athens for her treasures of education and wisdom. In his *Ad iuvenes* he argues the need to study profane literature and philosophy in order to obtain the tools for a better understanding of Holy Scripture: those who dye fabrics must first get their dyes together and, one must first look at the reflection of the sun on the surface of water before attempting to look at the sun itself. If there is some kinship between philosophical views and Christian doctrine, this will help the students. If not, the difference will confirm the knowledge of that which is better. The relationship between both is like that of the leaves and the fruits of a tree.

Basil himself is influenced by Platonism and Neoplatonism. In his *Hexaemeron* 1.4 he argues that the Greek philosophers did not know about God. For this reason they did not derive the origin of the universe from an intelligent cause. In this passage Plato is not mentioned by name; Basil may be arguing against the Epicureans. He adds that God did not use matter as material but created it.

Basil's brother, Saint Gregory of Nyssa, was well acquainted with Greek philosophy.[51] He wrote his works in the context of a syncretism

---

49. This correspondence between Plato and the Christian faith is pointed out in *PE* 12. Eusebius also draws attention to Plato's doctrine of divine providence.

50. *PE* 15.1.

51. See Heinrich Dörrie, in H. Dörrie, et al., eds., *Gregor von Nyssa und die Philosophie* (Leiden: 1976), 22.

that had Platonism as its most powerful component. For a while Platonism was even proposed as a scientifico-religious alternative to the Christian faith. As a matter of fact, the emperor Julian (from 359) attempted to use it as such against the Church. Gregory's view of Platonism is that of Porphyrius.[52] Pagan moral philosophy can sometimes be of help, he says, but it alone is not sufficient. Additionally, whatever is not true and good must be cut out. Sometimes philosophers have good doctrines but they deform them by their errors.[53] With regard to the soul they tend to say whatever they chance to think, but Christians accept only what conforms to Holy Scripture. For that reason they give up Plato's comparison of the soul with a chariot, two horses, and the coachman.[54] Gregory also discards the opinion that the soul is an emanation from God, and opposes Platonic and Pythagorean theories of transmigration and preexistence, calling this view impious because it asserts that man's individual soul comes into being through sin. He criticizes those who consider the soul mortal or explain it by means of the material elements of which it would be composed.[55] He points out, over and against Platonic views, that God is a personal being. On the other hand, Gregory accepts the classical and predominantly Aristotelian view of the cosmos, with its spheres and elements. He also uses the Platonic theory that the material world is an image of what is higher.

Before we consider the attitude of the Christian authors with regard to Aristotle, a few general observations may be helpful. All the authors use philosophy and acknowledge implicitly or explicitly its function for the training of the mind, a systematic explanation of the faith, and the defense against dissidents. Many of them say that some philosophers reached valuable insights into the truth. Positions such as that of Hippolytus are the exception rather than being common. In their view of the cosmos, all Christian authors accept some basic ideas from Greek thought, for example, that the world consists of four elements and is finite, and its marvellous order witnesses to the existence of God.[56]

In most cases the discussion of philosophical positions depended not so much on objective considerations as on more contingent events such as vicious anti-Christian attacks by philosophical writers and the appeal by heretics to philosophical authorities. In their zeal to defend

52. See ibid., 29. Dörrie reminds us that Prophyrius had edited the works of Plotinus about 300.
53. *De vita Moysis*, PG 44.336–37.
54. *De anima et resurrectione* 8.2: PG 46.49–52.
55. Ibid. 14.2–8.
56. See E. Minnerath, *Les Chrétiens et le monde (I° and II° siècles)* (Paris: 1973).

the Faith the Christian authors occasionally resorted to strong language. On the other hand, when they were led to seek support from philosophers, almost all Christian authors show a tendency to a closer association with Platonism than with any other philosophical system. This must be explained by the religious nature of Plato's thought, and its accessibility, as well as by its intrinsic merits. Consider the appeal of Plato's theory of an immaterial supreme reality, his account of the spiritual nature of the soul, and his description of moral life as a struggle to detach oneself from the world of becoming. However, very serious obstacles made an even partial assimilation of Platonism impossible: its tendency to monism; its divinization of the cosmos; its disregard of the world of becoming, of history, and the body. The ὁμοούσιον became the insurmountable barrier between Christianity and Platonism. Opposing the view of Protestant authors who speak of a hellenization of the Christian faith, Heinrich Dörrie argues that, as to its substance, Platonism has never been accepted by the church.[57]

III. THE CHRISTIAN APOLOGISTS AND ARISTOTLE

Tatianus's *Oratio ad Graecos* is a diatribe intended to pour ridicule on Plato, Aristotle, the Cynics, and the other philosophers. He blames Aristotle for asserting that there is no Providence for beings in the sublunar region, and that health and good fortune are required for man's happiness.[58] He adds that Aristotle also denies the immortality of the soul.[59] As we shall see, the same objections keep returning in Patristic writings. Apparently Tatianus reads Aristotle through the spectacles of his enemies. The Stagirite's considered view is quite different: in the *Nicomachean Ethics* (1100b8–10) fortune and external goods are not constituents of happiness but external conditions. The allegation that Aristotle excluded providence from the lower part of the cosmos is probably based on the *De mundo*.[60] For this doctrine, however, there is a basis in Aristotle's metaphysics. Tatianus does not yet use the argument that Aristotle's philosophy leads to shallow dialectics as some later Christian authors say it does.

Athenagoras of Athens is better acquainted with the theories of the different philosophers than Tatianus is. Aristotle, he says, holds that God, although being one, consists of body and soul: The ether and

57. Dörrie, 37.
58. *Ad Graecos*, 2.
59. Ibid. 25.
60. See A.-J. Festugière, "Aristote dans la littérature grecque chrétienne jusqu'à Théodorète," in *L'Idéal religieux des Grecs et l'Evangile* (Paris: 1932), 223ff.

the celestial spheres are God's body. God's soul supervises their motions without moving itself.[61] The source of this passage seems to be the *Placita* of Aetius, perhaps through the mediation of the *Epitome* of the pseudo-Plutarch.[62] Festugière sees in this concept of God some traits of the divinity of the Stoa and the *De mundo*.[63] The lost Aristotelian dialogue *On Philosophy* is likely to be the remote source of this interpretation, which was so widespread that it was even found in Peripatetic circles.[64]

Athenagoras furthermore notes that Aristotle excluded Divine Providence from sublunar things because of the inequality in fortune among men.[65] There is a certain dependence on Aristotle in Athenagoras's view that purpose is maintained in the universe and that despite occasional failure each specific order of things manages to achieve its own end.[66] This also applies to his use of the doctrine of the four causes and the principle of causality. Athenagoras makes an allusion to philosophy as dialectic, a critique which later Christian authors will frequently level against Aristotle.

Aristides begins his *Apology* with a concise argument to prove God's existence; the material for his proof is derived from Aristotle's demonstration from movement.

Justin mentions that in his quest for truth he also visited the Aristotelians, but because his teacher demanded a salary, he decided to go elsewhere. This teacher probably instructed his students in dialectic and elementary knowledge about the cosmos. Some other passages in the *Dialogue with Trypho* show the influence of Aristotle: the soul is not life itself but shares in life, for if it were life itself, it would make something else be alive, not itself.[67] A second doctrine is that the soul consists of soul-matter and life-giving spirit. This soul-matter evokes the fifth element, the material from which the stars are made. However, this view also depends on the Stoic doctrine that the pneuma is the essence of the soul.[68]

The pseudo-Justinian work *Cohortatio ad Gentiles* notes that Plato and Aristotle are far more respected than other philosophers; both are considered to have led a morally perfect life. But the author is sharply

---

61. *Oratio pro christianis* 6–7.

62. This dates to approximately 150. See also Eusebius, *PE* 14.16.8.

63. Festugière, "Aristote dans la littérature," 232.

64. See G. Lazzati, *L'Aristotele perduto e gli scrittori cristiani* (Milano: 1937), 69–73.

65. *Oratio* 25. As was pointed out in Section I, this critique is probably based on *De mundo*, although it does have a basis in the *Corpus aristotelicum*.

66. *De resurr.* 25. See Barnard, *A Study*, 120.

67. The passage recalls *Met.* 990b30, as R. M. Grant argued, "Aristotle and the Conversion of Justin," *Journal of Theological Studies* 7 (1956): 246–48.

68. *Stoicorum veterum fragmenta* 1: 521; 2: 272.

critical of Aristotle's attack on Plato. Moreover, Aristotle placed divinity in the fifth element and had a confused idea of God, contradicting himself. This critique probably refers to *On Philosophy*.[69] The author says that Aristotle made matter together with God the principle of all things and had no use for the Ideas. The soul has no corruptible parts, as Plato says it has; there is only intellect in it. But since the soul is the ἐντελέχεια of the body it is mortal. It is prior to movement and therefore it is unmoved itself.[70] The author of the treatise probably draws on the exoterical Aristotle, but seems to have some knowledge of *On the Soul*.

In his *Irrisio* (1–10), Hermias asserts that Aristotle knows two principles, acting and undergoing. There is no development in that which acts, but that which undergoes has four properties (the four main cosmic qualities). Hermias combines, it would seem, the doctrine of act and potency with that of a division of the cosmos into an always active part and the sublunar region characterized by the four qualities.

In his *Refutatio*, Hippolytus mentions Aristotle on several occasions, in particular in descriptions of philosophical schools presented in the first and seventh books. Aristotle gave a more scientific form to philosophy and made it argumentative. He developed the theory of the ten categories of being: the main constituents of all things are substance and the nine accidents. In the greater part of his views Aristotle agrees with Plato: He teaches the doctrine of the fifth element. After death the soul survives for a certain time until it is dissolved in the fifth element.[71] The world-soul is immortal, and the world itself eternal.

In chapter nine of book six Hippolytus quotes the magician Simon's view that visible fire is produced by an invisible one; Aristotle called this δύναμις and ἐνέργεια, and Plato αἰσθητόν and νοητόν.

In book seven Hippolytus intends to show that Basilides was misdirected by Aristotle, from whose doctrines he got his heresy together. Aristotle divides οὐσία into genus, species (εἶδος), and individual. The species are separated off from the genus which, he says, is just a heap of species. Hippolytus considers this genus a self-subsistent reality and the principle of all species. He seems to confuse genus with matter. In *Refutatio* 7.19 Hippolytus mentions the division of οὐσία into mat-

69. See Cicero, *De natura deorum* 1.13.33; *De finibus* 5.5.12. Cf. Minucius Felix, *Octavius* 19.9 ("Aristoteles variat"), and L. Alfonsi, "Traces du jeune Aristote dans la *Cohortatio ad Gentiles* faussement attribuée à Justin," in *Vigiliae christianae* 2, 65–88.

70. This observation is repeated by other Christian authors. It might ultimately go back to Aristotle's view that an unmoved point of support must be the starting point of any local movement (see his *On the Progression of Animals*).

71. This view is patently Stoic.

ter, form, and privation. The cosmos is divided into sections: the sublunar part of it is not governed by God and left to itself, but the rest of the universe is well ordered and extends to the outer circumference. According to Hippolytus the subject matter of physics is this sublunar part, whereas metaphysics considers what is above the moon.

He mentions a treatise by Aristotle on the fifth element, and a book on the soul in three parts. Hippolytus notes that it is not easy to tell what Aristotle means by soul, for his definition of soul as the ἐντελέχεια of an organic body needs much explanation. God is far more difficult to consider than even the soul. Aristotle defines God as "thinking of thinking." It is impossible to understand this definition, for it implies that God is mere not-being. The world is eternal and without error, for it is governed by νοῦς. Aristotle wrote works on ethics by which he changed his disciples from bad to good. In *Refutatio* 7.20 Hippolytus observes that Aristotle also wrote on homonyms and the categories, but this is no reason to connect Aristotle with Basilides.

The sources used by Hippolytus are contaminated and reflect the popular knowledge of philosophical systems in his day. Hippolytus is apparently not a philosopher himself, for he has great difficulty with abstract definitions. According to him, Basilides would have taken over from Aristotle the theory of homonyms and applied it to God whom we do not really know, for God is ineffable. As we have seen, Hippolytus believes that Aristotle's definition of God as "thinking of thinking" deprives God of being, so that one ends up with the unknowable God of the Gnostics. Furthermore, Basilides said that God created a seed of the world, from which all things developed. Surprisingly, Hippolytus connects this "seed" with Aristotle's genus. It is hardly necessary to point out the various misunderstandings which led Hippolytus to arrive at this reduction. To make some excuse for him, Festugière recalls that even Seneca was mistaken with regard to the precise meaning of the Aristotelian categories of being.[72]

It is perhaps not uninteresting to leave the Greek Christian authors for a moment to see what Tertullian has to say about Aristotle. In his *De praecriptione haereticorum,* chapter seven, the African apologist writes: "Wretched Aristotle, you taught the Gnostics dialectic which is a mistress of construction and destruction with its many proofs. It treats everything and finally nothing." But in chapter 3 of his *De anima* he praises Aristotle's logical consistency. In chapter 5 he argues against Plato and (the exoteric) Aristotle that the soul must be a body because it perceives the affections of bodies. In chapter twelve he attempts to

---

72. Festugière, "Aristote dans la littérature," 251. See Seneca, *Epist.* 6.58.6ff.

show that the νοῦς cannot be impassible as Aristotle asserts it is. In chapter thirty-two Tertullian adds more critical remarks on the atoms of Epicurus, the numbers of Pythagoras, the Ideas of Plato, and Aristotle's ἐντελέχεια.

IV. THE THIRD-CENTURY AUTHORS AND EUSEBIUS OF CAESAREA ON ARISTOTLE

When we return now to the Greek Christian authors, we must first deal with Clement of Alexandria. Clement draws attention to some blatant errors of the philosophers, such as the limitation of Divine Providence to the higher spheres of the cosmos.[73] On this point Aristotle was misled by a psalmtext.[74] Clement's *Protreptic* was intended to replace the famous treatise of the same name by Aristotle.[75] Clement goes back to before Thales, brings in the beliefs of other nations and has a more pessimistic view of the history of thought than Aristotle.[76] The influence of Aristotle's *Protreptic* shows in Clement's distinction between "to live" and "to live well," in his insistence on the importance of music, and the saying that not doing philosophy is still doing philosophy.[77] Clement writes that the founder of the Peripatetic school did not acknowledge the Creator of all things but considered the world-soul the highest god. Aristotle asserts that matter is a principle, but he does not indicate that the only true principle is but one. While Clement mentions Plato repeatedly and credits him with some knowledge about the Scriptures, Aristotle is seldom referred to by name. At *Protreptic* 5.66.4, Clement considers him the father of heresy. In a more positive text he calls Chrysippus a dialectician, Aristotle the specialist in physical science, and Plato the philosopher.[78]

References to Aristotle's ethics are more frequent. Clement quotes the Stagirite to the effect that health is best for man.[79] Aristotle and his school say that man's last end is a virtuous life, but that in order to attain happiness three goods are required.[80] He recounts that according to Aristotle the precept "know yourself" came from the Py-

73. *Stromata* 5.14.
74. *Stromata* 5.14.
75. Lazzati, *L'Aristotele perduto*, 34.
76. See J. Daniélou, *Message évangélique et culture hellénistique* (Tournai: 1961), 58.
77. *Stromata* 1.18, 162. On this question see Lazzati, *L'Aristotele*.
78. *Stromata* 7.16. In 8.9 he refers to Aristotle's logic. In 6.16 there is a reference to the biological works (Aristotle's theory of the embryo), but it looks as if Clement did not have the precise text himself.
79. *Stromata* 4.5.
80. *Stromata* 2.21.

thagoreans.[81] H. A. Wolfson has drawn attention to a text where Clement, appealing to Aristotle, writes that the judgment that follows on knowledge is πίστις (faith).[82] Clement also quotes the Aristotelian saying that a husband should never display affection for his wife when his servants are present.[83]

In conclusion one may say that Clement probably knew more of Aristotle than most other Christian authors of his time. However, the suggestion by Daniélou that Clement had firsthand knowledge of the school writings of Aristotle is not convincing.[84] The evidence is too scanty, and Clement may have relied on secondhand information. At best he knew the *Nicomachean* and the *Eudemian Ethics*, as well as some pages from *On the Soul*.

In his *Contra Celsum* (3.75) Origen writes that despite their love of wisdom, the Christians keep themselves away from Epicurus (who rejects Providence and places man's highest good in pleasure) and from the Peripatetics who deny Divine Providence and all relations between God and man. Both philosophers would have benefitted if they had listened to Moses, but Origen concedes that Aristotle is somewhat less impious than Epicurus.[85] He quotes a passage of Celsus that is sharply critical of the Jews who gave God the name of "the highest." Origen raises the question of whether names are a product of convention, as Aristotle has it in *De Interpretatione* 2.16–27. He speaks of the followers of Aristotle who are involved in the study of the question of the names of God.

Origen mentions twice that Aristotle criticized the theory of Ideas.[86] He adds that Aristotle denied the immortality of the soul. Aristotle's defection from Plato does not mean that Plato was wrong but that Aristotle was ungrateful. Likewise the defection of heretics cannot be used as an argument against Christianity.[87] According to the Peripatetics, prayers, just like the victims one offers, are of no use.[88]

---

81. *Stromata* 1.14.

82. *Stromata* 2.4. See H. A. Wolfson, *The Philosophy of the Church Fathers* (Cambridge, Mass.: 1956), 112ff. However, Aristotle does not apply πίστις to scientific knowledge, but he uses the term in the sense of a judgment that the knowledge we have corresponds to the reality of things. Cf. *On the Soul* 428a19–23, where Aristotle states that opinion implies faith, faith implies persuasion, persuasion implies reason. "Faith" would seem to mean the awareness of the certitude of one's knowledge. In this sense it denotes a function of the speculative intellect. It may be "faith" with regard to what is perceived by the senses, but also with regard to what is demonstrated by argument. In Stoic philosophy the meaning of the term became wider.

83. *Paedag.* 3.12.

84. Daniélou, *Message*, 121.

85. *Contra Celsum* 1.21.

86. *Contra Celsum* 1.13 and 2.12. He probably has his information from Diogenes Laertius 5.9 and not from *Posterior Analytics* 83a33.

87. *Contra Celsum* 2.12.

88. *Contra Celsum* 2.13. To the contrary cf. *Politics* 7.8.

The *De principiis* of Origen has few references to Aristotle. In book
1, chapter 7, he mentions that some Christians accept the immutability
of the stars. But Origen sees a difficulty: are not all things other than
God open to good as well as to evil? In his examination of this problem, Origen first accepts that the stars may be ensouled because the
Bible says that they execute God's commands, then observes that if
they do, they are capable of good and evil. Origen argues against the
existence of the fifth element: this is not known in Christian doctrine
and has no basis in Scripture. In the resurrection at the end of time,
we will not be given wholly new bodies, but our former bodies will be
transformed.[89]

A number of passages are reminiscent of texts in the *Corpus aristotelicum*,[90] but compared to the numerous dialogues of Plato quoted by
Origen, references to Aristotle's works are very few. Let us close our
remarks on Origen with two passages from *De principiis* 2.11: the first,
"all men seek knowledge," obviously refers to the opening sentence of
the *Metaphysics*; the second, a description of the three ways of life (the
life of pleasure, of effort, and of spiritual pursuits), evokes *Nicomachean Ethics* 1.3.

When we discussed Eusebius's *Praeparatio evangelica* in Section II
above, treatment of his attitude toward Aristotle was postponed. In
book fifteen Eusebius mentions some of the stories about Aristotle's
life and character in order to brush them aside as slander and ridic-
ulous gossip: Contradictions in these stories show that they are ficti-
tious. Eusebius handles the question of slanderous information about
Aristotle's private life in a gentlemanly way—the criticisms concerned
Aristotle's marriage with Pythias, Hermias's sister and his "defection"
from Plato. Eusebius shows acquaintance with the secondary literature
about Aristotle but, as will appear from the following, he shows little
if any understanding of the content of the school writings.

In chapters four to thirteen Eusebius quotes Atticus's and Plotinus's
rather devastating critique of a certain number of important points
of Aristotle's philosophy. The section is introduced by a passage on
Aristotle's view of happiness. Happiness is said to consist of three
goods. Without health, for instance, virtue alone is insufficient. Eusebius adds that the following pages will show how Plato's disciples
fight these views. Atticus vehemently opposes the Aristotelian idea of

---

89. De prin. 3.6.
90. *De prin.* 2.8 to *On the Soul* 411b7; *De prin.* 2.8 to *On the Soul* 405b29; *De prin.*
2.11 to the opening sentence of the *Metaphysics*; and in *De prin.* 3.1.13 there is question
of hidden evil being purified which might be a reference to the theory of κάθαρσις of
the *Poetics*.

happiness insofar as it denies that virtue alone is sufficient and attributes an influence to chance. Atticus apparently chose to start his attack with a critique of this point so that he could argue that, since Aristotle has the wrong view about the end of human life, the remainder of his philosophy is also bound to be wrong: This embittered and sly beast, Aristotle, cannot ascend to the sublime heights of Plato's doctrine! Platonists and Aristotelians have nothing in common. Neither in the works of Aristotle himself nor in those of his disciples do we find anything that tells our youth how to attain perfection by mastering their passions. Aristotle's books on ethics are insignificant, down-to-earth, and vulgar. In his stress on virtue and his disregard of other values, as well as in his lack of understanding of the concept of "knowledge for the sake of knowledge," Atticus seems closer to the Stoa than to Plato.

Eusebius turns next to the view that Divine Providence stops short at the moon, a theory which contradicts what Moses and the Prophets as well as Plato say. Atticus argues that the denial of Divine Providence undermines happiness: Aristotle destroys the divine order of nature, cuts the soul from its hope. Without belief in an afterlife there is no reason to be virtuous.[91]

Aristotle asserts that the world is eternal, Plato, on the other hand, says that it was made. Atticus knows that there are Platonists who think that even Plato considered the world to be eternal. But, he says, if you carefully read Plato, you will have to concede that he speaks of the god bringing about order in the world. Atticus mentions the arguments of Aristotle without analyzing them in depth ("what has come into existence, is perishable"; "what is eternal, has not been made") but, he says, if you consider the power of God rather than the nature of things, these objections lose their strength. God rules the world; he is more powerful than any created cause that makes things exist.[92] As appears from these chapters, Atticus's critique remains superficial and does not take into consideration the real problems. One can nevertheless understand why Eusebius felt he could use it to strengthen the position of Christian doctrine.

In the next chapter of the *Praeparatio evangelica* Eusebius quotes Atticus's attack on the theory of the fifth element: In his conceit, Aristotle introduced the superfluous fifth οὐσία which has only the name but none of the normal properties of bodies such as weight, temperature, and humidity. According to Atticus, Aristotle concocted this theory by borrowing from Plato the idea that there is an intelli-

91. *PE* 15.5.   92. *PE* 15.6.

gible immaterial substance and the idea that the celestial bodies are divine and incorruptible.[93]

In chapter eight Aristotle is said to deprive the celestial bodies of their souls, whereas Plato ascribes their circular movement to the causality of a soul. Moreover, Aristotle differs from Plato in his appraisal of what is above and what is below. Plato does not call the circumference of the world "above." At this juncture Eusebius notes that Moses and the Scriptures of the Hebrews do not concern themselves with these questions because they do not contribute to the correct conduct of one's life.

A discussion of the soul follows: According to Plato the soul is immortal and the source of all motion; all knowledge is ἀνάμνησις, so that one does not really learn new things. Atticus believes that Plato's entire philosophy and all his views depend on his conviction of the soul's divine nature and immortality. Those who do not accept this, bring down the edifice of Plato's doctrine, for the soul is the principle and cause of all process; it is the offspring of God. However, according to Aristotle the soul itself is unmoved, and it does not have the body as its seat. He believes that such activities as deliberation, thought, and expectation are of the body and the soul together. The Peripatetic Dicaearchus went even further and denied the self-subsisting nature of the soul altogether. But the activities of the soul are not those of the body. Through an analysis of them we learn something about the nature of the soul itself. If someone would try to defend Aristotle saying that he admits the immortality of the νοῦς, we answer that this is correct, but that he does not explain how the intellect arises. Apparently he does not know, and tries to cover up his ignorance. Plato, on the other hand, made it clear that the intellect must be always in a soul.[94]

In chapter ten Eusebius quotes Plotinus's criticism of the theory that the soul is the ἐντελέχεια of the body. If Aristotle's view were true, we would never be able to oppose ourselves to concupiscence, for the soul would be the subject of one and the same disposition and not of two conflicting ones. Even sleep would become impossible because certain other activities of the soul continue. Plotinus concludes that the soul which has sense cognition and desire cannot be the ἐντελέχεια of the body. Even when applied to plants, Aristotle's view faces difficulties because sometimes a plant's soul withdraws itself from the body of the plant into its roots. The soul, Plotinus writes, is a real being, whereas the body belongs to the world of becoming and

93. *PE* 15.7.   94. *PE* 15.9.

process. It is not difficult to answer Plotinus's criticism by pointing out that he failed to distinguish between substance, quantity, faculties, etc. Surprisingly, Eusebius did not see the disastrous conclusions that follow from Plotinus's thesis with regard to the nature of the souls of animals and plants.

Eusebius wants to drive some more nails into Aristotle's coffin. To this effect he now quotes from Porphyrius: if the soul is unmoved, whence come the movements of the living beings? Whence come volitions, cognition, reflection? It is shameful to say that the soul is the ἐντελέχεια of a physical body: on the contrary, it is a self-moving being and substance.[95] Eusebius closes this section by saying that according to Plato the soul brings order into the entire world, but that according to Aristotle there is no such comprehensive cause of order. Eusebius quotes a passage from Atticus in which this author bitterly attacks Aristotle for rejecting the Ideas: according to Plato the Ideas are reality itself, and eternal truth and man's happiness consists in reaching them and partaking in them.

In the following chapters of his *Praeparatio evangelica* Eusebius quotes from Zeno, Arius Didymus, Porphyrius, and Numenius. In chapters twenty-one and twenty-two he presents a refutation by Longinus and Plotinus of the Stoic theory that the soul is corporeal. In the final pages of his book he gives some reference to the views of the Presocratics about the celestial bodies. Let us end this section with Atticus's somewhat sarcastic qualification of Aristotle as the self-styled "secretary of the world of nature."

What prompted Eusebius to present this concerted attack on Aristotle by some of his opponents and enemies? Strangely enough, Eusebius did not see the dangers inherent to Platonism and Neoplatonism. He concentrated on some of Aristotle's errors, incapable of making a distinction between principles or basic tenets and derived theories.

V. THE FOURTH-CENTURY HERETICS, THE GREAT DOCTORS, AND ARISTOTLE

One of the most astonishing features of Christian life in the Church of the fourth century is the rise and rapid expansion of heresies. Leaving aside the third-century Gnostics, Sabellius, and Paul of Samosata, we must deal with Arius, who accused his bishop of falsehood when the latter preached that the Father begot the Son. Arius and his followers, in particular Aetius, had a close connection with the Aris-

95. *PE* 15.11.

totelian school, which was noted for training its students in subtle dialectic. The students were taught to discover the flaws in their opponents' arguments and show, with the help of syllogisms, the impossible conclusions which would follow from their position. These teachers were actually closer to the Sophists than to Aristotle, but they claimed Aristotle as their main authority. Arius was supremely skillful in this type of disputation; his follower Aetius belonged to the school of an Aristotelian teacher in Alexandria, and Eunomius was his disciple.

Saint Basil and the two Gregorys protested against the intrusion of this sort of dialectics into theology. In a similar vein of thought, Epiphanius calls Aristotle the bishop of the Arians.[96] As John Henry Newman writes, the error of the ancient Sophists had consisted "in their indulging without restraint or discrimination in the discussion of practical topics whether religious or political" without caring about the particular nature of the subject discussed. "The rhetoricians of Christian times introduced the same error into their treatment of the highest and most sacred subjects of theology."[97] Their minds were bent on the consideration of what is material only and not open to the contemplation of the supernatural order. Rules and criteria "grounded on physics were made the basis of discussion about the possibilities and impossibilities in a spiritual substance."[98] Epiphanius says of a sect of Arians that "aiming to exhibit divine nature by means of Aristotelian syllogisms and geometrical data, they are led to declare that Christ cannot be born from God."[99]

A few examples of this way of arguing may perhaps be helpful. Saint Basil quotes the Arians as saying that things dissimilar in their nature are caused in dissimilar ways; hence, that which is caused in a dissimilar way, is dissimilar according to its nature. Because Saint Paul says that all things are from the Father through the Son, the Father and the Son cannot be similar.[100] Another example is quoted by Epiphanius: Aetius argues that what is produced is different from that which produces it. This excludes the consubstantiality of the Father and the Son. God must be above all becoming.[101] In book one of his *Contra Eunomium*, Basil recounts another argument: since a privation is posterior to the *habitus* of which it is a privation, the "not-born" cannot be an attribute of the First Principle.

96. *Adversus haereses* 69.69.

97. John Henry Newman, *The Arians of the Fourth Century* (edit. of 1908), 327.

98. Ibid., 34.

99. *Adversus haereses*, PG 42:338C.

100. *De Spiritu Sancto* 2.4; PG:32, 73AB.

101. *Adversus haereses*, PG 42:533C. See G. Bardy, "L'Héritage littéraire d'Aëtius," in *Revue d'histoire ecclésiastique* 24 (1928): 814–15.

As appears from these quotations, the sharp criticism of Aristotelian dialectics by the great Doctors of the East has a rather accidental cause. We would be inclined to assume that the *Organon* is the most harmless part of the *Corpus aristotelicum* insofar as the Faith is concerned. But it so happened that heretics such as Aetius and Eunomius appealed to Aristotelian categories and distinctions in order to adulterate the Faith. In this way they provoked an aversion to dialectics among orthodox Christians.

While in the second century the Stoa had the name of being the main school of dialectics, the Aristotelians being considered as interested in physics,[102] Saint Basil and Saint Gregory of Nazianzus attribute this infatuation with dialectics to both the Stoa and the Aristotelians.[103]

Under these circumstances it is not surprising that Marcellus, the bishop of Ancyra and a staunch defender of orthodoxy writes that the heretical sects are all derived from pagan philosophy, from the doctrines of Hermes Trismegistos, Plato, and Aristotle.[104]

We must now consider the position of the three great Doctors of the fourth century. Together with his friend Saint Gregory of Nazianzus, Saint Basil studied in Athens where he attended the classes of the sophist Himerius and those of Proheresius. Himerius was an eclectic who considered Plato and Aristotle the greatest philosophers, Plato being the first. Gregory describes the education of Basil, who studied the arts and sciences with great success and became a superb dialectician. However, at the school of Himerius all these studies remained subordinated to the art of arguing.[105]

Among Basil's major works is his *Homilies on the Hexaemeron*. The sources for a good number of his comments on the first chapters of Genesis are Aristotle, Plato, Posidonius, and Plotinus.[106] Saint Basil begins by saying that we need not refute Greek views on the origin of the world because the philosophers contradict one another. Nevertheless, he turns his guns on atomism. Somewhat further on, without

102. See Clement of Alexandria, *Stromata* 7.101.4.

103. In the West a similar debate shaped up somewhat later. In view of certain excesses and deformations in the expressions of the faith, some Fathers declared that they could not accept that the faith be subject to the rules of human language. God knows grammar much better than Donatus and Quintilianus. See Saint Gregory the Great, *Épist. miss.*, chap. 5: "Indignum vehementer existimo ut verba caelestis oraculi restringam sub regulas Donati" (*Patrologia latina* 75:516B; hereafter *PL*). One may recall that Saint Anselm likewise speaks of the *nefasta temeritas* of modern dialecticians (*De fide Trin.*, chap. 2), and one of his disciples, Honorius, sees in philosophy and in dialectics a wine "qui mentes omnium inflat et in jactantiam elevat" (*In cant.:PL* 173:361D; 422B).

104. *De sancta Ecclesia.*

105. See Y. Courtonne, *Un Témoin du IVme siècle oriental: Saint Basile et son temps d'après sa correspondance* (Paris: 1973), 48–54.

106. See J. Quasten, *Patrology* (Westminister, MD 1990), 3:217.

mentioning Aristotle by name, he warns his auditorium that they should not think that the body which moves in a circular orbit does not have a cause.[107] It needs a cause to have given it its center and circumference. Another interesting argument is the following: since part of the universe is corruptible, the entire cosmos must be so.

In this first *Homily* Saint Basil gives an enumeration of the different meanings of the term ἀρχή that evokes Aristotle's *Metaphysics* 5 and the division given in *Physics* 2. He also stresses that there is finality in the world: everything is directed to the well-being of man. The world is a school to instruct rational souls in the knowledge of God. The philosophers, on the other hand, do admit a certain causality of God with regard to the world, although they hold that God did not create it. Subsequently Saint Basil speaks of time, using Aristotelian material (46C–D). He mentions the view of some who say that the world coexists with God as his shadow (48C).

In this *Homily,* Basil appears to admit Aristotle's image of the world: the heavens are made of a different element because they show no contraries and have an always equal movement. He also takes over the Aristotelian idea of the center and the circumference of the world as that which is up. Finally the text presents the division of sciences and arts into theoretical, technical, and moral disciplines.

In the third *Homily,* details of the structure of the world are discussed. The author wonders if our heaven (the expanse) is different from the first heaven and thinks that the answer is affirmative. One might describe his commentary as an attempt to combine a fairly literal exegesis of Holy Scripture with acceptable Greek cosmology (while it discards dualistic, materialistic, and atomistic interpretations). Throughout the treatise, the beauty of order is stressed. Further on in his commentary Saint Basil uses the Aristotelian expression of man as a microcosmos, and speaks of the marvels of man's nature.[108]

In one of his letters he writes that Plato used dialogues to express his thoughts, whereas Aristotle and Theophrastus, who were aware of Plato's shortcomings in this respect, wrote treatises.[109] With an appeal to Aristotle, Eunomius objected to ascribing "not having been made" to the Son; only the Father is not-made. Saint Basil attributes the "not-made" to divine being as such and exclaims: "Do we really need an argument from Aristotle or Chrysippus to know that the unborn has not been born?"[110]

107. *Hexaemeron* 9B.
108. *Hexaemeron* X 3. Cf. *Physics* 252b27.
109. Letter 105, addressed to Diodorus.
110. *Contra Eunomium* 1.5: *PG*, 516.

Petavius quotes a saying by Saint Basil, as recorded by Saint John Damascene, that the entire philosophy of Aristotle is distasteful to Christians and hostile to Christ.[111] However, such a saying would give a wrong impression: philosophy in general, and Aristotle's philosophy in particular, is a tool used by Basil. In his *Commentary on Isaiah*, chapter one, he writes that the power of dialectic is as a wall protecting the *dogmata*. In his Letter 38 to Saint Gregory of Nyssa he presents a fine dissertation on the meanings of οὐσία and ὑπόστασις in the theology of the Holy Trinity. Without the philosophical training of its author this letter would have remained unwritten.[112] However, philosophy is subordinated to the Faith: if a doctrine conflicts with the Faith it must be rejected.

As we have seen, Saint Basil was obliged to denounce the heretical views of Eunomius of Cyzicus who became the champion of Arianism. As is apparent from his *First Apology*, written against Saint Basil, Eunomius's philosophy shows Neoplatonic and Aristotelian traits. However, his entire work is dominated by a tendency toward rationalism and nominalism.[113]

Saint Gregory of Nyssa reproaches Eunomius for using a decoction of Aristotle's syllogistics.[114] In this connection he also rebukes Aristotle for excluding Divine Providence from the sublunar world (*Contra Eunomium* 2.411). Eunomius is threatening with the spear of Aristotle (ibid. 2.620). Gregory reproaches Aristotle for τεχνολογία but he himself uses the Aristotelian theory of opposition to refute Eunomius (ibid. 12).[115]

---

111. *Theologica dogmata*, Prolegomena, chap. 3; p. 18, 1885 edition.

112. As H. Dörrie has shown, the clarification of the term ὑπόστασις and the fixation of its use in the doctrine of the Faith owe the most to Athanasius (Dörrie, *Hypostasis: Wort und Bedeutungsgeschichte* [Göttingen: 1955]). We have not discussed Saint Athanasius's attitude toward Aristotle, because there is little to say. His *Ad gentes* contains some references to Pseudo-Aristotle's *De mundo*. The *Orationes contra diversas haereses* has some more. A possible reference to Aristotle's definition of time occurs in *Contra Arianos* 1.11. According to Wolfson, *Philosophy of the Church*, 307, a passage in *Contra Arianos* 1.14 ("What the Father engenders must be of the same nature as the Father himself ") recalls Aristotle's maxim "man engenders man." In his *Contra Macedonianum* (which may not be authentic) Athanasius writes that according to Aristotle things with the same but equivocal names have a different definition of their essence. Athanasius observes that one does not have to follow Aristotle but truth itself to know that equivocals do not have the same essence. On Athanasius's position with regard to philosophy, see E. Meyering, *Orthodoxy and Platonism in Athanasius: Synthesis or Antithesis?* (Leiden: 1968), 26–27, 30–33, 58–61, 80–81. In general, Athanasius is hardly interested in philosophy, even if he occasionally borrows from it (e.g., the description of God as the ὄντως ὄν). Cf. C. J. de Vogel, "Platonism and Christianity: A Mere Antagonism or a Profound Common Ground?" in *Vigiliae christianae* 39 (1985): 50–54.

113. See J. Quasten, *Patrology* 3:308.

114. *Contra Eunomium* 1.46.

115. *PG* 45:906–08.

The other works of Gregory also recall Aristotle on numerous occasions. In his edition of the *Commentary in Canticum Canticorum*, Langerbeck has collected about forty instances where the terms used may have been borrowed from Aristotle's works, in particular the *Nicomachean Ethics*, *Metaphysics*, *On the Soul*, *Parts of Animals*, and *Generation of Animals*. There are no references to the *Organon*, the *Physics*, or *On the Heavens*. In his *De virginitate*, Gregory takes over the Aristotelian definition of virtue being the mean between excess and deficiency (chapter 7.2). In this work some twenty passages evoke Aristotle, but references to Plato's works are much more frequent.

Even more than Basil and his brother had done, Saint Gregory of Nazianzus saw in Eunomius's writings a counteroffensive of Greek rationalism.[116] The heretics reduced religion to a mere question of human reasoning.[117] Saint Gregory liked to oppose to this wrong use of reason the positive contribution of philosophy to theology. Faith had to be conveyed in the language of Greek culture. In particular, what had been expressed in the manner of fishermen had to be reformulated in an Aristotelian way.[118] Moreover, philosophy must help to refute the arguments and principles of the heretics. Finally, philosophy prepares the mind for theological knowledge.

Positive appraisals of the role of philosophy are, however, accompanied by warnings. In his *Oratio* 28 Saint Gregory invites us to forsake useless speculations and to follow the narrow road to salvation. In a short paragraph he recalls the mistaken and sometimes preposterous conclusions of a number of philosophers: the silence of Pythagoras; The Ideas of Plato, his theory of transmigration and of ἀνάμνησις, and his belief that through the view of beautiful bodies, a (not-so-beautiful, according to Gregory) love is produced in the soul. He mentions next Epicurus's disregard of divinity and his unphilosophical theory of pleasure. With regard to Aristotle, Gregory recalls the latter's limitation of Divine Providence, his ἔντεχνον (artificial) dialectics, his "mortal way" of speaking about the soul, and the purely human dimension of his teaching (τὸ ἀνθρώπινον).

But this *Oratio* is also a fine piece of philosophical theology which shows a considerable Aristotelian influence. To mention a few points: Gregory draws a distinction between the *an sit* and the *quid sit*. He says that we cannot directly know God, but must ascend to him from created things. He rejects the Stoic theory that God is a body and the

116. See J. Plagnieux, *Saint Grégoire de Nazianze, théologien* (Paris: 1951), 282.
117. *Oratio* 31.18.
118. *Oratio* 23.12. See J. Mossay in the preface to his edition of Grégoire de Nazianze, *Discours* 24–26 in *Sources chrétiennes*, 284), p. 96–99.

atomism of the Epicureans. He also writes that some authors, whom he does not name, consider God to be the fifth element. Now there may be a fifth element, and you may even consider it incorporeal, but you go beyond all reasonable limits if you assert that the thing which moves in a circle is the Creator. There must be a cause of movement. If they say the cause is this or that thing, we ask again from whence it has its power, and so on. In this passage Saint Gregory shows that God is incorporeal.

Another Christian author, Epiphanius, says that heretics argue about God and Christ with syllogisms and subtleties. They assert, for instance, that if the Father engenders the Son willingly, the Son is later; how could Christ be already when he is engendered?[119] These "new Aristotelians" let the contagious power of this philosopher develop in themselves. Instead of taking refuge with the Holy Spirit, they prefer Aristotle and the rest of the dialecticians of this world. Aetius wants us to leave the truth of the fishermen to become disciples of Aristotle.

In this connection we should also mention Nemesius whose book *De natura hominis* had such a pervasive influence in the Middle Ages. It is significant that the author does not use the Aristotelian title *On the Soul* but the more biblical one *On the Nature of Man.* Although his approach to the study of man is more dualistic than that of Aristotle, Nemesius nevertheless feels it is important to consider the human body, and discusses the importance of the various organs. He follows Aristotle in his theory of the faculties and of free choice, refers to the *History of Animals,* and follows Aristotle in his account of the importance of the human hand. There are influences from the *Parts of Animals* and the *Generation of Animals.* With regard to the composition of man, Nemesius looks for a solution that holds the middle between Plato's dualism and the theory of the soul as ἐντελέχεια.

VI. THE FIFTH-CENTURY CHRISTIAN AUTHORS AND ARISTOTLE

In book two of his *Historia ecclesiastica* the historian Socrates has praise for Aristotle's works, in particular the *Sophistical Refutations.*[120] Aetius, he says, never had a good teacher, and did not go beyond the

119. *Adversus haereses* 2.2, PG 42:315A. One will find other examples in book 3. In the Latin West, Saint Ambrose writes with regard to this enthusiasm for dialectics: "Haec quae simplicibus verbis sacra Scriptura exprimit, magno quodam cothurno Aristoteles et Peripatetici personant" (*PL* 14:490C).

120. *PG* 67:300AB.

study of sophistical arguments nor understand the real intention of Aristotle in this book. Aristotle only wanted to propose exercises to train his students to unmask the false arguments of the Sophists.

Socrates has a balanced view of Greek philosophy: The disciples of Christ do not consider philosophy as inspired by God, nor do they entirely reject it as dangerous. Many Greek philosophers were not far from the knowledge of God and they opposed themselves against Epicurus and contentious sophists who denied Divine Providence. By their books the philosophers were very helpful to pious men, but they did not reach the real core of religion, the mystery of Christ.[121]

It would seem that Socrates' position reflects a new awareness of the importance of philosophy; it is much more positive toward Aristotle and dissociates him from the heretics.[122] We see this attitude also in the agreement between Athanasius II, the patriarch of Alexandria, and Ammonius (about 490) allowing Christian students to attend Ammonius's lectures.[123] The growing self-certitude of Christians in philosophical studies comes to the fore in Philoponus's critique of the Aristotelian doctrine of the eternity of the world and of time.

But let us return to the first decades of the fifth century. About 425 Theodoretus of Cyrus wrote a detailed refutation of paganism, the *Graecorum affectionum curatio*. In this book, which was written shortly before the council of Ephesus, the learned author places side by side the pagan and Christian answers to various problems. Although paganism had already lost much of its influence, occasional attacks were launched against the Faith, and pagan authors proposed a new religion and such models of sanctity as Apollonius of Tyana.

In the first book of his treatise, Theodoretus enumerates the different schools. Speaking of the Faith, he refers to Aristotle's definition of πίστις as the criterion of knowledge. In the second book the author mentions some theories of principles, omitting that of Aristotle. The following pages point out intimations of the doctrine of the Holy Trinity in Middle Platonism and Neoplatonism. Speaking about matter in book 4, Theodoretus has one sentence on Aristotle's doctrine: Aristotle considers matter corporeal, the Stoa calls it a body. Speculations about the size of the universe are of no value. Theodoretus seems to draw his information from Plutarch and Aetius. He insists on the

---

121. *PG* 67:410C.

122. Sozomenus, on the other hand, writes in his *Historia ecclesiastica* (*PG* 67:1083) that Aetius did study the entire philosophy of Aristotle.

123. See G. Verbeke, "Some Later Neoplatonic Views on Divine Creation and the Eternity of the World," in D. J. O'Meara, ed., *Neoplatonism and Christian Thought* (Norfolk, VA: 1982), 45–63.

endless variety of philosophical views of matter, the nature of man, and the human soul. Even Plato contradicts himself repeatedly. Intelligent people, like the Persians, grasp the meaning of difficult arguments and do not need to be acquainted with the labyrinths of Aristotle and Chrysippus.[124] A next step consists in developing truth from the positions of the philosophers: what they could only dimly see, is expressed more clearly in the Gospel.

He quotes Aristotle as excluding Providence from the lower region of the cosmos and surrendering the earth to fate.[125] For Theodoretus, Plato is the philosopher. In book 8 he justifies the cult of the martyrs and reminds his readers that even Aristotle used to offer sacrifices in honor of his dead wife. In book 11 he gives a survey of philosophical opinions with regard to man's last end: According to Plato it is the imitation of God. However, Aristotle did not use the doctrine of his master to his advantage, but declared that happiness comes about through three factors: the goods of the soul, those of the body, and external goods. In book 12 the author recounts some malicious stories about the Stagirite's attachment to valuable things. But he also makes critical remarks on the life of Plato and Socrates.

In conclusion one can say that Theodoretus has a good knowledge of Plato's dialogues. He seems to have read Plotinus and Porphyrius, unless he copies from other sources. He is not, however, a great thinker. His knowledge of Aristotle is superficial. In the first decades of the fifth century Aristotle was far from having a wide circle of disciples.

VII. THE GENERAL INFLUENCE OF ARISTOTELIANISM ON CHRISTIANS

In the course of this discussion we have pointed out that the Christians borrowed some terms and concepts from Aristotle. One may recall here the theories of the categories of being, the four causes, and analogy, and the definition of virtue. But there is more: E. Hatch has argued that under the influence of Aristotelianism a school of realistic, nonallegorical exegesis developed in Antioch. Unfortunately, it became entangled in a christology that had no eye for the central mystery of the Faith, so that it was rejected by orthodox Christianity.[126] However, according to A. Wistrand, Hatch fails to show to what extent

---

124. *Graecorum affectionum curatio*, 5.72.
125. Ibid. 6.7.
126. E. Hatch, *The Influence of Greek Ideas on Christianity* (Harper Torch: 1957), 81ff.

Theodorus of Mopsuestia was really influenced by Greek philosophy.[127] One may nevertheless speak of a Greek philosophical climate which, as Harnack argued, led Origen and others to a systematic and scientific elaboration of Christian doctrine.[128]

One may furthermore call attention to the fact that in the consideration of God's unity and the oneness of Christ, the modes of being one outlined by Aristotle in *Metaphysics* 5.6 played a certain role. To shed some light on what the Faith teaches in this respect, analogies were sought in the created order. In this connection philosophical positions began to exercise a greater influence.[129]

While the ideological background of Arianism is found in the Middle-Platonic theory of the descent of all beings, through various stages, from an ineffable First Principle, it has been argued that Nestorianism was caused by the intrusion of a more Aristotelian way of thinking into theology.[130] One may describe this influence as follows: Human nature, as it is now, is not the result of an ontological fall or sin, but it is a meaningful whole in which the mind must exercise control. Immortality insofar as it lies within the reach of man is not an extra gift of God and does not go beyond man but consists in rational knowledge, the rule of reason, virtue, and the contemplation of the universe.[131] As a matter of fact, Aristotle does not propose any other end to human life than that which can be reached by human means. His motto is ἀνθρώπινα φρονεῖν.[132] When a person possesses extraordinary virtue and reason has reached perfection in him, we call him divine.[133] Now this is precisely the way in which Theodorus of Mopsuestia looks upon Christ—because of his extraordinary virtue Christ deserved to be called the Son of God.

Von Ivanka reminds us that in the geographical area of Syria the works of Aristotle were translated into Syriac to become the foundation for the flourishing studies of Aristotle in the Islamic world. Considering the rise of Nestorianism from a certain distance, it is obvious that it is not Aristotle who is to be blamed for this heresy, but those Christians who were thinking too much in the horizontal dimension. It is an altogether different question whether Aristotle's philosophy in

127. A. Wistrand, *Die alte Kirche und die griechische Bildung* (Bern: 1967), 66.

128. A. Harnack, *Lehrbuch der Dogmengeschieble*, 5th ed. (Tübingen 1931), pp. 347ff.

129. See Wolfson, *Philosophy of the Church Fathers*, 374ff. It would seem, however, that Wolfson does not sufficiently take into account the influence of the given data of revelation and the intrinsic urge in Christians to seek greater understanding.

130. See E. Von Ivanka, *Hellenisches und Christliches im frühbyzanthinischen Geistesleben* (Vienna: 1948), 84ff.

131. Aristotle, *NE* 1177b33.

132. *NE* 1177a32.

133. *NE* 1145a27–29.

general, and his ethics in particular, shows a compatibility with and an opening toward the supernatural. Saint Thomas Aquinas was convinced that this is the case.[134]

Sixth century authors such as Maximus Confessor and John Damascene show Aristotelian influences, but to describe these in detail would take us beyond the limits set to this paper.[135] They played an important role in making the works of Dionysius accepted. Saint John Damascene considers logic and metaphysics prerequisites for the study of theology.[136]

VIII. THE CHRISTIAN WRITERS AND THE EXOTERIC ARISTOTLE

We must finally say a few words on the Christian authors as a source of Aristotle's lost exoterical works. In his new edition of the *Fragments*, O. Gigon lists the following quotations: in his *Apology* 6.124–25 Athenagoras writes that for Aristotle the divine is soul and body at the same time; the soul is the cause of movement, but it is itself unmoved. A second fragment deals with Divine Providence (*Apol.* 25).

Clement of Alexandria (*Paedag.* 2.18.2–3) quotes Aristotle as saying that a certain fish has its heart in its stomach. Clement also quotes Aristotle as saying that one should never show one's love for one's wife in the presence of servants (*Paedag.* 3.12). In *Protrepticus* 5 we read that Aristotle called the world soul God. Gigon presents some quotations from works on politics and the text (*Strom.* 5) according to which Aristotle excludes divine providence from the sublunar world.

Epiphanius writes in *Adversus haereses* that according to Aristotle there are two worlds; the sublunar one has no νοῦς, the world above is incorruptible.

IX. SOME CONCLUSIONS

When we consider the evidence presented, it would seem that the relationship between the Christian authors and Aristotle was not a very easy one. Certain teachings ascribed to Aristotle, such as the exclusion of Providence from the sublunar world, and his perceived confusion about the concept of God made Christians wary of Aristotle.

134. See my "St. Thomas Aquinas's Commentary on the Nicomachean Ethics," in L. Elders and K. Hedwig, *The Ethics of St. Thomas Aquinas* (Città del Vaticano: 1984).

135. See A. Riou, *Le monde et l'Eglise selon Maxime le Confesseur* (Paris: 1973), 51. Riou points to the view that all things tend to God as to their end and to the distinction between immanent and transient action.

136. *Fons scientiae*, pars 1 (= *Dialect.* 1: *PG* 94, p. 521ff).

Theology had not yet been developed to such a degree that the need was felt to make use of the tools which Aristotle provides. Another reason for this lack of enthusiasm for Aristotle is the highly technical level of the school writings which, moreover, seem removed from religious inspiration. Recourse to Aristotle by the heretics—however unjustified—also helped to turn the orthodox away from the Stagirite. Finally, the state of learning in the first four centuries made it difficult to gain personal access to, and acquaintance with, the *Corpus Aristotelicum*. To understand Aristotle and to use the insights he offers, a school tradition is necessary. It is only much later in the Latin West that Aristotle will take on his essential role in the development of theology.

The Christian authors of the first centuries were all very wary of resorting to a philosophy that they thought was not in agreement with the tenets of the Faith. They felt that it would corrupt Christian doctrine, as in fact it did in the heretics. Their attitude invites us to consider if, and to what extent, the intrusion of modern philosophical views into theological thinking has negatively influenced the expression of Christian doctrine.

7   Hippolytus, Aristotle, Basilides

IAN MUELLER

I. INTRODUCTION

In book seven of the *Refutation of all Heresies* (hereafter, *Refutatio*)
Hippolytus offers his "refutation" of one Basilides by attempting to
show that he holds the opinions of Aristotle of Stagira rather than of
Christ. Hippolytus supports this charge by giving an exposition of
Aristotle's philosophy (7.15–19) and then (7.20–27) of Basilides' theories in a way intended to stress parallels. We cannot determine the
accuracy of Hippolytus's presentation of Basilides,[1] but that is a question which I am going to bypass. For me "Basilides" will simply be the
name of the person whose views are described by Hippolytus. Similarly, I shall not discuss the identity of Hippolytus,[2] but simply use
"Hippolytus" as shorthand for "the author of the *Refutatio*." For my
purposes the *Refutatio* itself provides all necessary information about
its author, namely that he was a Christian writing in Greek in Rome
in the early third century. Although Hippolytus gives an account of
Aristotle before applying it to Basilides, it has seemed to me best to
describe Hippolytus's representation of Basilides as a means of explaining what he has to say about Aristotle; for Hippolytus obviously
shapes his account of Aristotle to substantiate his charges against

---

1. There is an English translation of the materials relating directly to Basilides in
Werner Foerster, *Gnosis* (Oxford: 1972), 59–83. For a brief discussion see the article
on Basilides by Ekkehard Mühlenberg in vol. 5 of the *Theologische Realenzyclopädie* (Berlin and New York: 1980). The full text of Hippolytus on Basilides and Aristotle is
translated in Catherine Osborne, *Rethinking Early Greek Philosophy* (Ithaca: 1987), 274–
309. Osborne's translation is based on Paul Wendland's text (*Die Griechischen Christlichen
Schriftsteller* vol. 26 [Leipzig: 1916]), which she reprints. Unless there is an indication
to the contrary, my translations follow the text of Miroslav Marcovich, *Patristische Texte
und Studien* vol. 25 (Berlin and New York: 1986).
2. I have done so in a paper, "The author of the *Refutation of all Heresies* and his
writings," to appear in *Aufstieg und Niedergang der Römischen Welt*. A useful brief discussion is the article on Hippolytus by Marcel Richard in the *Dictionnaire de Spiritualité*, vol.
7, part 1 (Paris: 1969).

Basilides. However, I shall not follow the exact sequence of Hippolytus's presentation, but will gather materials together by Aristotelian topic.[3]

II. HOMONYMY

Basilides apparently came down very hard on the idea that in the beginning there was nothing, but he was troubled by Parmenidean difficulties in talking about nothing:

[Basilides] says, "When I say 'was' I do not mean that it was but I say this to indicate what I want to show, that there was entirely nothing." And he says that what is called ineffable is not ineffable without qualification (ἁπλῶς); for what we call ineffable is not ineffable, and the non-ineffable is called non-ineffable, but it is beyond every name that is named. For neither do names suffice for the cosmos but they fall short because it is split into many parts. And, he says, I do not undertake[4] to find correct names for all things, but it is necessary to grasp mentally in an ineffable way and not from the names the peculiarities of things named; for homonymy has created confusion and error about things for listeners. (7.20.2–4)

Basilides' position here seems to be a now familiar, although not particularly Aristotelian one: language is necessarily tied to mundane experience so that it is impossible to talk in a literal way about the deepest matters; in such discussions understanding involves grasping things not conveyed by the literal sense of the terms used. Hippolytus (7.20.5) seizes on the word "homonymy" to assert that Basilides simply promulgates as his own the doctrine of homonyms put forward by Aristotle in the *Categories*. The truth underlying Hippolytus's charge is that Aristotle is probably the first person to include in the very term "homonymy" the idea that homonymy involves not just two things having the same name, but also the name being applied equivocally in the two cases. However, I see no reason to suppose that Basilides' application of the notion of homonymy[5] to discussion of the highest deity is in any substantive way dependent on Aristotle.[6]

---

3. I also leave out of account the last part of the discussion of Basilides (*Refutatio* 7.25–27), which is more purely religious and seems to have nothing particular to do with Aristotle.

4. Trying to read οὐ δέχομαι with the manuscript.

5. It is, of course, not out of the question that Hippolytus gives Basilides the word "homonymy" in order to "expose" his larceny.

6. Origen quotes (without attribution) the *Categories* definition of homonymy in a passage discussing predication of god (*Homilies on Jeremias* 20.1). On Origen's commonplace knowledge of Aristotle see G. Bardy, "Origène et l'aristotelisme," *Mélanges Gustave Glotz* vol. 1 (Paris: 1932), 75–83.

III. THOUGHT-OF-THOUGHT

Hippolytus proceeds to Basilides' description of the bringing into being of a world out of this nothing, now referred to as the god-which-is-not (οὐκ ὢν θεός):

When nothing was, not matter, not substance, not nonsubstance, not a simple, not a composite, not an intelligible, not a sensible, not a human, not an angel, not a god, and in general not something which is named or apprehended through sense or is an intelligible thing, but all things were absolutely circumscribed in this way and even more minutely, the god-which-is-not . . . willed to make a cosmos, acting unintelligibly, insensibly, without counsel or choice or passion or desire. (7.21.1)

In the words indicated by the ellipsis dots Hippolytus says that the Basilidean god-which-is-not is Aristotle's thought-of-thought (νόησις νοήσεως), that is, the prime mover of *Metaphysics* 12. It is tempting to read this identification in the light of Albinus's treatment of the highest of his three *hypostases* as a god that is like Aristotle's prime mover, but is unspeakable; not capable of being directly apprehended by humans; not a genus, species, or differentia; not good, bad, or indifferent; not having qualities or lacking them; not a part or a whole; not the same or different (*Epitome* 10.4). Unfortunately, Hippolytus contents himself with the suggestion that a thought-of-thought and a god-which-is-not are equally unintelligible:

Aristotle's treatise *On the Soul* is unclear; for on the basis of the entire three books it is not possible to say clearly what Aristotle thinks about the soul. For it is easy to state the definition he gives of the soul, but hard to find out what the definition means. For he says that the soul is the actualization (ἐντελέχεια) of a natural body with organs. But to find out what this is would require much discussion and considerable investigation. The god who is the cause of all these beautiful things is more difficult to apprehend than the soul even for someone carrying on a lengthier investigation. And, although it is not difficult to say the definition which Aristotle gives of god, it is impossible to understand it. For he says it is thought-of-thought, that is, an absolute non-being. (7.19.5–7)

Aristotle does not, of course, "define" god as thought-of-thought, but he does identify the prime mover as pure activity, an activity he characterizes as thought-of-thought. Although this conception of god's mental activity is of fundamental importance in ancient philosophy, the doxographers and others discuss Aristotle's conception of god in terms more of governance of the world than of self-thought.[7] In this

---

7. See, for example, Aetius 1.7.32 with the other texts cited by Diels, or Lactantius, *Divine Institutes*, 1.5.22.

sense Hippolytus's characterization is unusual, but it seems to me un-likely that his charge of unintelligibility against Aristotle is his own invention; he is perhaps building on some critical reaction to an ac-count of the highest divinity like that of Albinus. On the other hand, one might well suspect that the paraphrase of thought-of-thought as "an absolute non-being" is Hippolytus's own, motivated by the sub-sequent "refutation" of Basilides' identification of the highest god with non-being. I doubt that any more underlies Hippolytus's charge than this correlation, which may be derived from someone's criticism of something like Albinus's description of the highest divinity.[8]

IV. INDIVIDUAL, SPECIES, GENUS

Hippolytus turns next to a lengthy description of the cosmos created by the god-which-is-not. This is not our ordinary cosmos, but the seed of that cosmos which in some sense contains all the things in the cosmos: "In this way the god-which-is-not made a cosmos which is not from things which are not, planting and giving reality (ὑπόστασις) to a single seed[9] containing in itself the whole *panspermia* of the cosmos. . . . [Basilides] says that this is what the seed-which-is-not planted by the god-which-is-not is like: an all together, polymorphic, and poly-substantial *panspermia* of the cosmos" (VII.21.4–5). It seems to me somewhat surprising that Basilides would treat the seed as well as god as a non-being, and it is a point that Hippolytus picks up on. For this seed containing the whole *panspermia* is, Hippolytus tells us, "what Aristotle calls a genus divided into infinitely many ideas (ἰδέαι) as we cut off ox, horse, human, from animal, which is a non-being." What Hippolytus has in mind here is made clearer in his initial exposition of Aristotelian philosophy.[10]

Hippolytus begins this exposition by mentioning the *Categories* di-vision of substance into genus, species, and individual.[11] He compares

8. I discuss the Aristotelian conception of divinity further in Section VI below. It is perhaps worth mentioning here the possibility that Hippolytus's idea that Aristotle's god is a non-being comes from the notion that Aristotle referred to god as nameless (ἀκατονόμαστος). See Cicero, *Tusculan Disputations* 1.10.22 and 1.26.65–27.66, and Pseudo-Clement of Rome, *Recognitions* 8.15 (*Doxographi Graeci*, p. 251).

9. Omitting the ⟨οὐκ ὄν⟩ of Marcovich.

10. Steven Strange has pointed out to me that the idea that for Aristotle the genus animal is a non-being probably comes ultimately from Aristotle's remark at *On the Soul* 1.1.402b5–8 that if there is a separate account of each species of animal, then the universal animal is either nothing or posterior to the species. I would like to thank Professor Strange for a set of detailed written comments on the basis of which I made several revisions of an earlier draft of this paper.

11. Hippolytus points out that something is an individual (ἄτομον), not because it is a small body, but because it is indivisible by nature.

the genus to a heap[12] of seeds from which all the species of things which have come to be are separated off. This formulation in terms of seeds is likely to be Hippolytus's own and aimed at Basilides. However, Hippolytus says that he will clarify matters by means of an example which will enable him to move on to a discussion of "the entire Peripatetic view." Although it is not inconceivable that Hippolytus actually read the *Categories*, what follows is probably derived from a critical exposition of Aristotelian doctrine written by a Platonist.[13]

To argue that the genus is a non-being Hippolytus uses the example of the genus animal, which he also calls "animal without qualification." He says that it is not any particular animal, such as ox, horse, human, or god, and that it is from the animal without qualification that the ideas of particular animals get their reality. But this animal without qualification is no one of ox, horse, etc., and therefore, according to Hippolytus, Aristotle makes the reality of things that come to be come to be from non-beings. "Not being one, [the genus] has become a certain one principle of beings."[14] Hippolytus turns next (7.18) to the relation of individuals to species in order to show that individuals, too, are constituted from non-beings. The species human, he says, is already separated from the many animals but it is still jumbled together (συγκεχυμένον) and not yet transformed into hupostatic substance; that is, individuals have not yet been discriminated, as they are when we give a human a name such as "Socrates" or "Diogenes," at which point no further division in accordance with nature is possible; hence the name "individual."

Hippolytus now (7.18.2) offers an account of chapter two of the *Categories*. The individual, what Aristotle calls substance in the fullest sense, is according to Hippolytus what is neither said of a subject nor in a subject. The genus is said of the species, that is, the same one being is said similarly of different species, since when horse, ox, and human are called animal they are each called a besouled, sensitive substance. Here Hippolytus is obviously retailing Aristotle's claim (*Categories* 5.2a19–21) that when something is said of a subject both

12. The term 'heap' (σωρός) is clearly imported from Basilides. It occurs seven times in Hippolytus's discussion of Basilides. See, e.g., *Refutatio* 7.22.16.

13. For early examples of such critical expositions by Platonists and Stoics, none of which, however, corresponds closely with Hippolytus's, see Paul Moraux, *Der Aristotelismus bei den Griechen* 11, vol. 6 of *Peripatoi* (Berlin and New York: 1984), pp. 519–27 (Eudorus), 532–63 (Lucius and Nicostratus), 585–601 (Athenodorus and Cornutus), and 608–23 (Pseudo-Archytas).

14. Hippolytus says he will indicate in the sequel who plants the principle, which is not, of the things which later come to be. He does not do so explicitly, but his account of Basilides (at *Refutatio* 7.19.5) makes clear that he has in mind Aristotle's ultimate non-being, thought-of-thought.

its name and its definition are predicated of the subject. Hippolytus next turns to the notion of "being in" and quotes Aristotle's account of what is in as "what is in something not as a part and is incapable of existing separate from what it is in." He says that this definition applies to all of the accidents (συμβεβηκότα), but adds that these are called quality, that with respect to which we are said to be qualified in a certain way. No quality, he adds, can be independent (αὐτὸ καθ᾽ αὑτό), but must exist in something. Hippolytus's examples are qualities in the strict sense, colors, virtues, and vices, but I suspect he is here taking "quality" to be a general term for items in all the nonsubstantial categories, i.e., accidents in general. He makes no mention of Aristotle's doctrine of ten categories in book seven, even though it is the first thing mentioned in his presentation of Aristotle in section twenty of his famous doxography, in book one of the *Refutatio*.[15] It seems likely to me that Hippolytus is following people—referred to in some of the commentaries on the *Categories*—who thought that the categories were adequately described as substance and accident.[16] The reduction of all accidents to qualities is strongly suggested by Plotinus in *Ennead* 2.6, which ends with the words, "What is never a form or species (εἶδος) of something else but always an accident is purely a quality, and only this is purely a quality."

The crucial point for Hippolytus is to underline the claim that for Aristotle beings come from non-beings: "But if neither animal, which I say of all particular animals, nor the accidents, which are found to be in everything to which they belong, can be independent, but individuals are brought to completion (συμπληροῦσθαι) from these things,[17] threefold substance is composed from non-beings rather than other beings" (*Refutatio* 7.18.6).[18] In the absence of direct knowledge of Hip-

---

15. There, however, neither the threefold division of substance nor the distinction between being said of and being in is mentioned. Elsewhere in the *Refutatio* (6.24.1 and 8.14.9) Hippolytus treats the doctrine of the ten categories as Pythagorean.

16. See Dexippus, *Commentary on the "Categories"* 31.13–14. Simplicius reproduces these lines in his own commentary at 63.24. Unfortunately the people in question are only referred to as "others."

17. The notion that Forms bring individuals to completion is a commonplace of Neoplatonism; see, e.g., Plotinus, *Enneads* 2.6.1. However, one would expect the doctrine to be applied only to the Forms of essential characteristics, not accidents; see Porphyry, *Commentary on the "Categories,"* 95.22–96.2. In the *Isagoge* (7.21–23) Porphyry characterizes individuals as collections (ἀθροίσματα) of *propria*. For an attempt to trace this characterization back to Middle Platonism see A. C. Lloyd, "Neo-platonic logic and Aristotelian logic—II," *Phronesis* 1 (1955–56): 158–59.

18. Immediately after this passage Hippolytus makes the curious assertion (7.19.1) that Aristotle also divided substance into matter, form, and privation, but that this division does not affect the previous argument that for Aristotle substance is dependent on non-beings. Here Hippolytus appears to have run together what Aristotle says about

polytus's source or sources, it is difficult to say on what basis he developed his account.[19] My suggestion is that Hippolytus's account derives from a criticism of Aristotle written from a Platonist perspective in which it is taken for granted that individuals depend on the forms for their existence.[20] Given this supposition, it would be an easy matter to criticize Aristotle's doctrine of the primacy of individuals by arguing that his denial of reality to universals commits him to constructing entities out of non-entities. The source could well have said that the genus contains all the species potentially and perhaps even made a comparison with seeds,[21] though, as I have suggested, the latter may well be Hippolytus's own polemically motivated innovation.

V. SOUL

After describing Basilides' cosmic seed, Hippolytus turns to more baffling gnostic elements of the creation (7.22.7). The cosmic seed is said to contain a trinity of sons consubstantial (ὁμοούσιος) with the god-which-is-not, a heavy son (παχυμερής), a light son (λεπτομερής), and a son in need of purification. The light one immediately shoots up out of the seed to the god-which-is-not. The heavy one remains in the seed, but he equips himself with a wing. Basilides calls this wing the Holy Ghost, but Hippolytus likens it to the soul's wing in Plato's *Phaedrus*, thereby enabling himself to point out that Aristotle was Plato's student. The Holy Ghost and the heavy son are not quite able to attain the realm of the light son and the god-which-is-not, but they remain close to it, at the outermost sphere of the heavens. The third son simply remains in the heap of the *panspermia*. The next phase of Hippolytus's report involves a distinction between this cosmos with the heavy son and the Holy Ghost at its outermost edge and the hypercosmos beyond it in which the light son and the god-which-is-not dwell

---

causes or principles (e.g., at *Metaphysics* 12.2.1069b32–34) with his doctrine of substance in the *Categories*. I suspect he has simply misconstrued a handbook statement of Aristotelian principles of the kind found in Aetius (1.3.22).

19. The fact that Hippolytus has the most to say about the *Categories* is not significant evidence of direct acquaintance with the work since it was the most studied and commented on Aristotelian text.

20. Plotinus takes this kind of position in *Ennead* 6.3, particularly in §§7–9, although he makes heavy use of the notion of the individual as a composite of form and matter. At the end of §8 he says, "And there is no need to object if we make sensible substances out of non-substances; for the whole [i.e., the composite] is not true substance, but imitates true substance [i.e., the intelligible Forms], which has its being without the others which attend on it, and the others come into being from it, because it truly is" (Armstrong translation). And in the next section he writes that "the more generic is prior, so that the species is also prior to the individual [ἄτομον]."

21. Cf. Plotinus, *Ennead* 5.9.6.8–20.

(7.23). In this cosmos there comes to be a great Ruler, who takes in hand the detailed construction of the heavens and makes a son— called Christ in a later passage (7.26.2)—much better and wiser than himself, all in accordance with the prior plans of the god-which-is-not.

Hippolytus stresses the superiority of the son to the father in order to make his last explicit and perhaps most unbelievable comparison with Aristotle:

> This is what Aristotle calls the actualization (ἐντελέχεια) of a natural body with organs, the soul which activates (ἐνέργειν) the body and without which the body can accomplish nothing greater or more illustrious or powerful or wise. So Basilides just elaborates for the great Ruler and his son the account that Aristotle gave earlier for the soul and the body. For according to Basilides, the Ruler generated the son, and Aristotle says that the soul is the product (ἔργον καὶ ἀποτέλεσμα) of the body, the actualization of a natural body with organs. And, just as the actualization governs the body, so, according to Basilides, the son governs the god who is more ineffable than the ineffables [namely, the great Ruler]. Thus all ethereal things, i.e., those down to the moon (since there air is separated from ether), are foreknown (προνοεῖν) and governed by the great Ruler. (7.24.1–3)

It looks to me as though Hippolytus's comparison is based on a straightforward misunderstanding of the Aristotelian formula for the soul. He takes it to mean that the soul is something that is actualized (brought into actuality) by the body rather than an actualization undergone by the body. I know of no clear parallel to this interpretation and am inclined to chalk it up to Hippolytus himself. Nothing in the text suggests that Hippolytus had any more information about Aristotle's discussion of soul than the formula and,[22] perhaps, the charge of obscurity, which he brings up in his exposition of Aristotle at *Refutatio* 7.19.5–6 (quoted above). His way of explicating the formula gives him a weak parallel to turn against Basilides.

---

22. The standard formula in the doxography is the fuller expression at *On the Soul* 2.1.412b5–6: "first actualization of a natural body with organs potentially having life." See Diogenes Laertius 5.32–33 and Aetius 4.2.6 (with other texts listed by Diels). Diogenes gives a long but garbled explanation of the definition, explaining actualization as incorporeal form. Pseudo-Plutarch explains it as ἐνέργεια, as does Theodoret. (Stobaeus has form and ἐνέργεια). Hippolytus may have misunderstood the word ἐνέργεια, taking it in its ordinary sense as activity or operation, rather than in its specifically Aristotelian sense. The word ἐντελέχεια seems to cease to be a part of active philosophical vocabulary in later antiquity. Plotinus uses it only in a discussion of Aristotle's definition of soul (*Ennead* 4.7.85) and in a reference to that discussion (4.2.1.3). Themistius introduces the term in his paraphrase of *On the Soul* 2.1 by saying, "If someone were to call this shape and form an ἐντελέχεια, he would not be justly criticized for using an alien word" (39.17).

VI. THE PARTS OF THE COSMOS

Although the comparison between Aristotelian soul and the Basilidean son of the great Ruler is the last explicit parallel made by Hippolytus, it is reasonably clear that he also has in mind as part of his attack the point mentioned in the passage just quoted concerning the role of providence in the celestial realm. For Hippolytus has said (7.23.7) that the seat of the great Ruler and his son is the boundary between this cosmos and the hypercosmos, the firmament, also called the *Ogdoad*, that is, the (eighth) sphere of the fixed stars. He goes on immediately after the passage just quoted to talk about a second Ruler/son pair for the sublunar realm, who inhabit the *Hebdomad*, that is, the planetary realm.[23] In the sublunar realm, "the things which come to be come to be naturally as previously made by someone[24] who calculated that things would happen which ought to and as they ought to and when they ought to. But of these things there is no governor or planner or fashioner; what suffices for them is the reasoning performed by the god-which-is-not when he made a cosmos" (7.24.5). Thus we have in the Basilidean system a hypercosmic god-which-is-not, a great Ruler who inhabits the sphere of the fixed stars and oversees the planets, and a second Ruler inhabiting the planetary realm who has something to do with the sublunar realm but does not really govern it. The following passage shows how Hippolytus tries to meet the challenge of assigning the origins of this system to Aristotle:

According to Aristotle the cosmos is divided into several different parts; this part from the earth to the moon is without providence or steering, its own nature alone being sufficient; that from the moon to the surface of the heaven is ordered in all order and providence and steering. The surface, which is a fifth substance, is separated from all the natural elements from which the cosmos is constructed. And this fifth substance is according to Aristotle like a certain hypercosmic substance.

And for him the treatment of philosophy is divided according to the division of the cosmos. For there is a treatise on physics by him in which he labors on things between earth and moon, which are ordered by nature and not by providence; and there is by him another special book of discussions with the title "Metaphysics" concerning things above the moon; and there is also a special discussion by him of the fifth substance, which is for him theology. Such, taken in outline, is the division of the universe and of Aristotelian philosophy. (7.19.2–4)

The parallelism with Basilides should be clear enough, but the same

---

23. That is, the domain of the seven wandering heavenly bodies, Moon, Sun, Mercury, Venus, Mars, Jupiter, and Saturn.
24. Omitting Marcovich's ⟨οὐκ ὄντος θεοῦ⟩.

cannot be said for the basis on which Hippolytus makes his claims about Aristotle. In discussing this question I shall have to consider several overlapping topics: the Aristotelian conception of god, his division of the cosmos, the nature and role of ether, the doctrine of providence, and Aristotle's so-called exoteric works.

It is well known that the ancients ascribed a multiplicity of conceptions of divinity to Aristotle, and sometimes said that he himself was inconsistent on this subject. The most famous accusation of this kind is from Cicero's *On the Nature of the Gods*; the Epicurean speaker is complaining about what Aristotle has to say in *On Philosophy*: "At one moment he assigns divinity exclusively to the intellect, at another he says that the world itself is a god, then again he puts some other being over the world, and assigns to this being the role of regulating and sustaining the world-motion by means of a sort of *replicatio*; then he says that the celestial heat is god—not realizing that the heavens are a part of the world which elsewhere he himself has entitled god" (1.13.33).[25] To avoid making similar charges about Aristotle's *On the Heavens*, modern scholars are prone to speak about textual insertions, particularly on the question of whether the heavens constitute a highest divine self-moving being or are moved by an external prime mover.[26]

The doctrines described by Hippolytus may be derived, at least in part, from lost exoterica such as the *On Philosophy*. The works he refers to are another matter: his description of the "*Physics*" and the "*Metaphysics*" do not seem particularly appropriate for the works we have under those names; and we have no other knowledge of a work called "*On the Fifth Substance*."[27] One might perhaps locate all three of the treatises mentioned by Hippolytus in book twelve of the *Metaphysics*: Hippolytus's "*Physics*" is chapters 1–5, his "*Metaphysics*" is chapter 8, and *On the Fifth Substance* is chapters 6, 7, and 9. It is perhaps also worth remarking that Hippolytus's division of the branches of philos-

25. I have used the Loeb translation except for leaving *replicatio* untranslated. The Loeb translator renders it "inverse rotation," but it may simply mean "rotation." See below, note 31.

26. See, for example, H. J. Easterling, "Homocentric Spheres in *de caelo*," *Phronesis* 6 (1961): 138–66. A good instance of ancient uncertainty about Aristotle's meaning is provided by Simplicius's commentary on *On the Heavens* 279a18–b3. Simplicius informs us that Alexander of Aphrodisias took the passage to be about the sphere of the fixed stars, whereas later interpreters took it to concern the movers of the heavens.

27. Aristotle's fullest discussion of ether is, of course, *On the Heavens* 1 and 2, but he does not refer to ether as a fifth anything in the extant works generally accepted as authentic. Terms like "fifth substance" perhaps come from *On the Cosmos* 2.392a8–9, where ether is described as an element other than the four. Cf. Plato, *Timaeus* 55c and the possibly spurious *Epinomis* 981c.

ophy corresponds to the *Metaphysics* 12.1 division of substances into sensible and perishable, sensible and eternal, nonsensible and unchanging.

The division of the cosmos into a sublunar realm of things subject to generation and corruption and a superlunar realm of eternally rotating heavenly spheres is, of course, standard Aristotelianism. However, there is stronger evidence that Aristotle's contemporary Xenocrates postulated the Hippolytean threefold division of the cosmos than that Aristotle himself did.[28] To get a parallel with Basilides' second Ruler, Hippolytus apparently thinks of the planetary realm as an Aristotelian quasi-ruler of the sublunar realm.[29] Hippolytus cannot, of course, directly identify the Basilidean great Ruler with the prime mover since the prime mover as thought-of-thought has already been identified with the hypercosmic god-which-is-not.[30] There remains the sphere of the fixed stars, the movement of which is transmitted to each of the planets in the Aristotelian world picture and which Basilides did make the home of the great Ruler. It is conceivable that in talking about Aristotle's theory Hippolytus has in mind the being Cicero mentions as "regulating and sustaining the world-motion by means of a sort of *replicatio*.[31] Sextus Empiricus (*Outlines of Pyrrhonism* 3.218) also ascribes to Aristotle the view that god is the limit (πέρας) of the heaven.[32] Sextus says that this god is incorporeal, but there is another ancient line of Aristotle interpretation which, probably under the influence of Stoicism, treats the heavens as the body of god and the mover of the heavens as god's soul: "Aristotle and those who follow

28. Aetius 1.7.30. For a cautious assessment of this and other evidence on Xenocrates, see Richard Heinze, *Xenocrates* (Leipzig: 1892), 73–78. On the ascription of such a tripartition to Philolaus, see Walter Burkert, *Lore and Science in Ancient Pythagoreanism*, trans. Edwin L. Minar, Jr. (Cambridge, Mass.: 1972), 244–46.

29. For the rudiments of the idea of the heavens as somehow ruling the sublunar realm see *Meteorology* 1.2, *On the Heavens* 2.3, *On Generation and Corruption* 2.10. The doctrine, which seems to have much more to do with a Stoic cosmos held together by sympathy than with an Aristotelian one, is fully developed as Aristotelian by Alexander of Aphrodisias in a treatise on providence preserved in two Arabic versions. See Hans-Jochen Ruland, *Die arabischen Fassungen von zwei Schriften des Alexander von Aphrodisias* (doctoral diss., Saarbrücken, 1976).

30. Hippolytus does not indicate any awareness of the doctrine of a multiplicity of astral movers.

31. Cf. A. J. Festugière, *La Révélation d'Hermès Trismégiste*, vol. 2 (Paris: 1949), 245–46, who takes the *replicatio* to be a motion opposite to that of the planets. Others who accept the association of this deity with the sphere of the fixed stars take *replicatio* to be simply a rotation; among these people Bernd Effe, *Studien zur Kosmologie und Theologie der Aristotelischen Schrift "Über die Philosophie"* in Zetemata no. 50 (Munich: 1970), 160–61, takes *replicatio* to render the Greek word ἀνείλιξις, whereas Enrico Berti, *La filosofia del primo Aristotele* (Padua: 1962), 382–83, distinguishes between the meanings of *replicatio* and ἀνείλιξις.

32. Cf. *On the Cosmos* 6.397b24–27 and *Physics* 8.10.267b6–9.

him, considering god to be one composite like an animal, say that god is composed of a body and a soul, considering the ethereal, that is, the planets and the sphere of the fixed stars, which moves in a circle, to be god's body, and the reason (λόγος) which applies to the motion of the body to be god's soul" (Athenagoras, *Supplication* 6).[33]

In this passage Athenagoras identifies the whole ethereal heaven with the body of god. For Hippolytus only the surface of the heaven is made of the fifth substance or ether, a claim which seems to have an echo in the celestial heat of the Cicero passage,[34] but flies in the face of *On the Heavens*, in which Aristotle clearly enough assigns the fifth element to the whole heavens down to and including the moon.[35] Hippolytus's assimilation of the material (non-ethereal) components of the heavens to those of the sublunar region perhaps reflects Stoic materialism, but I know of no Aristotelian analogue of the contrast between the make-up of the planetary realm and that of the outer sphere.[36] His suggestion that the ether is "quasi-hypercosmic" is obviously intended to stress the analogy with the Great Ruler who lives at the "boundary" of the god-which-is-not.[37] In *On the Heavens* Aristotle himself speaks of the heaven as divine, and even seems to say it is the ultimate deity.[38] Equally relevant are the passages in Cicero in which Aristotle is said to have identified the ether with the stuff of the mind.[39] Hippolytus makes no mention of this identification in book seven, although it probably underlies his attributing to Aristotle in the doxography of book one (20.4) the essentially Stoic view that after

33. Cf. Aetius 1.7.32 (Pseudo-Plutarch *apud* Eusebium).

34. On the difficulty of being sure what Cicero's celestial heat is, see David E. Hahm, "The Fifth Element in Aristotle's *De Philosophia*: A Critical Re-examination," *Journal of Hellenic Studies* 102 (1982): 74.

35. See also the pseudo-Aristotelian *On the Cosmos* 2.392a5–31 and, indeed, the brief doxography taken by Hippolytus from Sextus Empiricus (10.7.4). Curiously Hippolytus assigns ether to the planetary realm in discussing Basilides (*Refutatio* 7.24.3, quoted above). For other ancient passages which assign a special status to the sphere of the fixed stars see Willy Theiler, "Ein vergessenes Aristoteleszeugnis," *Journal of Hellenic Studies* 77 (1957): 128–29 (reprinted in Theiler's *Untersuchungen zur antiken Literatur*, Berlin: 1970).

36. In the *Epinomis* (987b), the sphere of the fixed stars is contrasted with the planetary spheres because it moves in a direction opposite to them and is most of all called a cosmos.

37. The word 'hypercosmic' (ὑπερκόσμιος) suggests Gnosticism and late Platonism rather than Aristotelianism. It is used by Philoponus in a description of theology in what passes as a fragment (number 8, Ross) of Aristotle's *On Philosophy*, and it is connected with Aristotelian theology in the *Vita Marciana* §39; see Ingemar Düring, *Aristotle in the Ancient Biographical Tradition*, Studia Graeca et Latina Gothoburgensia no. 5 (Göteborg: 1957), 105.

38. *On the Heavens* 1.3.270b1–25, 1.9.279a11–b3, 2.1, and 2.3.286a9–12.

39. *Academica* 1.7.26 and *Tusculan Disputations* 1.10.22, 17.41, and 26.65–27.66. Cf. Aristotle, *Generation of Animals* 2.3.736b29–737a12.

death the soul disappears into the ether.[40] It seems, then, that a great variety of allegedly Aristotelian ideas enter into Hippolytus's representation of the outermost sphere as a special kind of body and divinity.

In the extant works Aristotle does not speak of providence in a cosmic or theological sense. And the self-contemplating deity of *Metaphysics* 12 would seem to be the antithesis of a providential god. However, in one of the two Arabic versions of Alexander of Aphrodisias's treatise on providence (D18) Aristotle is quoted as saying that providence extends down to the sphere of the moon. Alexander argues rather tendentiously that what Aristotle means is that providence exists in the superlunar sphere but affects the sublunar one.[41] It seems clear that Alexander is combating the kind of interpretation of Aristotle we find in Hippolytus, while accepting the idea that sublunar providence is an effect of superlunar providence. The origins of the Hippolytean interpretation are not easy to determine.[42] Alexander does not give

40. H. J. Easterling, "Quinta Natura," *Museum Helveticum* 21 (1964): 73–85, has argued that there are two fifth natures in Aristotle; an incorporeal psychic stuff described in the lost early works, and the heavenly stuff described in *On the Heavens*. The assimilation of these two in the doxographical tradition would do much to explain Hippolytus's nebulous description of the ether.

41. See Ruland's dissertation, pp. 59–62. I quote Ruland's translation of the passage in the other Arabic version (D15) in which the distinction between two kinds of providence is made clearly: "Die Leitung [i.e., Providence] besteht aus zwei Arten, von denen die eine die Leitung der Himmelskörper vom äussersten Himmel bis zum Himmel des Mondes und die andere die Leitung der sublunarischen Welt ist. ⟨Was⟩ aber die Leitung der ersten Körper ⟨angeht⟩, so rührt sie vom ersten Urheber her; die Leitung der irdischen Welt aber rührt von den ersten Körpern her durch das, was es in ihnen von der ersten Kraft gibt. Und der Philosoph erwähnt das und sagt: 'Der Mensch bringt Menschen hervor und die Sonne' [*Physics* 2.2.194b13], d.h. dass die Sonne ihm dabei hilft." R. W. Sharples, "Alexander of Aphrodisias on Divine Providence: Two Problems," *Classical Quarterly* 32 (1982): 200–04, questions whether Alexander believed in a superlunar providence.

42. Fritz Wehrli, *Die Schule des Aristoteles*, vol. 10 (Basel and Stuttgart: 1959), 64 and 66, proposes Critolaus as the originator. The proposal depends mainly on Epiphanius's ascription (*Panarion* 3.31, *Doxographi Graeci*, p. 592) of the conception to Aristotle, and his subsequent statement that Critolaus held the same opinions as Aristotle. Between the two passages, however, Epiphanius has said that Theophrastus agreed with Aristotle, and Praxiphanes with Theophrastus. This is really not very much to go on. Wehrli also suggests (p. 73) that a comparison between the king of the cosmos and a ruler who focuses only on important things in fragment 37a (Plutarch, *Precepts of Statecraft* 811c) is Critolaus's, but the comparison and the citation of Euripides seems more likely to be Plutarch's own. In any case, the comparison hardly provides independent evidence for a theory of providence. The claim for Arius Didymus (fr. 9, Stobaeus 1.22.1c) as originator is as strong as the case for assigning anonymous material in Stobaeus to Arius. For general discussion of this topic, see Paul Moraux, *Der Aristotelismus bei den Griechen* 1, vol. 5 of *Peripatoi* (Berlin and New York: 1973), 259–71. Fragment 9 satisfies three of the ten criteria for assignment to Arius constructed by Diels, *Doxographi Graeci*, pp. 73–75, namely: occurrence of an initial δέ suggesting a broader context; discrepancy in doctrine or order with "Aetius"; and mixture of Stoic and Aristotelian formulations.

the source of his quotation. Theophrastus suggests the absence of purpose from the sublunar realm (*Metaphysics* 10a22–11b23),[43] and the idea may have been developed further in the mechanistic aspects of the philosophy of his successor as head of the Lyceum, Strato (fr. 32–39, Wehrli). In any case, the conception is standardly ascribed to Aristotle in doxographies.[44] Among authors earlier than Hippolytus who make it are Atticus (fr. 3 and 8, from Eusebius, *Preparatio evangelica* 15.5.800a, and 15.12), and Tatian (*Oration to the Greeks* 2). Hippolytus, then, is retailing another doxographical commonplace, although his attempt to fit the commonplace into his account of the Peripatetic Basilides helps to produce an apparently unique picture, the cosmological scheme of which is indicated by the following hierarchical list:

Basilides' god-which-is-not / Aristotle's prime mover
The great Ruler / the sphere of the fixed stars
The second Ruler / the realm of the planets
The sublunary realm from which providence is absent

VII. CODA

This completes my discussion of *Aristoteles apud Hippolytum* except that for completeness I shall quote the brief additional doxographical information with which Hippolytus completes his account of Aristotle before he turns his attention to Basilides:

The cosmos is imperishable and eternal according to Aristotle.[45] For there is nothing inharmonious in it, since it is steered by providence and nature. Aristotle produced treatises not only about nature and cosmos and providence and god, but there is also a work of ethical treatises by him, which are called the ethical books; through these he changed the character of his students from bad to good.

I am loath to base a chronological hypothesis on so weak a foundation. The Arius fragment is worth quoting in part since it shows the same unclarity about spheres and transcendent deities as Hippolytus: "The four elements are surrounded by the ether. This is where divine things are settled distributed among the spheres of the so-called fixed and wandering stars. There are equally many spheres and gods moving them. And the greatest god is the one which surrounds all the spheres; it is a rational and blessed creature, holding the heavens together and being provident of them."

43. Cf. Giovanni Reale, *Teofrasto e la sua aporetica metafisica* (Brescia 1964), 156–61.

44. The most detailed discussion is in A. J. Festugière, *L'Idéal religieux des Grecs et l'Evangile* (Paris: 1932), 221–63. See also A. P. Bos, *Providentia Divina* (Assen and Amsterdam: 1976). (At the time of writing I had not seen Bos's book *Cosmic and Metacosmic Theology in Aristotle's Lost Dialogues* [Leiden: 1989].)

45. Hippolytus does not indicate whether Basilides intended a temporal creation of the world, but he makes clear that Basilides was unwilling either to allow for creation in any literal sense (*Refutatio* 7.21–22) or to speak of an emanation (7.22.2).

If, then, Basilides is found, not just implicitly, but in his very statements and words, to have read the opinions of Aristotle into our gospel and saving Word, what will be left but to give up these importations and show to Basilides' disciples that, since they are heathens, "Christ will be of no advantage to them." (7.19.7–9)

Hippolytus's treatment of Basilides as a proponent of Aristotelianism must seem to most modern readers a bizarre interpretation of a bizarre doctrine. But, whatever one thinks of the reliability of Hippolytus's account of Basilides, there can be no doubt that doctrines equally bizarre were in the air in the second and third century. The Aristotle from whom Basilides allegedly borrowed is for the most part not our Aristotle, except for a sentence here and there. And I doubt that he was ever the Aristotle of any one person except, of course, the author of the *Refutatio.* We cannot know where Hippolytus got his Aristotle, but it certainly looks as though he relied on handbooks for the quotations specifying Aristotle's "definitions" of god and of the soul, information which he misunderstood but tried to use as a weapon. He clearly knew more about the *Categories,* but nothing that would not be available in secondary sources. His conception of the Aristotelian cosmos is a blending of ingredients that may well all have their origin in Aristotle although not in the now extant Aristotle; but they certainly are to be found in other later treatments of Aristotle's world view. Everything is, as we have seen, distorted by Hippolytus's polemical aims. I cannot, then, conclude by promoting Hippolytus as a second Alexander of Aphrodisias nor even as one among many interpreters of Aristotle. He can, however, serve as a reminder of how immediate intellectual concerns can lead people to misconstrue and misuse the words of even the greatest authors. And that, perhaps, is a reminder no less important today than it ever was.

8   The Aristotelianism of Photius's Philosophical Theology

JOHN P. ANTON

I. PHOTIUS AND THE PHILOSOPHICAL TRADITION

Photius (820–91) is discussed in this paper as a philosopher rather than as architect of the spiritual policy of orthodoxy, or as one of the protagonists in the controversy that led to the Great Schism over the *filioque* clause, or as the inspired statesman of the great apostolic missions to the Slavs, or the principal agent who persuaded the emperor to end the iconoclastic heresy and restore the holy icons to their rightful place of worship.[1]

My main objective is to explore Photius's Aristotelianism as we find it in his commentary on Aristotle's *Categories,* and relate this strand of thought to his philosophical theology. The emphasis falls on the way Photius recast the concept of *ousia* after the model of Christian Neoplatonism to accommodate the intellectual demands of revealed theology. Curiously enough, nowhere in his writings, especially in the *Bibliotheke,* does he mention Plotinus or give a hint that he has read the *Enneads.* His use of Neoplatonic terminology did not require intimate familiarity with the principal writings of the Neoplatonists since much of their philosophical vocabulary had become comfortably assimilated by the middle of the ninth century into the rhetorical style and the stock of expressive means of the ecclesiastic writers in the Byzantium.

The recent book of the French scholar Paul Lemerle (1971), and prior to this the works of V. Grumel and F. Dvornik—both noted Catholic clergymen—have done much to restore Photius's place in history, something the great scholar and editor of the *Patrologia,* Cardinal Hergenroether, was hesitant to do. We can easily imagine his reluctance when working on volume 101 of the *Patrologia graeca* to

---

1. The translations of Photius's text and of the citations from secondary sources are mine.

favor the inclusion of Photius in the series as he wrote: "Doctrina celebris, at facinoribus, quibus diu ecclesiam perturbavit, et teterrimum schisma inauguravit . . . callidus hypocrita, ambitiosus, falsarius, schismaticus, tyrannus."[2]

Hergenroether's three-volume work in 1867–69 improved things only slightly. It was not until the middle of the twentieth century that intensive studies of Photius's works began. Cyril Mango (1958) and Basil Laourdas (1959) published splendid studies on the *Homilies*. Professor G. L. Kustas's 1953 Harvard dissertation and his subsequent publication of articles on Photius as literary critic (1960) and theorist of rhetoric and history (1964), along with the recent definitive edition of the *Amphilochia* by Professor L. G. Westerink (1986 [1967]), have given all that scholars need for a renewed effort to asses Photius's contribution to the history of Western culture. To this list I must add the contributions of K. Ziegler (1941), Francis Dvornic (1953, 1960), Klaus Oehler (1964), B. Tatakis (1967, 1968), and Linos Benakis (1971). My own theme is limited to an attempt to assess the Aristotelianism in Photius's philosophical theology.

Since Photius seems to follow the interpretative approach of Ammonius and John Damascene the questions that need to be explored are: (*a*) in what respect he shows originality, (*b*) what are his Neoplatonic leanings, (*c*) what he selects from Aristotle to articulate his philosophical theology, and (*d*) what are the limits of his Aristotelianism. In essence, we need to determine the relationship of his Aristotelianism to the Church dogma and how it affects his theoretical stance. It has been established that John Damascene is a common source from both Saint Photius in the ninth century and Saint Thomas Aquinas in the thirteenth century. Yet the scope and the uses of their respective Aristotelianisms differ as do their modes of assimilating the philosophy of Aristotle, and this in spite of their common indebtedness to Neoplatonism. A detailed study of the differences and similarities between the two thinkers is still lacking. Prominent in Photius's interest in Aristotle is the *Categories*, because of a special emphasis on the genus *ousia*. His concern is mainly related to redefining *ousia* along neoplatonist lines to suit the Christian demand for a philosophical theology. It appears that he was also aware of the Stoic reformulation of this concept as *apoios ousia* and of the Plotinian shift to the Platonic *megista genē* of the *Sophist*.

These two views, the one materialistic the other idealistic, were available to Photius, but he worked mainly with the Pauline doctrines in

2. Quoted in Lemerle 1971, chap. 7, n. 1.

trying to bring together the universal, *spermatikos logos* of the Stoics and the transcendent *ousia* of the Neoplatonic Good. With Photius, *being* becomes *hyperlogos* and *hyperousios theos*.

Next to Leon the Mathematician, Photius stood at the helm of the renaissance movement of the ninth century.[3] Tatakis (1967) refers to Photius as the greatest representative of the ninth century: "the theses he formulated became essential features of the mind of Byzantium" (104); a wise man even if he lacks "the originality of an Aristotle." According to Tatakis, Photius succeeds in bringing together the science of Hellas and the Christian vision of life, and his development is best understood in conjunction with the "outside *paideia*" or the Greek conception of education, literature, science, and philosophy (103).[4]

Photius wrote the *Amphilochia* between 867 and 877 as a series of epistles in which he dealt with religious topics and questions in theology, mainly philosophical problems related to Aristotle's *Categories* with regard to the ontological status of species and genera. The question of Photius's originality as a philosopher cannot be separated from his theological stance. His interest lies not in creating an independent system of thought, for his mode of philosophizing was certainly not that of a Presocratic, not even of the Hellenistic tradition. The stance he adopted required the adjusting of select intellectual pre-Christian traditions to the Christian outlook. He worked within the framework of his theological dogma as set by the ecumenical councils and the apologetic writers. Inquiry, in his case, was not a call to discovery but rather a process of understanding and confirming. Discursive thought entered only to the extent that intellectual engagement was needed either to avoid disconfirming or to strengthen agreement with the fount of religious truth: Revelation.

3. Niketas, the biographer of Patriarch Ignatius and opponent of Photius, acknowledges that "Photius stood out among his contemporaries not only for his command of grammar, poetry, rhetoric and philosophy, but also of medicine and every science of nature, and compared favorably with his counterparts in antiquity" (paraphrase mine). See *Vita Ignatii*, PG 105, 509 A, B.

4. Tatakis 1967 writes that Photius's contribution is a landmark in that he initiates a new phase in the dialogue between Greek education and Christian life (106). Unlike Basil, Photius did not have firsthand experience of the Greek mind and the Greek tradition, the reason being that the Christianization of the ancient world had by that time been completed (107). Tatakis's point is that ever since Photius reintroduced the wisdom of classical Greece, each subsequent generation had to take a stance and evaluate for itself the Hellenic heritage, face the challenge and give its own answer. By initiating this on-going dialogue, Photius formulated the problem of Christian humanism (107): "Underlying this attitude is a philosophical theory of civilization which Psellus will clearly formulate in the tenth century; it is a theory that accepts the progressive development of civilization. It is an attitude that assigns a just place to the ancient world" (119). Thus, the victory of the iconolatric movement is essentially "a Hellenic triumph over the invading oriental elements" (104).

In examining the thought of Photius, I will begin with his way of stating basic theological theses and then proceed to review his use of Aristotelianism as it relates to his philosophical theology. The basic issue here is to identify his mode of understanding logic and ontology in seeking to effect agreement with the truths of faith. Photius's approach is one of problems, projected queries needed to adjust logic to revealed truths. These problems called for discursive resolutions to settle differences and assimilate significant truths of reason to the superior axioms of faith.

Photius would not, even if he could, conform to the Greek mind, nor was he ever tempted to consider such an objective. His response to the philosophical heritage of Greece was that of an eclectic. It would be fair to say that Photius was not looking to find in Aristotle's texts ways to verify the dogmatic claims of Orthodoxy. He needed no authority for his beliefs other than the two Testaments and the writings of Paul. Basically, the role of philosophy was limited to his quest to settle issues concerning the difference between the ways of natural orders and the ways of God. This explains why he seems eager to add to the distinctions he finds in Aristotle and to amplify the original uses of key philosophical expressions to serve the needs of his religious commitment. The fact remains that he does not try to defend Aristotle's system.[5] He merely uses it to whatever extent he can without compromising the truths of the dogma. Hence we do not find in the speculative pieces he wrote a theoretical concern to develop a position comparable to the Thomistic doctrine of the double truth.

Photius is an erudite Christian, knowledgeable, urbane, but still in the main a Christian both in culture and conviction.[6] He remains devoted to his commitment to the established religious tradition which viewed both Judaism and Hellenism as propaedeutic to the drama of salvation, the Christian's "philosophy of history." Judaism and Hellenism were understood to be related to the drama only indirectly through the advent of Christianity and its institutions, not as direct and complete anticipations.

The determining line separating the Testament of the Hebrews from the *logos* of the Greeks is evident in all his *Homilies* and the

5. Photius's "lost philosophical writings" are listed in Hergenroether 1869, 3.258–60. The extant philosophical writings afford no indication that he may have attempted such a defense in the "lost" writings.

6. Photius describes the Christian religion in PG 66B as follows: Ὅσον οὖν μεγέθει καὶ κράτει καὶ κάλλει καὶ ἀκριβείᾳ καὶ καθαρότητι καὶ ἐν τῇ ἄλλῃ πάσῃ τελειότητι τῶν ἐν τοῖς ἔθνεσι δοξασμάτων ἡ τῶν Χριστιανῶν πίστις ("The faith of the Christians is by far superior to the beliefs of all the nations in greatness and in power, in beauty and in exactitude, in purity and in every perfection"; translation mine).

writings that comprise the body of the *Amphilochia,* where thematics and expositions purport to illumine complex issues, be they in theology or philosophy. They are written exclusively from the Christian perspective, even when the issues originate in the Hebraic or the Hellenic tradition. Hence, Photius is neither a defender of the wisdom of the Greeks and their humanistic outlook, nor a strict exegete of the biblical literature as the fountain of infallible guidance. Rather, his spiritual allegiance belongs almost exclusively to Paul, and only secondarily to Gregory of Nanzianzus and John of Damascus.

Photius uses *logos* as the stepping stone to reach the realm of the *hyperlogon,* and he uses the obedience to God, when not for purposes of worship, always to restate and reconfirm the Christian dogma of salvation as the only true path that leads to the hypercosmic peace of life eternal. In both cases, Photius, following the tradition of the Eastern Church Fathers, concentrates on the supreme value of the person, especially the perfect person, Christ. This fundamental tenet undergirds the essays in question 77 of the *Amphilochia,* in which he analyzes the concepts of genera and species and where he also states his opposition to Platonism and argues against the theory of forms. The refutation is also central to understanding why he is critical of Aristotle's theory of second *ousia* that is wanting in existence, i.e., deficient in ontic power. This ontology compromises the Christian principle that demands the centrality of person to be above fact and above concept. For Photius, the dogma of the Trinity concerns the ultimacy of the person-God, and as such it needs no theoretical justification and demonstration. Trinity and divine incarnation are fundamental facts, the former of hyperlogic faith, the latter of history located between the beginning and the end of time in the cosmos.[7]

Photius understood the need to respond to the ongoing cultural confrontation with the past, and hence to reevaluate for his generation the place of the Hellenic mind in the intellectual politics of Byzantium and the church affairs of Eastern Christianity. He knew well how careless and hasty contacts with Greek philosophy lead to acceptance of unwanted values and how facile concessions to *logos* tend to compromise the supreme article of the *Christos qua* person. Lack of proper preparation easily condones the intrusion of conceptualizations that distort the meaning of the Passion, the uniqueness of the cross and

---

7. See Kustas 1964 for Photius on the meaning of history as confirming the triumph of the truths of the Church. He notes that "Appeal to history is only one weapon in his [Photius's] theological armament. Three elements are habitually stressed throughout his works: (1) Scripture; (2) the Church Fathers and Church Councils convened [in past centuries]; and (3) logical demonstration" (p. 38).

the ultimacy of the Resurrection. Concessions to the rational demands of the Hellenic *logos* when made from time to time in the East as well as in the West affected seriously, always negatively, the historicity of Jesus as personal savior and as a unique person. Those who made the concessions shifted the responsibility of the Christian from a life of worship to one of civic and impersonal duty in the service of the state and worldly affairs.

However, since Byzantium was close to the Hellenic philosophical heritages, both in language and other related cultural traditions, this proximity made easy access to ways of transforming the *Christos* from person to *logos*, or to put it differently, from *pathos* to concept and from savior to ideal. It should be of no surprise that repeated intrusions of a humanistic strand took place with the aid of philosophy, literature, and especially art.

Whenever intrusions were left unexposed there was always the danger that they could converge into a dominant intellectual attitude. Seen in this light, the type of humanism that was rooted in the Greek tradition, surviving through the centuries as a cultural undercurrent, retained its potency and appeal to develop into a movement with sufficient force to bring about a "renaissance" of classical antiquity. However, the established Christian ethos was so deeply entrenched by the ninth century in all the activities of the state and its culture that it seems inconceivable that the surviving elements of Greek humanism could generate sufficient momentum to inaugurate radical changes and effect such a renaissance.[8]

Given the prominent role of sin in the salvational life, the conservative sector of the Church viewed the intrusions of humanist elements as being fraught with spiritual risk. Photius's goal was not tied to policies to prevent the intrusion of Hellenic humanism but to the new designs to secure the balance of values in the wake of the subsiding of the turmoil that had brought misfortune to the icon-worshippers during the iconoclastic period. The threat to a rich religious life had been real. The icon-worshippers had long been deprived of the daily bread needed to sustain the absorption of symbolic imagery.[9]

8. Kustas 1964 has aptly noted this aspect: "The particular form which the alliance of past and present takes in the ninth century is partly to be explained by the fact that Christianity had by now advanced temporally to the point that its own past had in the eyes of Photius and his contemporaries taken on the aura of a classical age" (63).

9. According to Kustas 1964: "The 'renaissance' of the ninth century is then not so much a rediscovery of the classics, as in the West, but a re-examination of their relationship to Christian life based on the fuller availability of texts and on the introduction of various modes of classicizing art promoted by the iconoclasts themselves as a substitution for the representation of religious scenes" (64). In note 87, Kustas gives valuable

Photius, the defender of the icons, wrote pieces dealing with philosophical concepts in order to draw attention to the following errors: (*a*) Absolutizing the genera and species to the point that the process of conceptualization would endanger the integrity of the person-*Christos* by replacing the person with a Platonic form even if supremely divinified; hence, the importance of the essay on genera and species.[10] (*b*) Legalizing negative attitudes toward the functions of icons, the artifacts whose contributive role is to alert the worshipper to the usefulness of symbolic means when abstractions cease to function dramatically. In this connection the essays forming the commentary on Aristotle's *Categories* provide the theoretical justification of a dimension of experience involving *ousia* and *sumbebekota* to defend iconolatry as part of the *paideia* of the Christian. *Ousia*, a key term for Photius, had also figured largely in the Arian controversy.[11] Thus, when Photius attacks the iconoclasts as heretics and compares them to the Arians, he employs theological uses of *ousia* in composite expressions as in *homoousion* and *homoioousion*, which Arius had claimed were not to be found in the Scriptures.[12] When reading Photius's commentary we need to keep in mind the Arian heresy and Photius's condemnation of it together with his attack on the iconoclasts. What explains Photius's concern for this Aristotelian treatise is that he finds in it a discourse that provides the terminology for the relevant case of homonymity pertaining to co-incidental properties of *ousia*, both human and super-human, especially the divine *ousia* of the ultimate person. The objective is not to map the system of essences in the natural world, i.e., to pursue natural science, but to identify the conceptual means to transcend the experience of the natural *onta* in their concreteness in order to envisage the divine person *qua* creator and savior.

Photius's Aristotelianism can thus be understood as a corrective tool and as a valuable philosophical procedure to underscore the fundamentals of orthodox faith as well as prevent aberrations and abuses of traditional religious discourse. That this Aristotelianism was also viewed as acceptable descriptive ontology of natural orders, was an

bibliographical references on "the features and philosophy of Byzantine art from Justinian to the tenth century."

10. See also Tatakis 1962, 165ff.

11. Especially *Homilies* 15 and 16 on the Arian Heresy, trans. Mango 1958, 244–81, with extensive bibliographies in the notes.

12. Photius writes: Οἱ ἀρειανοί, ἄγραφός ἐστιν ἡ τοῦ ὁμοουσίου φωνή. οἱ εἰκονομάχοι, ἄγραφός ἐστιν ἡ τῶν εἰκόνων προσκύνησις. Again: οἱ ἀρειανοί, οὔτε γὰρ ἂν τοῖς εὐαγγελίοις τὰ κυριακὰ λόγια, οὔτε ἡ παλαιὰ γραφὴ παραδέδωκεν ὁμοούσιον ἢ ὁμοιοούσιον ἢ οὐσίαν λέγειν ὅλως ἐπὶ πατρὸς καὶ υἱοῦ. Text in Laourdas 1959 (155.26ff).

extra feature that strengthened its appeal. His was a selective Aristotelianism with modifications. Its usefulness improved strikingly once certain amplifications were introduced to comply with the Christian dogma of the supreme being *qua ousia*. Thus the most significant part of the commentary as it relates to Photius's philosophical theology is question 137 of the *Amphilochia*. In essence it contains no argument. It is written as exposition, not demonstration. In view of these considerations, the question is not whether Photius is "Hellenic," or whether he conforms to the Greek mode of philosophizing, but rather how he anthologizes from the Greek sources of philosophy to forge intellectual tools for upholding the values of his faith.

The substance of Photius's thought is Christian, and so is his commitment. The theoretical side of his outlook in its use of the classical tradition employs a model that is Hellenistic in character and "Hellenizing" in its modality, but not classical. However that may be, Photius found it necessary to reassess the mind of Greece on a selective basis and borrow only what he regarded as valuable ways and means to defend and restore the cherished practices of his faith that were distorted during the iconoclastic period and threatened through the *filioque* addendum. What is of special interest in the context of his Aristotelianism is that in the case of the *filioque* controversy, he had no occasion to appeal to his reformulation of the Aristotelian *ousia*. He fought the battle through strict appeal to the *traditio* of the Church, especially the council of Nicea, confident that history was on his side. The finality and completeness of the Creed was declared in his own Council in 879–80.

Photius's religious guiding principles were of the standard Christian version: (*a*) *Christos* as person, (*b*) the Holy Trinity, (*c*) man's relation to God as determined by the end of salvation, and (*d*) reason in the service of the truths of faith. All that he deemed pertinent in Aristotle, and the Greeks in general, came under the last item. In his effort to turn Aristotelianism into a working theological ontology, he had to supplement his borrowing with elements from Neoplatonism—not Plato but Plotinus. Actually both traditions remained conceptually and axiologically subservient to the Christian commitment. The Incarnation altered nothing in the *ousia* of the divine *logos*; it only affected the history of humanity by making salvation available. It was this part that brought the worldly preoccupation of elucidating Christianity ineluctably close to Greek philosophy, but without concessions to the ontology and humanistic ethic of the latter. Photius's Aristotelian essays and especially his homilies make this abundantly clear.

To the Christian theorist, heresy is not a Greek problem. Only ab-

errant Christians can commit heresy by deviating from the fundamentals of the dogma, which is to think and act otherwise than what
the truths of faith permit. Yet for a Christian to select from Hellenism
or any other outlook on life, is not heresy.[13] In the context that interests
us here denouncement for heresy would be forthcoming only if the
selection is heedless, or worse, intended to subvert. Neither case applies to Photius. His philosophical theology moved in a different direction from that of an apologetic writer logged in confrontation with
the institutions of a pagan world.[14] He is a theoretical leader emerging
within a Christian world at the crucial moment after a long period of
turmoil. Aside from the work related to the restoration of the icons,
he also shaped and implemented a policy to revitalize the apostolic
principle and secure the spiritual loyalty of the areas to the north that
were available to the orthodox part of what was formerly the Eastern
Empire. To do both successfully he had to move boldly, renew the
educational institutions of Byzantium and assume a leading role for
the apostolic mission. Hence the value of the preparatory work of the
Bibliotheke. As for the restoring, this was mainly done through the anti-
iconoclastic policies he helped formulate and execute. The apostolic
task was carried out by the brilliant missionaries Methodius and Cyril,
who did the proselytizing in the vast regions of the Slavs. The controversy with the Church in the West during this period was but a bitter
and consuming chapter in this long and harmful dispute.

Throughout its long history, the Orthodox Church in Byzantium,
continuing the tradition of the enlightened apologetic writers, exercised authority over the use of pre-Christian cultural and intellectual
traditions, especially the classical. There never was a time when theoretical problems did not engage the attention of the leadership in the
Eastern Orthodox Church and play a role in the political life of Byzantium. Church leaders often sought assistance from the secular wisdom of the past. It was the changing problematic of the place of the
Church vis-a-vis the other institutions that decided what features of
the classical and Hellenistic periods of philosophy were useful to doctrinal exposition. Rarely, if ever, did the church officially question

13. Arianism, according to Photius, is not reverting to Hellenism; rather it is Christian being misled by the Hellenic folly. See *PG* 102, 633C, 633D. Kustas 1964, interprets
Photius to have taken the view that Arianism was based on a "Greek system," and hence
open to the charge of polytheism (69).

14. Kustas 1964 notes: "Whereas the vast reservoir of pagan learning supplies the
externals, the standard is always Christian and the vocabulary of paganism is itself
adjusted to serve Christian purpose" (64–65). And in note 88 he draws attention to the
way this phenomenon takes place in connection with literary criticism. See also Kustas
1960, where he writes that Photius's habit "is more to use the pagan reference to define
and illumine the Christian" (132–39).

seriously and without qualifications the relevance of the classics. This explains why the classical works were preserved during the long period of the Byzantine Empire.

Photius was confronted with a host of problems that advocated the extensive reintroduction of the classics. The sustained and fruitful response he initiated has been conveniently labeled "the ninth century renaissance." To a certain extent this is accurate but it should not be understood to imply that the ninth century was also a creative period of enlightenment or that Photius was a model humanist and philosopher. Actually, he was a brilliant statesman of the Church and a cultural diagnostician who carefully selected from a rich reservoir of available materials the means to face the tasks at hand: internally to restore a cherished richness in the worship and externally to proselytize the tribes in the north who were posing a formidable danger to the Empire. Both tasks proved to be immensely complex, and in the process he encountered resistance both from within and without.

The obstacles he faced and the consequences of the policies he sought to implement are well known. They are part of the history of Byzantium, its political, cultural, intellectual and religious record, and in this regard they render defensible the thesis that, in contrast to the West, Byzantium did not go through a period of "dark ages" in the seventh and eighth centuries. By way of influence during this period, the policies of Byzantium, religious and cultural, point in three directions: to the Slavic people in the North, to the Latins in the West, and to the Arabs in the East.

II. TOWARD A PHILOSOPHICAL THEOLOGY

The main texts that show Photius's knowledge and use of Aristotle's philosophy are the occasional references to Aristotle in the *Bibliotheke* —however, these lack specificity and depth, and hence have limited value[15]—and three sections in the *Amphilochia* (a later work composed during the period 868–72): (*a*) question 75, "How it is said that the divine is in all and how to dispense with the doubts that some advance against this hypothesis." This is a theological doctrine; (*b*) question 77, dealing with questions and solutions about the genera and the species, as a response to a logical and ontological problem; (*c*) ques-

15. Plato is often mentioned in this monumental work, but the fact is that Photius nowhere undertakes the analysis of a Platonic dialogue or of an Aristotelian treatise. Hence it is not possible to determine what Aristotelian doctrines he had mastered at the time he composed those essays. Nevertheless, the *Bibliotheke* is an important source of information for the history of philosophy. For instance, it preserved whatever we have from the writings of the sceptic Aenesidemus and the Neoplatonist Hierocles.

tions 137–47, being a synopsis of the ten categories, mainly a brief essay on ontology, in which Photius develops in some detail his views on *ousia* by extending and reformulating basic Aristotelian distinctions.[16]

The place to begin a discussion of Photius's indebtedness to Aristotle is a statement in question 75 related to his philosophical theology. Certain doctrines expounded in this question receive further attention in his commentary on the *Categories*, where he amplifies the concept of *ousia*. In lines 27–30, he states: "The divine is at once wise and beyond wisdom (ὑπέρσοφον), and God is both powerful and beyond all godliness (ὑπέρθεος), predominantly *ousia* and also above *ousia* (ὑπερούσιον), the good itself and also above the good (ὑπεράγαθον), and thus God is said to exist in all (τὸ παντί) and above the all (ὑπὲρ τὸ πᾶν)." Accordingly, he adds further down, that "to be in all does not cancel that which is above the all; instead, it indicates agreement and certainty" (lines 33–34). The explanation is that "the divine in all is both according to actuality and essence (*ousia*)" (lines 44–45). What is introduced here is a special meaning of the term "*ousia*," or rather a special case of what it is to be always in actuality and never in potentiality. "We must understand the divine as intuitive reason (νοῦς), always in actuality," meaning that process or actualization does not pertain to the divine mind, whose self-actuality is also self-substance as such. This divine being, always total actuality and substance, "keeps active the cohesion and endurance of all beings, grants them existence, and governs the nature of all things it has created" (lines 50–52).

These basic tenets of Photius's ontology of the divine set forth the parameters within which he uses the conceptual apparatus of the Aristotelian tradition of metaphysics. One of the issues he must settle before he can elucidate the ontic features of the divine, is the meaning of what it is to be in accordance with *ousia*, not in the sense of Aristotelian concrete individuals but as genera and species, *second ousiai*: τὸ κατ' οὐσίαν ὑπάρχον.

Question 77, on "*aporiai* concerning genera and species," shows how fundamental to Photius's philosophical theology is the rejection of the Platonic ontology. The argument there is constructed to refute the Platonic theory of the Ideas on the ground that Platonism compromises the omnipotence of divine creativity:

Many a time did we discuss the problem of genera and species and sought to clarify the ancient disputes. It was the opinion of those who attended the discussions that the inquiry went deep enough as to leave no question un-

16. All references to the *Amphilochia* are to the recent edition of the text by L. G. Westerink 1986–87; the translations are mine.

answered. Plato's Ideas came up for special consideration because they could not be predicated of individuals. I will not recount the argument, namely that admitting the preexistence of perfect types and exemplars, which will be used by a creator, forces us to admit that there exists a creator who does not have the power to create through the unqualified apprehension of what he wills to make. Nor will I bring up here the argument that to seek to pose the existence of preexisting perfect types, the Ideas, on account of the endless series of types it necessitates, leads to infinite regress. (lines 3–11)

God's creative power needs no assistance. This is a thesis based on dogma. Logically, Photius finds the Platonic doctrine unacceptable since it leads to infinite regress. He subscribes to Aristotle's criticism based on the third-man argument. What is equally objectionable in Plato's theory is that the Ideas cannot function as genuine predicates in the sensible world, which is God's creation: "If we admit the existence of perfect types residing in the divine mind, assuming they partake in serenity, being motionless and unshakable, how could they be attributed as predicates to things that are in constant motion, in flux and emanation?" (lines 17–20).

This brings him to discuss a related problem: the determination of the mode of existence of the genera and species. He reminds Amphilochus that this problem was solved in the past, when they were discussing the issues; then he summarizes the position: "However, the great dispute refers to the three-dimensional substances (*hypostaseis*), namely bodies. Is it indeed necessary to call their genera and species also bodies, or is it better to regard them superior to objects of sensation and place them in the class of bodiless beings?" (lines 40–44). The genera as entities, being predicates and genuine referents, are themselves non-material and bodiless. "It should be evident then that the formulas of the bodiless beings with reference to genus, being determinative of the subject, are themselves bodiless" (lines 49–50).[17]

In brief outline, Photius's solution is as follows: The notion 'man,' for instance, is not by nature something bodily or somatic. Actually, it stands for a *hupokeimenon* or subject "in itself not bodily but indicative of a subject possessing a body." Photius comes nearest to Aristotle's position when he states his solution to the problem in the following passage: "The genera and the species of these bodies are not really

17. Tatakis 1968 has pointed out that Photius posed in this brief essay the problem of nominalism versus realism, which two centuries later in the West was to figure prominently in the writings of William of Champeux (1070–1121) and Roselinus (1050–1123). In his 1967 essay, he notes: "As far as I know, Photius is the first to face vividly, clearly, and profoundly, reflecting deep knowledge of the history of the problem, what will become the object of interminable dialectical investigations of the *aporiai* associated with this fundamental philosophical theme. The answer he constructed shows that he used essentially original elements" (126).

bodiless beings, yet they do not go so far with respect to bodily existence as to manifest bodily mass, nor do they have matter like their
carrier through which three-dimensional fullness can be subsumed.
In general, they are said of bodies and are called 'bodily' (σωματικά).
What they suggest is body and what they assert is a subject" (lines 55–
60). The gist of the solution is that genera and species are somatic
without being bodies. They state the substance or *ousia* of subjects
without themselves being subjects, that is, sensible carriers of properties. They indicate and display the *ousia* of subjects but do not constitute it. They appropriately indicate the *hypostasis* or underlying
existence of subjects without adding or giving something to the subjects, for the latter are deficient in their being. Hence, the subjects do
not receive anything sensible from the species and the genera. The
problem was posed by the Platonizing Christians, the solutions came
from an Aristotelianizing Christian. The positions Photius refuted
were extreme. Whereas realism assigned existence to the supreme
genera, independently of the individual entities in which they inhere,
nominalism counterposed the view that these supreme genera as such
are nothing more than mere symbols or names.

Before leaving question 77 of the *Amphilochia*, Photius pauses to pay
high tribute to Aristotle. It is worth quoting: "Aristotle whose birth-
place was Stagira gave back to all Greece a delightful miracle: his own
wisdom" (lines 202–24). Next Photius claims that his own reflections
on the mode of existence of the genera and species, compared to
Aristotle's, do not fall far behind. He offered the Christian solution
to a thorny problem that was bound to be raised after the Christian
theologians introduced their own understanding of the principles of
classical ontology.

III. EXPANDING THE ARISTOTELIAN CONCEPT OF *OUSIA*

The commentary on the *Categories*, questions 137–47, consists of a
pithy analysis of select Aristotelian doctrines needed to complement
his philosophical theology. The text offers a pointed yet complicated
elaboration on what Photius takes to be Aristotle's theory of predication. Photius views the doctrines of this treatise as being in need of
correction and reformulation before he can use them to elucidate
ontological issues related to the Christian doctrine of being, the concept of God, the idea of Trinity, and bodiless substantial beings.

The *Synopsis decem categoriarum* is a rich and difficult text; its significance has not been sufficiently recognized although it is one of the
most important philosophical documents of the medieval Byzantine

period. The remarks presented here, admittedly short of offering the full treatment the *Synopsis* deserves, are limited to his expanded conception of *ousia*. My main concern has been to help make clear the ground for Photius's expansion of the meaning of *ousia*, beyond its initial Aristotelian boundaries, and to indicate how the new aspects he introduced were designed to serve his religious commitment.[18]

Photius begins with comments on the well-known distinction of *homonyma, synonyma, paronyma,* to which he adds *polyonyma* and *heteronyma,* noting that "in a certain way" *polyonyma* are opposite to *homonyma* and *heteronyma* opposite to *synonyma.* The arrangements are used later in the commentary to settle issues of the classification of entities beyond the types Aristotle had recognized. In the case of *homonyma* Photius enlarges the meaning of *logos tes ousias* by way of (*a*) omitting the word *ousia* in line 7, only to include it in line 18 to avoid misunderstanding, and (*b*) insisting that *logos* stands either for definition or description (ὑπογραφή). This amplification is not to be found in Aristotle, but Photius remains silent about his departure from the original. The practice, by no means exclusively his, is an important one in that it enables him to attach to Aristotle's text the addendum "description" (ὑπογραφή) originating with the Hellenistic commentators.[19]

After summarizing the early chapters of the *Categories,* Photius takes up the centerpiece of the treatise in a separate essay that constitutes the theme of question 138: "On *ousia.*" *Ousia* is a "*pollachos legomenon,*" it has many meanings, and refers to (1) matter, (2) form, and (3) the efficient agent (μορφωτικὸν καὶ εἰδοποιὸν) that gives form to matter. In a metaphorical sense (4) it indicates possessions and money. It is said (5) of the existence and substantiation of each being, the opposite of which is non-being, but (6) in a totally different trope, *ousia* is "*hyperousia* and productive of all beings.*" The reader recognizes here the *ousia* Photius has reserved exclusively for the divine. The word 'God' does not occur in the text. However, he states clearly that the *theoria* of the supreme *ousia* is not the subject of a study such as the treatise titled *Categories* undertakes, but belongs to a totally different inquiry: First Philosophy. Evidently, the reference is to Aristotle's *theologia* in the *Metaphysics.*

Further down (lines 18–20), he states that none of the aforementioned meanings of *ousia* is really a predicate, a *kategoria.* The rule

18. Kustas 1964 states that "His [Photius's] interest in logical reasoning is but part of a larger involvement with philosophy," and also that "the techniques of logical reasoning are made to serve his theological purposes" (39).

19. I have discussed this and other related topics in several articles, chiefly in my 1968 "The Meaning of ὁ λόγος τῆς οὐσίας in Aristotle's *Categories* 1a," and 1969 "Ancient Interpretations of Aristotle's Doctrine of 'Homonyma'."

applies most strictly to the extraordinary case of ὑπερούσιος *ousia* that holds all beings together (συνεκτικὴ τῶν ὄντων), itself above all concepts and names, and residing in ineffable greatness. But next comes the puzzling part of Photius's amplification of Aristotle's *ousia* (lines 26–40). First he hints that the list is incomplete and then, working his way through the concept of self-subsistence, he draws a distinction between self-subsisting beings, the ones Aristotle called *protai ousiai* ("first substances") consisting of form and matter, and the self-subsisting beings consisting of what are only analogues of form and matter. The latter make up a distinct class. We are in the realm of angels and of immaterial reason or *nous*.

As the paragraph is about to close, he states that the self-subsisting beings in this new class have escaped the conditions of bodily mass by virtue of possessing a bodiless nature. The expository account suddenly stops and the author announces that "this topic, being so different and profound, belongs to another inquiry." Presumably, the type of discourse that deals with sensible reality cannot cover the whole of *ousia*. In the remainder of the essay Photius instructs Amphilochus on select topics of the doctrine of the categories without returning to the topic of *theologia*. Nevertheless, the theologian has made his point.

Photius's comments in *Amphilochia* on genus and species (also on the "categories"), appear to be based on notes from discussions that took place with friends at Photius's residence before he became patriarch. The questions examined here are: (*a*) What reality do the genera and species possess? and (*b*) What is the relation between genera and species?

Genera and species are "somatic" but as such they are not bodies, nor do they denote subjects that are bodies. Since Tatakis (1967) has discussed in some depth the problem of genera and species (129–30), and has drawn attention to the objections Photius raises against the Aristotelian view of *ousia*, I will discuss his analysis and add certain reservations and critical remarks.

Photius proceeds to examine *ousia* independently of Aristotle, although he uses the text of the *Categories* as a basis. He recasts the meanings of *ousia* to accommodate his own Christian theory of being by adding two new items, as I have already indicated: (*a*) the case of the divine as οὐσία ὑπερούσιος καὶ προακτικὴ τῶν πάντων οὐσία, and (*b*) the case of the angels, as ἀσώματος οὐσία.

Photius disagrees with Aristotle that the distinction between first and second *ousia* is limited to individual versus universal *ousia* (ἄτομον, μερικόν versus καθόλου). According to Photius the individual, first *ousia,* and the universal, second *ousia,* cannot be predicated synonymously either with regard to themselves or with regard to *ousia* (οὐχὶ συνωνύμως οὔτε πρὸς ἑαυτὰς οὔτε πρὸς τὴν οὐσίαν). Clearly the objection is to predicating synonymously first *ousia* and second *ousia* of individuals. It rests on the assumption that the individual and the universal, although they share in the name *ousia,* each calls for a different determination (προσδιορισμός); for what determines first *ousia* is totally different from what determines second *ousia.* Tatakis (129–30) is right in pointing out that the issue is embedded in Photius's approach but he falls short of explaining the reasons for Photius's strong objections to Aristotle's formulation. There can be no doubt that the opposition to Aristotle stems from Photius's theological position.

Photius also objects, contrary to what Aristotle says, that we cannot "predicate synonymously" of a concrete individual (*tode ti*) what is included in the "*propria*" of *ousia.* Such a predicative allowance is nothing but a useless superfluity since "what is *proprium* belongs only to the first *ousia* that has been named in accordance with it." Tatakis notes that "these expressions show that Photius disapproves of the Aristotelian distinction between first and second in the category of *ousia*" (130). But again, Tatakis does not elaborate on the reason for this objection.

As I understand it, Photius's concern is to extend the denotation of the concept of the individual, the *tode ti,* to cover in some qualified way other meanings of first *ousia,* demanded of his philosophical theology. No doubt he is aware why this cannot be done once the restriction of *ousia qua* first and second is accepted. Clearly, if angels *qua ousiai* are special cases of *tode ti,* i.e., if they have concreteness, the feature of *proprium* cannot be predicated synonymously of both human beings and angels, let alone of human beings and God.

An equally important objection is raised against another Aristotelian expression: "more and less *ousia*" (μᾶλλον οὐσία, ἧττον οὐσία). For Photius, the former covers the case of individuals, the latter of universals, a reading he obtains by way of comparing the species and the genus on the basis of the proximity of each to what is first *ousia.* The pertinent text of Photius reads: "Therefore, from what Aristotle argues so far we are allowed to conclude that what he calls 'more' *ousia,* as being more indicative and explanatory of what lies before us, actually does this poorly. However, it is not our present intent to examine how it is possible to conceive of that which is more indicative and explanatory either as total *ousia* or more *ousia.* Let what has been discussed so far about *ousia* end at this point" (lines 212–18). Tatakis' comment is limited to the following observation:

Photius, when discussing the category of *ousia,* is doing only logic. However, the thesis Aristotle projects is also one which controls his metaphysics, and hence not only logical. Therefore, Photius does not agree with the extended uses of Aristotle's logic; these constitute a theme for a different investigation. Had Photius accepted the position that what is "more indicative and explanatory of what lies before us" is also "more *ousia,*" he would have reached the terrifying conclusion that God's "*ousia*" is less *ousia,* since as a Christian he also admits that the divine is ineffable and incomprehensible. In other words, for Photius *ousia* is independent of the definition we give it. To be able to speak of "more" and "less" *ousia* is something that is not to be decided on the basis of what is "more indicative and explanatory of what lies before us" (131).

Admittedly, "the issue that separates Photius from Aristotle on this topic is indeed a great one" (130). However, the interpretation Tatakis introduces, aside from his keen remark on the greatness of the issue and the gulf that separates the two thinkers, is not without difficulties. A more plausible alternative would be one that understands Photius doing both logic and ontology when counterposing his own to Aristotle's logic and ontology. In other words, it is misleading to view Photius as separating logical doctrines from ontology, even when he reads Aristotle with alternating emphases between logical and ontological issues. Lurking in the background of the text under consideration are the following:

(*a*) A shifting of terminology and expressions; e.g., for Aristotle's expressions for "definition" (ὅρος, ὁρισμός, λόγος τῆς οὐσίας), Photius substitutes one of his own: "determination" (προσδιορισμός).

(*b*) The introduction of new uses of the term *ousia* with a novel conceptualization, even if this practice is not new with Photius. Thus πρώτη οὐσία not only stands for the individual *tode ti* of the *Categories,* but the paradigm case is mainly the human person understood religiously, a meaning designed to cover far more ground than Aristotle's definition of *anthropos.* But more importantly, the new meaning includes the case of the divine, God *qua* person, whose fullness requires more than the definition to apprehend its ineffability. Here, the ontological grounds of logic, of the theory of soul and the four causes, fall short of meeting the demands of the Christian view of man and God. Photius has in mind the theology of God, the creator and maker of man in His image and likeness.

(*c*) Photius introduces his non-Aristotelian *ousia* in *Amphilochia* question 138, in order to go beyond second *ousiai* and indeed above them. This move creates a problem when the discussion turns to the meaning of "more and less" *ousiai.* By bringing in new and different substantial types, for which Aristotle did not provide, the distinction itself becomes irrelevant, if not systematically misleading from the Christian perspective. Thus Photius finds it necessary to question the relevance and use of the distinction between *ousia* as *tode ti* and what is "more or less" *ousia* in the case of the second *ousiai*, especially as one approaches the more inclusive case of *ousia*, i.e., the genus, which in Aristotelian terms is said to be even less *ousia* than the species. For Photius, making what is a higher ontic concept less revelatory than *ousia* as *tode ti*, is to devalue *ousia* irreparably when the reference is to higher beings, namely, angels. Presupposed here is a hierarchy of being in relation to the way revelation discloses the nature of the human *tode ti*.

(*d*) Aristotle's conception of God does not adequately provide for the proper understanding of the human *tode ti*, the paradigmatic instance of Aristotelian concrete individuals, even when Aristotle uses the term "*ousia*" in contexts richer than the *Categories*.[20] There is no reason to doubt that Photius knew of the uses of *ousia qua* first, as found in the *Metaphysics*, yet such uses are hardly what Photius could have regarded as adequate to serve the conceptual needs of his philosophical theology. The radical use of *ousia* occurs in the opening lines of *Amphilochia* question 138, to which I have already referred: ἡ τῶν ὄντων συνεκτικὴ καὶ ὑπερούσιος οὐσία ὡς πολλῷ κρείτων τῶν τοιούτων φωνῶν καὶ ἐννοημάτων καθισταμένη, μᾶλλον δὲ ὡς ὑπερβολῇ ἀρρήτῳ ἐξηρτημένη τε καὶ ὑπεριδρυμένη.

We are now in the realm of the *hyperousia*, where the Aristotelian *more-less* loses all relevance. The theological conception of *ousia* provides Photius with a new basis from which to criticize the classical conception of being. The use of the reference to the "more and less" *ousia* pertaining to genus and species, is recast to conform to the religious conception of reality.[21]

It has been maintained by a number of scholars that Photius's philo-

---

20. E.g., *Met.* 12.7.1072b22: τὸ γὰρ δεκτικὸν τοῦ νοητοῦ καὶ τῆς οὐσίας. Also *Met.* 12.9.1074b21–22: εἴτε νοῦς ἡ οὐσία αὐτοῦ εἴτε νόησίς ἐστι, τί νοεῖ.

21. It is on this basis then that I conclude that Tatakis has overlooked the deeper reason that led Photius to criticize Aristotle. I think that Tatakis has misconstrued the passage in Photius's commentary where the "more-less" distinction is discussed. He writes that "Aristotle distinguishes between more *ousia* and less *ousia*. By more *ousia* he means the *ousia* of the individual while by less *ousia* that of the universal" (130). Tatakis follows Photius in accepting this reading, yet nowhere does Aristotle use the expression μᾶλλον οὐσία in relation to *tode ti*. Instead, the expression he employs for the latter is κυριώτατα οὐσία. Photius reverses the order of the comparative and puts at the apex his own *hyperousios ousia*. Tatakis is on better grounds when he turns to Photius's own understanding of the Greek philosophers in general and notes in passing the following: "The place where the disagreement with Aristotle is openly declared is in the case of the metaphysical projections, or rather the metaphysical foundations upon which Aristotle's logic rests. There Photius does not follow Aristotle's rationalism to the end. He is closer, even when he does not seem aware of the dependence, to Plato, who believed that at the end of the dialectical process the soul envisions the Idea. The idea, while something that the soul intuits, is at the same time ineffable" (131).

sophical works have been lost.[22] Even without the benefit of his complete writings in philosophy it is still possible to reconstruct in general outline the basic theses he sought to support in his philosophical theology. His contribution was not in the form of an original theology; rather, it was to the understanding of the place which philosophical method should be granted for the scrutiny of ontological issues raised in theological discourse. This is not to say that Photius is not a philosopher.[23] It would be more to the point to say that philosophy holds his interest primarily if not exclusively for the sake of philosophical theology. The dominant tone in his writings in this area shows that his thinking was not aiming at constructing demonstrations to defend the "truths of faith," to render them immune to theoretical dispute, or even less to show that fundamental religious beliefs can be established independently with the help of the intellectual tools of natural reason. Photius was primarily a man of faith and only secondarily a systematizer, a worker of religious harmonies, a concerned scholar with the ability to effect a synthesis of ideas. Unshaken in his belief in the superiority of the Christian values and ideas, he saw nothing in his faith that called for improvement.

It has been suggested, and correctly so, that the study of the problem of *ousia* in the theological essays may yield rich rewards. However, this is not to say that the theological writings are the only texts that contain philosophical ideas, nor does it offer support to the view that the texts in which Photius presumably developed his philosophical views were lost. One suspects that Photius saw no compelling reason to write a "purely" philosophical treatise on *ousia* and other related topics, if only on the ground that such works could not possibly add anything novel to the doctrines he had espoused. I have not been able to discern in his writings any indication that philosophy can introduce principal theses capable of improving on what theology could not assert on its own. Photius gives no clues that he ever entertained the view that the problem of *ousia* in its theological setting had to be solved through an appeal to philosophy.

Thus to understand what Photius had to say on the subject of *ousia* the reader must go first to the "truths" as stated in the context of the dogma and only then proceed with the exploration of the implications they have for the proper employment of theoretical distinctions such

22. Tatakis 1967 (119); Lemerle 1971, chap. 7; Hergenroether 1869 (3:258–60), has provided a list of these "lost" works.

23. So with Tatakis 1967 (119), who sees Photius's contribution mainly in literature and philosophy by reviving interest in the study of classical texts and being a precursor to the renaissance of classical learning; hence the monumental significance of the *Bibliotheke*.

as those of *ousia-hypotaseis* and *ousia-idiotetes*. Plainly put, in order to form an adequate picture of his ontology one must first consult the theological theses contained in the articles of faith and Revelation. For instance in question 180, beginning with line 17, we find the following:[24] "It is through the denial of all beings that we rise to the vision of the *ousia* and divinity that is above all beings. For what is not as one among all beings but better than all, this is what God is, who brought out from non-being into being everything and who thoughtfully cares for the continuance and the harmonious movement of all the things he created." This and other passages like it in the *Amphilochia*, leave no doubt that Photius's philosophical theology explored and used traditions that had worked out terminologies far beyond the limits of the concept of being in classical ontology.

IV. THEOLOGICAL ONTOLOGY AND
NEOPLATONIC AESTHETICS

Aristotelianism gained a prominent place in the theological ontology of Photius but was denied a comparable place in another and equally significant part of his thought, the aesthetic appreciation of icons as art. Here the prize went to Neoplatonism.

On March 28, 867, he delivered his famous *Homily* at the celebration of the return of the icon of the Mother of God to the Church of Hagia Sophia.[25]

It is in these things that the deed which is before our eyes instigates us to take pride. With such a welcome does the representation of the Virgin's form cheer us, inviting us to draw not from a bowl of wine, but from a fair spectacle, by which the rational part in our soul, being watered through our bodily eyes, and given eyesight in its growth toward the divine love of Orthodoxy, puts forth in the way of fruit the most exact vision of truth.[26]

24. Ἀλλὰ γὰρ καὶ ἐξ ἀποφάσεως τῶν ὄντων ἁπάντων εἰς θεωρίαν ἀναγόμεθα τῆς ἐξῃρτημένης τῶν ὄντων οὐσίας τε καὶ θεότητος. ὁ γὰρ μηδέν ἐστιν τῶν πάντων, κρείττων δὲ τοῦ παντός, τοῦτ᾽ ἂν εἴη θεός, ὃς προήγαγέν τε ἐκ μὴ ὄντων εἰς τὸ εἶναι τὸ πᾶν καὶ τῶν προηγμένων διαμονῆς καὶ ἐναρμονίου κινήσεως τὴν πρόνοιαν ἔχει. Compare *Amphilochia*, Questions 181–92, where Photius elaborates on his theological theses.

25. Homily 17, trans. Mango 1958, 286–96. In the note, Mango writes with reference to the main topic of the sermon, the restoration of the images in St. Sophia: "It would not be an exaggeration to say that no other text expresses the re-establishment of 'Orthodoxy' with equal authority and eloquence. The underlying theory is given in almost Platonic terms. In the eyes of Photius, painting is the most direct form of instruction, for a picture that is in agreement with religious truth contains the *eidos*, or essence, of the prototype, which is in turn apprehended by the faculty of sight and indelibly imprinted upon the mind. A painter is guided by divine inspiration, so that his work is not merely mimetic, but contains an actual share of the prototype. One would look in vain for a better expression of Byzantine art theory" (282).

26. Homily 17.ii, 31ff.; text in Laourdas, 1959, 298; trans. Mango 1958, 290.

It is noteworthy that Photius did not employ Aristotle's theory of art or the particular view on mimesis in the *Poetics* when he described the source of the beauty and attractiveness of the icon of the Mother Virgin. This comes as a surprise since art was at the center of the iconoclastic controversy. For instance, he declares that the icon was made through divine inspiration and that it depicts a divine theme; it imitates the real archetype with exactitude.[27] The educative value for religious education reigns supreme as the icon elicits irresistible consent and grants to the soul of the beholder the *ousia*, the *eidos* of the visible. Thus, the viewers, by seeing the perfect sensible form, which is what the beautiful icon is, are granted "a grace of the eyes, and a grace of the mind, carried by which the divine love in us is uplifted to the intelligible beauty of truth" (Mango, 295).

But stronger than the affinity in language between Photius and Plotinus is the similarity of views regarding the creative act, the source of power of the icon, and the transcendent nature of the archetype with its immediate revelatory effectiveness. The latter is admittedly not Plato's position. Although Photius knew Plato's works, the meanings these expressions took on in Photius's writings are conspicuously closer to the way Plotinus employed them, especially in *Ennead* 5.8.[28]

Photius borrowed from the Neoplatonic theory of beauty, although he never mentions Plotinus, to explain the ontic status of a painting and the activity of the artist. His use of this theory of art, Neoplatonic rather than Platonic, made it possible for his theory of being to blend comfortably with a Platonizing vision of aesthetic experience.

It may seem somewhat unorthodox to say that if the entire culture of Byzantium, Photius's contribution included, is in itself an attainment of *techne*, better still political *techne*, if one prefers, it may be

27. "With such exactitude has the art of painting, which is a reflection of inspiration from above, set up a lifelike imitation" (text in Laourdas, ii.299.12); again: "Neither is the fairness of her form, but rather is it the real archetype" (ii.299.21).

28. Laourdas 1959 notes that the expressions τὸ εἶδος, ὁ ἐν ἡμῖν θεῖος ἔρως, τὸ νοητὸν τῆς ἀληθείας κάλλος, remind us of Plato. He cites the following texts of Photius: p. 171 (=ii.305.32–35, and ii.306.22 to 307.27) in his edition of the *Homilies*. He also observes that Photius's use of Platonic terminology to project his own aesthetic ideas is an exception, especially in view of the fact that most and the best Christian theorists of the art of icons appealed to Aristotelian principles. Laourdas stops short of explaining in detail in what ways Photius "platonizes" in his aesthetics, nor does he suspect the gap between this aspect of Photius's thought and the Aristotelianism of his logic and ontology. In the same vein, Tatakis 1967 (131) follows Laourdas in seeing Photius's Platonism surfacing fully in Homily 17, and attributes to Photius a Platonic aesthetic. There are numerous passages in the *Enneads* where the phraseology tempts us to suspect that the font of Photius's expressions may well understandably be in Plotinus. Cf. *Ennead* 1.6.1.49: κάλλος μὲν οὗ ψυχῆς πᾶσα καὶ κάλλος ἀληθινώτερον ἢ τὰ πρόσθεν. Also in 2.9.16.45–56; 5.8.3.1–2. The title of 5.8 interestingly enough is Περὶ τοῦ νοητοῦ κάλλους.

compared to a work of art. If so, the aesthetic theory we should employ to understand it is not to be found in Aristotle's writings. To do justice to Photius's aesthetic theology we should probably go to Plotinus, just as Photius did when he invoked what was needed to appreciate the intelligible beauty of the great icon of the Virgin Mother. The last word, and the highest, came from the mixture of the Platonic and the Plotinian; only the logic of the ontology was Aristotelian. The crown of the achievement, not surprisingly, was Christian, namely, a Christian work of art.

V. APPENDIX: A BIOGRAPHICAL AND HISTORICAL NOTE

Photius (820–91), Patriarch of Constantinople, called the Wise, was for most of his life a layman deeply committed to the Christian faith. His father's brother, Tarasius, served as Patriarch, and the family enjoyed close ties to the Imperial Court. In 858 Photius was appointed Patriarch of Constantinople, an office he held for eleven years. In 867 he was deposed and exiled by the new emperor, Basil of Macedon. Photius was reinstated to the patriarchal throne in 878, and held the office of the Patriarch for another period of eight years (878–86), at the end of which he was deposed again. He died in 893 at the age of seventy-two.

Photius is regarded as the most important link in the history of the transmission of classical letters in Byzantium, initiating a strong movement that brought about a renaissance of Greek letters. However limited its intellectual scope, it was the first such revival of ancient literature since the sixth century A.D. He admired and loved classical antiquity for its elegance, style, and power of expression rather than for the veracity of its philosophical ideas.

Photius was first and foremost a Christian. While totally devoted to service in the Faith and the inculcation of religious values, he also attempted to combine natural wisdom and revealed theology with the aid of new elements by taking the position that philosophy is not merely a servant to theology but a separate discipline that can rightfully claim to be human wisdom as dialectic and logic. Concerning Photius's relationship to classical philosophy, Laourdas (1959) has remarked that "it would be a mistake to interpret this interest of Photius in the classical writers as admiration also for their ideas. . . . Compared to the ideas of the Apostle Paul, Photius believed, the ideas of the classical writers offer no help at all to the human soul" (14–15).

Photius's family had sided with the iconophiles and suffered under the Isaurians. The conflict between the two factions played an important role in his development and in many ways defined the issues of his times. The movement to return to the worship of the icons succeeded but did not restore its defenders to full political power. Many of the leaders and members of the iconoclast party were still in positions of power and resisted removal. Because of their lingering influence the tensions between East and West deepened. Rome and the pope were on the side of the iconophiles.

The struggle between iconoclasts and iconophiles ended in favor of the restoration of the icons in 843, but its consequences did not stop there. Understandably enough, the iconoclast movement gave rise to a number of heresies, but the scene was even more complicated at the level of international politics and ecclesiastical affairs. Charles the Great, a supporter of the iconoclastic movement, was crowned in 800 in Rome instead of Constantinople, where the emperor resided. The polarization that ensued became a factor in the weakening of the power of the Eastern church.

During the last phase of the iconoclastic movement in the first half of the ninth century, the emperor Theophilus (829–42) had ordered "reopened" the centers of learning—the "universities" which Leon Isaurus (717–41) had disbanded, destroying the buildings and burning the books. Education was reorganized on a new basis once the conflict over the dogma had subsided and interest in the classical writers returned. Theophilus gave protection to two outstanding intellectuals, John the Grammarian and Leon the Mathematician.[29]

When the new regime of Michael III (842–67) consolidated its position, Caesar Bardas, brother of Theodora, the Emperor's mother, implemented the decision to reopen the university, known as the "School of Magnaura." He appointed Leon its first head, and professors Theodore to the chair of Geometry, Theodeghios to the chair of Astronomy, and Comitas to the chair of Grammar. All were students of Leon, as were Photius and a certain Constantine, who later changed his name to Cyrillus and together with his brother, Methodius, completed the conversion of the Slavs to Christianity.

Thus, next to the two existing priesthood schools in Constantinople, a third and secular one was created and located in the palace of Magnaura. It was reconstituted for the education of talented young people planning to enter into government service or pursue diplomatic ca-

---

29. Leon had the reputation of a great thinker and philosopher. As bishop of Thessaloniki, he preserved the works of Archimedes. These manuscripts were moved to Italy in the twelfth century and in 1266 they became the possession of the pope, and then were lost in the sixteenth century.

reers and other administrative positions. It was this school that Photius, a layman with a brilliant mind, was asked by Bardas to lead.[30]

Tensions and antagonisms between East and West, Constantinople and Rome, were nothing new. But they became increasingly intense during the latter part of the ninth century, eventually causing a serious rupture in the unity of Christendom. Part of the background was the lingering ideological and doctrinal element of the *filioque*. It was Photius's misfortune to be one of the protagonists in the dispute.[31]

The formulation of the doctrine of the Trinity Photius employed to counter the *filioque* clause occurs in *Homily* 16.[32] It employs philosophical terms (*idiotes, heterotes, ousia, diaphora, hypostasis*), but the content is obviously unrelated to philosophy, especially Aristotle's. In working with the tradition that supplied useful concepts to theological work, Photius appears to have drawn liberally from the writings of others.

Aristotelianism in Byzantium may be said to go back to Leontius (475–534/4).[33] It is quite likely that Photius had Porphyry's work before him when he wrote his own commentary. There are strong indications that he follows Ammonius and John Damascene. The question of his originality, whatever the answer, cannot be decided apart from the problems, including those of logic, he sought to explore and solve in the texts that deal with issues in philosophical theology.

30. See Laourdas 1959, 5–6 and notes.
31. See Dvornik's 1974 monumental work on the schism for a full account of the issues, as history and legend. A brief account of the origins of the *filioque* is given in Magoulias 1972: "The Creed, as originally composed by the church fathers who sat in the First and Second Ecumenical Councils, states that the Holy Spirit proceeds from the Father. In the sixth century, however, in Spain, theological controversy between Spanish Catholics and Arian Visigoths was intense; to defend the orthodox position that Christ was consubstantial with the Father against the Arian position that he was a deified creature, not of the same essence as the Father, and, therefore, inferior and subordinate, the Catholics inserted the filioque formula into the Creed so that it now read: '. . . the Holy Spirit, the Lord and lifegiver, Who proceeds from the Father *and* the Son [*filioque*] . . .' When the Arian Visigoths were finally converted to orthodox Christianity under their King Reccared in 589, the *filioque* clause was retained in the Nicene-Constantinopolitan Creed" (97).
32. ὁ μὲν (πατὴρ) ἐγέννησεν, ὁ δὲ (υἱὸς) ἐγεννήθη. τὸ δὲ (πνεῦμα) ἐκπορεύεται, οὔτε τοῦ πνεύματος τῇ τοῦ θεοῦ γεννήσει συνεγγραφομένου, οὔτε τοῦ θεοῦ τὴν ἐκπόρευσιν τοῦ πνεύματος συγκληρουμένου, ἀλλ᾽ ἑκατέρου τὴν ἰδιότητα καθαρὰν καὶ ἀσύγχυτον διασώζοντες, τῆς ἑτερότητος τῶν ἰδιοτήτων καὶ τῶν κλήσεων οὐχ ἑτερότητα τῆς οὐσίας παρεισαγόντων, τὴν διαφορὰν δὲ τῶν ὑποστάσεων ἐπιδεικνύντων. Text in Laourdas 1959, 161, last 3 lines, to 162 line 1.
33. Referring to Leontius, T. P. Sheldon-Williams 1967 writes: "Although his [Leontius's] work shows that he was well-grounded in the Aristotelian logic and was particularly familiar with Porphyry's *Isagoge* and a commentary on the *Categories* written either by Porphyry or a disciple, and is sometimes called the founder of Byzantine Aristotelianism, the substance of his teaching is Platonist or Neoplatonist" (490, and notes 1–2). See also David Beecher Evans 1970.

BIBLIOGRAPHY

Alexander, Paul. 1958. *The Patriarch Nicephorus of Constantinople*. Oxford: Oxford University Press.

Anton, John P. 1968. "The Meaning of ὁ λόγος τῆς οὐσίας in Aristotle's *Categories* 1a." *The Monist* 18: 17–27.

Anton, John P. 1969. "Ancient Interpretations of Aristotle's Doctrines of 'Homonyma'." *The Journal of the History of Philosophy*, 7 (no. 1): 1–18.

Baldwin, Barry. 1978. "Photius and Poetry." *Byzantine and Modern Greek Studies*, 4: 9–14.

Benakis, Linos. 1971. "Η σπουδὴ τῆς Βυζαντινῆς φιλοσοφίας" (The Study of Byzantine Philosophy). *Philosophia* (Athens) 1: 390–433.

Benakis, Linos. 1977. "From the History of Post-Byzantine Aristotelianism in Greece." *Philosophia* (Athens) 7: 416–54.

Dvornic, Francis. 1931. "La Carriere universitaire de Constantin le philosophe." *Byzantinoslavica* 3: 59–67.

Dvornic, Francis. 1948. *The Photian Schism, History and Legend*. Cambridge: Cambridge University Press.

Dvornic, Francis. 1950. "Photius et la reorganization de l'Academie patriarchale." *Analecta Bollandiana* 68 (Melange Peeters, II): 108–25.

Dvornic, Francis. 1953. "The Patriarch Photius and Iconoclasm." *Dumbarton Oaks Papers* 7: 69–97.

Dvornic, Francis. 1960. "Patriarch Photius Scholar and Statesman," *Classical Folia* 13: 3–18.

Dvornic, Francis. 1970. *Byzantine Missions Among the Slavs, s.s. Constantine Cyril and Methodius*. New Brunswick: Rutgers University Press.

Evans, David Beecher. 1970. *Leontius of Byzantium: An Origenist Christology*. Dumbarton Oaks, Center for Byzantine Studies, 13. Washington, D.C.

Florovsky, G. 1950. "Origen, Eusebius and the Iconoclastic Controversy." *Church History* 19: 77–96.

Grabar, Andre. 1957. *L'Iconoclasme byzantin*. Paris: Dossier archeologique.

Hergenroether, J. 1960 [1867–69]. *Photius, Patriarch von Constantinopel: Sein Leben, seine Schriften und das griechische Schisma*. 3 vols. Regensburg. Reprint Darmstadt: Wissenschaftliche Buchgesellschaft.

Kustas, George L. 1960. "The Literary Criticism of Photius: A Christian Definition of Style." *Hellenika* 17: 132–69.

Kustas, George L. 1964. "History and Theology in Photius." *The Greek Orthodox Theological Review* 10 (no. 1): 37–74.

Ladner, G. B. 1953. "The Concept of the Image in the Greek Fathers and the Byzantine Iconoclastic Controversy." *Dumbarton Oaks Papers* 7: 1–43.

Laourdas, Basil, ed. and commentary. 1959. Φωτίου Ὁμιλίαι (*The Homilies of Photius*). Monograph Series no. 12. "Hellenika" Thessaloniki.

Lemerle, Paul. 1971. *Le Premier Humanisme Byzantin*. Paris: Presses Universitaires de France.

Martin, E. G. 1931. *A History of the Iconoclastic Controversy*. London: Society for the Promotion of Christian Knowledge 1931.

Magoulias, H. J. 1982. *Byzantine Christianity: Emperor, Church and the West*. Detroit: Wayne State University Press.

Mango, Cyril, trans. and commentary. 1958. *The Homilies of Photius Patriarch of Constantinople*. Cambridge, Mass.: Harvard University Press.

Myerdorff, John. 1956. *Orthodoxy and Catholicity.* New York: Shed and Ward.

Meyerdorff, John. 1974. *Byzantine Theology: Historical Trends and Doctrinal Themes.* 2nd ed. New York: Fordham University Press. Especially chapter 7, "The Schism between East and West," pp. 91–102.

Oehler, Klaus. 1964. "Aristotle in Byzantium." *Greek, Roman and Byzantine Studies* 5: 133–46.

Photii Patriarchae Constantinopolitani. 1986 [1967]. *Epistulae et Amphilochia,* vol. 4.6.1, ed. L. G. Westernik. Teubner Verlagsgesellschaft.

Sheldon-Williams, T. P. 1967. "The Greek Christian Platonist Tradition from the Cappadocians to Maximus and Eriugena." *The Cambridge History of Late Greek and Early Medieval Philosophy.* Cambridge: Cambridge University Press, pp. 425–533.

Tatakis, Basil. 1949. *La Philosophie Byzantine.* Paris: Presses Universitaires de France.

Tatakis, Basil. 1951. Θέματα Χριστιανικῆς καὶ Βυζαντινῆς Φιλοσοφίας (*Christian and Byzantine Philosophical Themes*). Athens: The Apostolic Mission of the Church of Greece.

Tatakis, Basil. 1967. Μελετήματα Χριστιανικῆς φιλοσοφίας (*Essays on Christian Philosophy*). Athens: Astir Publishers.

Tatakis, Basil. 1968. "Ὁ Φώτιος ὡς φιλόσοφος" (*Photios as Philosopher*). *Poly-chordia, Festschrift Fraug Dolger,* 3. Amsterdam, pp. 185–90.

White, Despina S. 1987. "The Hellenistic Tradition as an Influence on Ninth Century Byzantium: Patriarch Photius' Letter to Boris-Michael, the Arcon of Bulgaria." *The Patristic and Byzantine Review* 6 (no. 2): 121–29.

Wilson, N. G. 1983. *Scholars of Byzantium.* Baltimore: The Johns Hopkins University Press.

Ziegler, K. 1941. "Photios." Article in *Real-Encyclopaodie der Classischen Alterums-wissenschaft.* vol. 20. Ed. A. F. Pauly and G. Wissowa.

9   Averroes: The Commentator and the Commentators

THÉRÈSE-ANNE DRUART

Ibn Rush, alias Averroes,[1] who lived from 1126 to 1198, was a Muslim, and did not even know Greek, may seem somewhat of an intruder in a series on "Aristotle in Late Antiquity," particularly since it was only in the thirteenth century that he began to replace Alexander of Aphrodisias as the Commentator par excellence. Yet, his influence as commentator of Aristotle was deep and long lasting. So it may be interesting to determine how Averroes understood his commenting task and what role he gave to the previous commentators in his own enterprise.

These two questions are not easy to answer. Averroes commented on most of the works of Aristotle so extensively that often he wrote two kinds of commentaries on the same text and in at least five cases even three (*Posterior Analytics, Physics, On the Heavens, On the Soul,* and *Metaphysics*). These three kinds of commentaries are traditionally known as short, middle, and long. The short commentaries are in fact epitomes in which Averroes takes such liberties with Aristotle's text that some scholars contend that they should not be considered "commentaries."[2] The middle commentaries are mainly paraphrases, whereas

1. For bibliography, see: George C. Anawati, *Bibliographie d'Averroes (Ibn Rushd)* (Algiers: 1978); Charles E. Butterworth, "The Study of Arabic Philosophy Today" and "Appendix (1983–87)," in *Arabic Philosophy and the West. Continuity and Interaction,* ed. Thérèse-Anne Druart (Washington, D.C.: 1988), 81–90 and 131–37; Philipp W. Rosemann, "Averroes: A Catalogue of Editions and Scholarly Writings from 1821 Onwards," *Bulletin de Philosophie médiévale* 30 (1988): 153–221; and Thérèse-Anne Druart and Michael E. Marmura, "Medieval Islamic Philosophy and Theology: Bibliographical Guide (1986–1989)," *Bulletin de Philosophie médiévale* 32 (1990): 106–11. For a recent general introduction to Averroes, see Miguel Cruz Hernández, *Abū-l-Walīd Ibn Rušd (Averroes): Vida, Obra, Pensamiento, Influencia* (Cordoba: 1986).

2. On Averroes' Aristotelian commentaries in general, see Helmut Gätje, "Averroes als Aristoteleskommentator," *Zeitschrift der Deutschen Morgenländischen Gesellschaft* 114 (1964): 59–65; Miguel Cruz Hernández, "El sentido de las tres lecturas de Aristoteles por Averroes," in Academia Nazionale dei Lincei, Rendicotti della Classe di Scienze

the long commentaries are literal, line by line, and at times extensive explanations of Aristotle's text.

Not all of these commentaries are still extant in the original Arabic and, therefore, some must be read in Hebrew or Latin translations. Furthermore, some have not been critically edited or even edited at all.

In addition to these problems, it is obvious that on some issues, such as his understanding of the eternity of the world, the nature of the material intellect, and the role of emanationism, Averroes changed his mind.[3] Thus, the different types of commentaries on the same text may present various positions. Still worse, not only did Averroes change his mind, but he also rather perversely revised and corrected some of his previous works, and this gave rise to different versions of the same commentary. This is clearly the case for the *Epitomes* of the *Physics, On the Soul,* and *Metaphysics.*

One may, therefore, ask:

1. What is Averroes' specific purpose in each kind of commentary?
2. How much does he use the Greek and Arabic commentators in each type of commentary? To make things easier we will limit ourselves to his explicit references to them and to his own way of understanding them.
3. According to him, what role did the various commentators, Greek and Arab, play in his own intellectual development and in his different interpretations of Aristotle?

Some scholars have already reflected on Averroes as commentator of the Greeks but still much more detailed work is to be done and can only be done systematically when critical editions are available and the texts have been carefully studied.[4]

---

morali, storiche e filologiche, 8th ser., vol. 28, fasc. 3–4, March-April 1973 (Rome: 1974), 567–85; Helmut Gätje, *Das Kapitel über das Begehren aus dem mittlern Kommentar des Averroes zur Schrift über die Seele,* Aristoteles Semitico-Latinus, Prolegomena et Parerga II; Verhandelingen der Koninklijke Nederlandse Akademie van Wetenschapen, afdeeling Letterkunde, n.s. 129 (Amsterdam: 1985), particularly pp. 23–35; and Miguel Cruz Hernández, *Abū-l-Walīd Ibn Rušd,* 59–69.

3. See Herbert A. Davidson, *Alfarabi, Avicenna, & Averroes, on Intellect: Their Cosmologies, Theories of the Active Intellect & Theories of Human Intellect* (Oxford: 1992), 220–356.

4. Besides Cruz Hernández's and Gätje's works referred to in note 2, see the following articles in the section titled "Averroes Commentateur des Grecs" in *Multiple Averroes* (Paris: 1978): Abdurrahman Badawi, "Averroes face au texte qu'il commente" (pp. 59–90), which discusses the *Long Commentary on the Metaphysics*; Muhsin Mahdi, "Alfarabi et Averroes: Remarques sur le commentaire d'Averroes sur la *République* de Platon" (pp. 91–103); Pierre Thillet, "Réflexions sur la paraphrase de la *Rhétorique* d'Aristote par Averroes" (104–16); and Charles E. Butterworth, "La valeur philosophique des

As Averroes distinguishes logical from philosophical works, I shall focus on the latter, but I can only consider some of them. Three of Aristotle's major works fascinated Averroes and led to much polemic in the Medieval Islamic and Medieval Latin worlds. They are the *Physics*, *On the Soul*, and *Metaphysics*. On each of these Averroes wrote the three types of commentaries. In each case he also revised somewhat his *Epitome*, and both versions may be found in the same two basic Arabic manuscripts.[5] I would like first to reflect on these three *Epitomes* and on the reasons why Averroes corrected and revised them. These *Epitomes* are particularly revealing because they are provided with an introduction which states their purpose, and the corrections at least in some cases indicate which commentator influenced Averroes' early thinking.

The first version of these *Epitomes* seems to be prior to Averroes being introduced in 1168–69 by Ibn Ṭufayl, philosopher and court physician, to the ruler Abū Yaʻqūb.[6] As a follow up to this visit, Ibn Tufayl told Averroes that Abū Yaʻqūb was complaining about the difficulty of expression of Aristotle and his translators and about the obscurity of his aims. The ruler wanted someone to paraphrase Aristotle's books and to expound their aims. So Averroes put himself to this task.[7]

The second versions are certainly posterior to this meeting and reflect Averroes' deeper knowledge of Aristotle's texts since all of them seem to refer to the *Long Commentaries* which were written by Averroes when he was old.[8]

---

commentaires d'Averroes sur Aristote" (pp. 117–26). See also, Christos Evangeliou, "The Aristotelianism of Averroes and the Problem of Porphyry's 'Eisagoge'," *Philosophia*, 15–16 (1985–86), 317–31. Averroes commented not only on Aristotle but also on Plato's *Republic* (Hebrew ed. by E. I. J. Rosenthal, *Averroes' Commentary on Plato's "Republic"* [Cambridge: 1969]; trans. Ralph Lerner, *Averroes on Plato's "Republic"* [Ithaca: 1974]), on Galen (Arabic ed. by M. de la Concepción Vázquez de Benito, *Commentaria Averrois in Galenum* [Madrid: 1984]), and on Porphyry's *Eisagoge* (Hebrew ed. by Herbert A. Davidson, *Averrois cordubensis commentarium medium in Porphyrii Isagogen et Aristotelis Categorias* [Cambridge, Mass.: 1969]; trans. Herbert A. Davidson, *Averroes. Middle Commentary on Porphyry's Isagoge* [Cambridge, Mass.: 1969]).

5. The early versions in Cairo, Dār al-Kutūb, Ḥikma wa-Falsafa 5, and the second in Madrid, Biblioteca Nacional, Arabic Manuscript 5.000.

6. Cruz Hernández, *Abū-l-Walīd Ibn Rušd*, dates them 1159 (p. 56). The dating of the *Epitome of the Physics* is the most secure since it follows the date of completion given in the Madrid manuscripts in the explicit of the *Meteorology*, the last of the physical treatises. See also Josep Puig, trans., Averroes, *Epítome de Física (Filosofía de la naturaleza)*, Corpus Commentariorum Averrois in Aristotelem, Versio Hispanica, A20 (Madrid: 1987), p. 65 and p. 92.

7. See Marrakushi, *Kitāb al-muʻjib fī talkhīṣ akhbār al-Maghrib*, 2nd ed., ed. R. Dozy (Leiden: 1885), 174–75; For English translation, see George F. Hourani, trans. Averroes, *On the Harmony of Religion and Philosophy* (London: 1976), 12–13.

8. Cruz Hernández, *Abū-l-Walīd Ibn Rušd* (p. 57) dates the earliest 1186 (by mistake

After examining these *Epitomes*, I shall contrast one of them with the two other types of commentaries on the same text. For practical reasons I had chosen *On the Soul*, the only work for which there are serious editions of the three commentaries, but it also turned up that for this text Averroes makes more use of the commentators than usual.

Finally, I must mention that in all types of commentaries Averroes expands on some issues while skimping on others. At times he corrects Aristotle's views, but generally only on matters of detail. He also adds numerous cross-references to other works of Aristotle and always organizes and systematizes his material, assuming that the traditional order of the *corpus* is both logical and systematic.[9] I shall, therefore, follow this order for my presentation of the *Epitomes*.

I. THE *EPITOME OF THE PHYSICS*[10]

This text is part of a unit including four physical texts, *Physics, On the Heavens, On Generation and Corruption,* and *Meteorology* which are preceded by a general introduction.[11]

The first version, written in 1159,[12] begins as follows: "In this work, we were intending to deal with Aristotle's books and to abstract from them the statements necessary to the attainment of human happiness."[13] Averroes goes on to explain that he will omit passages raising doubt, except for those well-known to his contemporaries. He justifies this procedure in claiming that Aristotle only included them because

---

he indicates a second *talkhis* or *Middle Commentary* of the *Physics* instead of the *tafsir* or *Long Commentary*).

9. The Arabic tradition which Averroes adopts differs from the modern one by including the *Rhetoric* and the *Poetics* among the *logical* works after *On Sophistical Refutations*. The Greek tradition was unsure whether the *Rhetoric* and the *Poetics* should be classified among the logical works or the works on practical philosophy. See Deborah L. Black, *Logic and Aristotle's "Rhetoric" and "Poetics" in Medieval Arabic Philosophy* (Leiden: 1990).

10. Critical edition by Josep Puig, ed., Averroes, *Epitome in Physicorum Libros*, Corpus Commentariorum Averrois in Aristotelem, Series Arabica, A 20 (Madrid: 1983); this edition will be cited hereafter as Puig, Arabic, followed by a page number and, where necessary, a line number. Spanish translation with introduction and notes by Josep Puig, ed., Averroes, *Epítome de Física (Filosofía de la Naturaleza)* (see n. 6); cited hereafter as Puig, Spanish, followed by a page number. Puig edited the second version, but the Arabic of the first version can be found in the *apparatus criticus*. A study of the differences between Averroes' text and Aristotle's can be found in the translation (pp. 31–59 and 93–95). In the same volume, Puig also examines the first version and compares it to the second (pp. 83–92).

11. See Puig, Spanish, 61–72.

12. As we already indicated in n. 6, the explicit of *On Meteors* in the Madrid manuscript states that it was written in 1159. See Puig, Spanish, 63–65 and 92.

13. See Puig, Arabic, 7, *apparatus criticus*.

in his time wisdom had not yet been perfected. Now wisdom has been perfected since no longer does anyone dispute the validity of philosophy and, therefore, we should now study philosophical sciences as one studies mathematics.[14]

Averroes then indicates that he will proceed with the first of Aristotle's books, i.e., the *Physics,* and paraphrase its scientific, i.e., demonstrative, statements.[15]

This version uses commentators to illuminate obscure passages or passages which gave rise to controversies. Averroes refers four times to Avicenna, often rejecting his views and contrasting them to those of others, particularly the Peripatetics.[16] On the other hand, he approves of another Arabic commentator, Ibn Bājjah, alias Avempace, whom he names only once but often follows without referring to him.[17] Among the Greek commentators, he cites by name Themistius (six times),[18] Alexander and Theophrastus (each once), and as we have seen at least twice the Peripatetics and the commentators.[19] Of course, it is not always clear whether he has really read these Greek commentators or simply knows of their views through Arabic sources.

The second version refers twice to his *tafsīr* or *Long Commentary*[20] and, therefore, the text was not revised before 1186.[21] Averroes rewrote his general introduction: "In this work, we were intending to deal with Aristotle's books and to select from them the scientific statements which make his doctrine necessary, i.e., the most secure statements," leaving aside most of the views of his predecessors.[22] "What

14. Ibid., 7–8, *apparatus criticus.*

15. Ibid., 8.12.

16. See Puig, Arabic, 12.7, *apparatus criticus,* which opposes Avicenna and the commentators on their views on the respective tasks of physics and metaphysics; 21.9–10 and 26.11–18 which both emphasize Avicenna's disagreement with the Peripatetics' view of the subject matters of physics and metaphysics (as the Spanish translation indicates the pagination of the Arabic text, we indicate only the latter); and 56.11 which discusses the different interpretations of Avempace and Avicenna of *Physics* 4.5 on the place of the celestial sphere.

17. For the reference, see Puig, Arabic, 116.13 on *Physics* 7.1. Further references in the second version illustrate how profound was the unacknowledged influence of Avempace on this first version. For this, see Puig, Arabic, 6–7 and nn. 24–25.

18. Puig, Arabic, 99.8 and 100.3 on *Physics* 6.4; 103.2, 105.16, and 106.2 on *Physics* 6.5; and 141.4 on *Physics* 8.5.

19. For Alexander of Aphrodisias, see ibid., 62.16 (a quotation: "if there were no soul, there would be no time and no motion") on *Physics* 4.14; for Theophrastus, see 105.16 (referred to along with Themistius) on *Physics* 6.5; for the Peripatetics, see 21.9–10 and 26.11–18 (see n. 15); and for the commentators, see 12.6 and 105.17 (see n. 15).

20. Puig, Arabic, 43.6 on *Physics* 3.8 and 135.10 at the end of the beginning of book 8.

21. Cruz Hernández, *Abū-l-Walīd Ibn Rušd,* 57, and Puig, Spanish, 92.

22. Puig, Arabic, 7.7–10.

moved us to this is that many people are busy refuting Aristotle's doctrine without truly understanding it and this leads to a lack of determination of what is true or false in it. Already Al-Ghazālī had very much wished to accomplish this in his book known as *The Intentions of the Philosophers* but he did not succeed."[23]

Averroes no longer focuses on human perfection and has lost his illusions about philosophy having reached perfection in his own time. On the contrary, because of actual ignorance, he wants to pursue the enterprise begun by al-Ghazālī who had so successfully attacked the philosophers in his next work, the famous *Incoherence of the Philosophers*. He also sternly reminds the readers that they had better study some logic by means of al-Farabi's introduction or his own before reading these philosophical *Epitomes*.[24]

Averroes had discovered that neither he nor his contemporaries really knew Aristotle, and a better knowledge of the text and of the commentators brought this ignorance to light. Averroes' recantations make this clear. For instance, concerning *Physics* 4.5, in which Aristotle discusses the place of the sphere of the heavens, Averroes' first version had implicitly adopted Avempace's interpretation. Now Averroes explicitly rejects Avempace's interpretation, which al-Fārābī had adumbrated, and he adds detailed comments on Avicenna's view. In book six he also rejects Avempace's explanation of instantaneous change, which he had previously adopted.

Yet, it will come as no surprise that the most extensive revision is at the beginning of book eight which discusses the controversial issue of the eternity of motion and its relevance for the eternity of the world.[25]

The first version ignores commentators and presents two alternatives: (1) the world and motion began, which is Anaxagoras' view; (2) a generic eternity of motion, defended by Empedocles, which involves an infinite succession of worlds that come to be and pass away. According to Averroes, this was the position Aristotle adopted in order to refute those who claim that the world began.

The new version asserts that the purpose of this chapter is to determine whether there is an eternal prime mover and to show that the eternity of primary motion is evident. Now Averroes attributes the view that the world began to Plato and to the Muslim and Christian theologians. Certain philosophers' mistaken interpretations confused

---

23. Puig, Arabic, 8.2–5.
24. Puig, Arabic, 8.8–10.
25. Puig, Arabic, 129–35 (first version is in the apparatus); Spanish translation in double columns, pp. 227–37.

people. The culprits are al-Farabi, Avicenna, and Avempace, who are all following John Philoponus who was the first to try refuting Aristotle. Averroes then confesses that he has abandoned the generic eternity of motion after writing the first version of his *tafsīr* or *Long Commentary*.

The second version of the *Epitome* shows more sophisticated discussions of disputed issues. It relies more on commentators, giving five new references to Avempace[26] and even introducing two new names, al-Fārābī and Philoponus,[27] and it exhibits a more critical approach to the commentators. Averroes is taking serious distance from Avempace who had been the main influence on his first version, even if rarely named. The new references in the second version often present a critical evaluation of his positions which had been previously accepted.

II. THE *EPITOME OF THE DE ANIMA*[28]

In the two basic manuscripts, the *Epitomes* of the physical treatises form a unit, and are followed by the *Epitomes* of *On the Soul* and the *Metaphysics*, which constitute another unit.[29]

Whereas the *Epitome of the Physics* was rather brief and divided into eight books according to the traditional division of Aristotle's text, the *Epitome of On the Soul* is much longer, provides a lengthy introduction, moves to a section on the substance of the soul and its powers, and then awards a chapter to each power of the soul. Needless to say, these

26. Puig, Arabic, 55.16 and 56.4 on *Physics* 4.5; 99.13 and 100.7 on *Physics* 6.4; and 134.11 at the beginning of 8.

27. For al-Fārābī, see Puig, Arabic, 8.9 in Averroes' introduction, which presents him as author of a good textbook of logic; 55.16 on *Physics* 4.5; and 134.10 at the beginning of book 8; for Philoponus, see 135.1 on *Physics* 8.1.

28. Arabic edition in Ibn Rochd, *Talkhīç Kitāb al Nafs (Paraphrase du "de Anima")*, *suivi de quatre textes*, ed. Ahmed Fouad El Ahwani (Cairo: 1950), 2–101 (the *apparatus criticus* allows one to keep track of the various versions); other Arabic edition, Averroes, *Epitome De Anima*, ed. Salvador Gómez Nogales, Corpus Commentariorum Averrois in Aristotelem, A 31 (Madrid: 1985), which is based on the second version and does not often include traces of the first version in the *apparatus criticus*; Spanish translation by Salvador Gómez Nogales, *La Psicologia de Averroes: Commentario al libro sobre el alma de Aristóteles* (Madrid: 1987), which speaks of two versions, inserts most of the first in brackets into the translation of the second and in the notes refers to the Arabic in El Ahwani's edition (sic).

29. There are no dates in the manuscripts, but Gómez Nogales (Arabic ed., intro. p. 17) and Cruz Hernández (*Abū-l-Walīd Ibn Rušd*, 56) give 1159 as the probable date of the first version, and the second version seems posterior to the *Long Commentary* which may be dated before 1190 (Cruz Hernández, *Abū-l-Walīd*, 57) or around 1190 (Manuel Alonso, S.J., *Teología de Averroes* [Madrid-Granada: 1947], 95–96).

neat and tidy divisions do not reflect the messy character of the text or the traditional division of *On the Soul* into three books, though Averroes adopts the traditional division in his *Middle Commentary* and, with a slight variation, in his *Long Commentary.*[30]

The two versions of the introduction to the physical *Epitomes* focused on Aristotle's books. Both versions of the *Epitome of On the Soul* share the same introduction, and it indicates a different approach: "The aim of this work is to establish from the statements of the commentators on the science of the soul what we deem to agree most with what was shown in physics and to be most appropriate to Aristotle's aim."[31] Averroes is substituting the work of the commentators for Aristotle's own text. He seems more interested in developing a science of the soul that is well integrated with physics than in explaining Aristotle's words. The introduction goes on selecting from each of the four physical books and from the *Book of Animals* the principles useful for the science of the soul.

The "explicit" common to both versions again puts more emphasis on the commentators than on the commented: "Here ends the discussion about the universal statements from the science of the soul according to the custom of the Peripatetics."[32]

The first version relies heavily on commentators and refers by name to Avicenna (twice),[33] Avempace (four times),[34] Alexander (four times),[35] Themistius (eight times),[36] and Galen (eight times).[37] It also speaks of

30. The *Long Commentary* at least in its Latin garb begins book 3 of *On the Soul* at book 3, chap. 4.

31. El Ahwani's ed., 3; Gómez Nogales, Arabic, 5 n. 1, and Spanish, 99.

32. El Ahwani's ed., 101; Gómez Nogales, Arabic, 139, n. 143, and Spanish, 230.

33. (1) On touch, El Ahwani's ed., 52; Gómez Nogales, Arabic, 70.1, n. 77, and Spanish, 161; (2) on the speculative intellect, El Ahwani, 83; Gómez Nogales, Arabic, 121.7, n. 122, and Spanish, 207.

34. (1) On taste, El Ahwani, 41; Gómez Nogales, Arabic, 57.4, n. 59 and Spanish, 149; (2) on material intellect, El Ahwani, 90 and Gómez Nogales, Spanish, 149 n. 132; (3) on material intellect, El Ahwani, 91 and Gómez Nogales, Spanish, 215 n. 132; and (4) on material intellect, El Ahwani, 92 and Gómez Nogales, Spanish, 217 n. 132.

35. (1) On sight, El Ahwani, 32; Gómez Nogales, Arabic, 46.9, n. 47, and Spanish, 133; (2) on taste, El Ahwani, 41; Gomez Nogales, Arabic, 56.5, n. 59, and Spanish, 149; (3) on taste, El Ahwani, 43; and Gómez Nogales, Arabic, 59.7, n. 62, and Spanish, 151; (4) on speculative power, El Ahwani, 86; and Gómez Nogales, Arabic, 123.15, n. 125 and Spanish, 209.

36. (1) On sight, El Ahwani, 32; Gómez Nogales, Arabic, 46.9, n. 47 and Spanish, 133; (2) on hearing, El Ahwani, 37; Gómez Nogales, Arabic, 51.17, n. 54 and Spanish, 141; (3) on taste, El Ahwani, 41; Gómez Nogales, Arabic, 57.5, n. 59 and Spanish, 151; (4) on touch, El Ahwani, 47; Gómez Nogales, Arabic, 64.3, n. 67 and Spanish, 157; (5) on touch, El Ahwani, 50; Gómez Nogales, Arabic, 67.14, n. 73, and Spanish, 160; (6) on intellect, El Ahwani, 81; Gómez Nogales, Arabic, 118.8, n. 117 and Spanish, 204;

the Peripatetics (three times),[38] the commentators (three times),[39] the specialists in physics (once),[40] and introduces the rather un-Aristotelian Muslim theologians. Among the latter are some disciples of al-Nazzam,[41] and those theologians who defend metempsychosis (mentioned twice)[42] —a view Aristotle did not discuss, but which Avicenna refuted in his *On the Soul*.

Both versions of the *Epitome of On the Soul* have rather lengthy chapters on taste and touch in which a fair number of the references to the commentators occur. The discussion of taste refers twice to Alexander and once to Avempace and Themistius. That of touch uses Themistius twice and Avicenna once but Galen seven times.

Yet, what really puzzled Averroes all his life was the nature of the material intellect,[43] an issue on which Aristotle was a man of few words and fairly obscure ones at that. The chapter on the intellect uses Alex-

---

(7) on material intellect, El Ahwani, 83; Gómez Nogales, Arabic, 121.4, n. 122, and Spanish, 206; and (8) on material intellect, El Ahwani, 84; Gómez Nogales, Arabic, 122.2, n. 123, and Spanish, 207.

37. (1) On nutritive power, El Ahwani, 16; Gómez Nogales, Arabic, 26.1, n. 21 and Spanish, 114; (2) on touch, El Ahwani, 47; Gómez Nogales, Arabic, 64.11, n. 68, and Spanish, 157; (3) on touch, El Ahwani, 48; Gómez Nogales, Arabic, 65.6, n. 68, and Spanish, 158; (4) on touch, El Ahwani, 49; Gómez Nogales, Arabic, 66.2, n. 70, and Spanish, 158; (5) on touch, El Ahwani, 53; Gómez Nogales, Arabic, 70.6, n. 78, and Spanish, 162; (6) on touch, El Ahwani, 53; Gómez Nogales, Arabic, 70.9, n. 78 and Spanish, 162; (7) and (8) on touch, El Ahwani, 53; Gómez Nogales, Arabic, 70.10, and Spanish, 162.

38. (1) On practical power, El Ahwani, 71; Gómez Nogales, Arabic, 101.15, n. 103, and Spanish, 190; (2) on speculative intellect, El Ahwani, 72; Gómez Nogales, Arabic, 106.1, n. 105, and Spanish, 195; and (3) explicit, El Ahwani, 101; Gómez Nogales, Arabic, 139.5, n. 143, and Spanish, 230.

39. (1) In his introduction, El Ahwani, 3; Gómez Nogales, Arabic, 5.4, n. 1, and Spanish, 99; (2) on common sense, El Ahwani, 56; Gómez Nogales, Arabic, 74.11 (*apparatus criticus*), n. 82, and Spanish, 166; and (3) on desiderative power, El Ahwani, 100; Gómez Nogales, Arabic, 138.13, n. 142, and Spanish, 230. (The Madrid version includes another reference on the desiderative power, El Ahwani, 100; and Gómez Nogales, Arabic, 138.12, n. 142, and Spanish, 230, which may have been dropped from the Cairo manuscript and be part of the original first version.)

40. On the acquired intellect, El Ahwani, 74; Gómez Nogales, Arabic, 109.8, n. 108, and Spanish, 197.

41. (1) The *mutakallimūn*, on common sense, El Ahwani, 56; Gómez Nogales, Arabic, 74.10, n. 82, and Spanish, 166; and (2) the defenders of the doctrine of latency, on the intellect, El Ahwani, 83; Gómez Nogales, Arabic, 106.10, n. 105, and Spanish, 196.

42. (1) On speculative intellect, El Ahwani, 74; Gómez Nogales, Arabic, 109.8, n. 108, and Spanish, 197; (2) on speculative intellect, El Ahwani, 79; Gómez Nogales, Arabic, 115.4, n. 114, and Spanish, 201.

43. For an extensive study of this issue and of Averroes' various positions and their chronological order, see Herbert A. Davidson, "Averroes on the Material Intellect," *Viator* 17 (1986): 91–137. See also Arthur Hyman's excellent "Averroes as Commentator on Aristotle's Theory of the Intellect," in *Studies in Aristotle*, ed. Dominic J. O'Meara, Studies in Philosophy and the History of Philosophy 9 (Washington, D.C.: The Catholic University of America Press, 1981), 161–91.

ander, Themistius, the physicists, the commentators, the Peripatetics, and Avempace. The part on the material intellect is most instructive. This first version adopts Avempace's view that the material intellect is a mere disposition in the imaginative power. It even includes a long excursus on Avempace's *On the Conjunction of the Intellect* and its implications.[44] In it Averroes claims not only that Avempace's views are true[45] but even demonstrative.[46]

This last statement may be the worm in the fruit of demonstrative statements since in his second version Averroes abandons these views, drops the excursus, and introduces a paragraph which explains more fully Alexander's and the commentators' interpretation.[47] In the conclusion to the whole chapter he indicates that he has changed his mind.

This recantation begins as follows: "What I have said of the material intellect is how it appeared to me previously."[48] He then goes on to say that after a thorough examination of Aristotle's words he realized this view was impossible. He adds "the first who defended this view is Avempace and he misled me. All this I have already shown in my commentary (*sharḥ*) on Aristotle's *On the Soul*."[49]

As in the *Epitome of the Physics*, Averroes ends up distancing himself from Avempace after having acquired more knowledge of Aristotle's own text. Yet, the *Epitome of On the Soul* seems to have relied originally nearly exclusively on the commentators and to be more free than the *Physics'*. I even wonder though I tremble to whisper such a suggestion whether Averroes had read carefully Aristotle's *On the Soul* before he wrote his *Epitome*.

III. THE *EPITOME OF THE METAPHYSICS*[50]

The four sections of this *Epitome* do not reflect at all the traditional divisions of the *Metaphysics* though Averroes uses them in his *Long Commentary*.[51]

44. El Ahwani, 90–95; Gómez Nogales, Spanish, 214–21.
45. El Ahwani, 90; Gómez Nogales, Spanish, 214.
46. El Ahwani, 91; Gómez Nogales, Spanish, 216.
47. There are three more references to Alexander: El Ahwani, 87 (twice) and 89; Gómez Nogales, Arabic, 125.14, 126.6, n. 128, 127.12, n. 131, and Spanish, 211 (twice) and 213. There are also two more references to the commentators: El Ahwani, 83 and 86; Gómez Nogales, Arabic, 121.4, n. 122, and 126.1, n. 128, and Spanish, 207 and 211.
48. El Ahwani, 90; Gómez Nogales, Arabic, 128–29, n. 132, and Spanish, 213–14.
49. El Ahwani, 90; Gómez Nogales, Arabic, 129.1–2, n. 132, and Spanish, 214. The reference to the commenatry (*sharḥ*) on *On the Soul* seems to be to the long commentary. See Gómez Nogales, Spanish, 258–59, n. 395.
50. Arabic edition by Uthmān Amīn, Averroes, *Talkhīṣ ma ba'da al-ṭabi'a.*, 2nd ed.

The introduction is common to both versions.[52] "In this work, we were intending to collect the scientific statements from Aristotle's sections dedicated to the science of metaphysics according to the way we proceeded in the previous books. We will begin with stating the aim of this science, its usefulness, its parts, its rank, and its relation. In sum, we will begin with things useful to understand before starting this science."[53] We are back to Aristotle's text rather than the commentators. Averroes' text goes on to provide information necessary to understand this science, i.e., it discusses what metaphysics is all about. Averroes of course cannot resist the opportunity to attack some of Avicenna's metaphysical conceptions. In one case he even justifies his criticism by stating that al-Ghazālī, in his *Incoherence of the Philosophers*, had already shown that Avicenna's position is impossible.[54]

In the text itself Averroes refers a dozen times to Avicenna, generally to oppose him,[55] once to al-Fārābī and to al-Ghazālī,[56] twice to the theologians,[57] but never to Avempace. This is not surprising since Avempace wrote on physics and psychology but not much on metaphysics. There are few references to the Greek commentators though the text is fairly lengthy: three to Alexander,[58] one each to Porphyry, Galen, the Stoics, Ptolemy, and Themistius.[59] It seems that at that time

---

(Cairo: 1958); German translation by S. Van den Bergh, *Die Epitome der Metaphysik des Averroes* (Leiden: 1924), reprint 1970. On pp. 274–321, Van den Bergh gives in parallel columns the differences between the Cairo and the Madrid manuscripts, but explains the differences as glosses. In his "Averroes on the Active Intellect as a Cause of Existence," *Viator* 18 (1987): 191–225, Herbert A. Davidson shows that some of these were not glosses but rather revisions.

51. In all manuscripts the text is divided into four parts. Yet, in the introduction, Averroes announces five chapters (Arabic, 6 n. 14; German, 5).

52. Again, Cruz-Hernández, *Abū-l-Walīd Ibn Rušd*, gives 1159 as the date of the first version (p. 56). About the existence of two versions, see Davidson's "Averroes on the Active Intellect," 193–94 and n. 11.

53. Arabic, 1 nn. 1–2; German, 1.

54. Arabic, 4 n. 8; German, 3–4.

55. (1) and (2), Arabic, 4 n. 8; German, 3; (3) Arabic, 4 n. 9; German, 4; (4) Arabic, 19 n. 15; German, 17; (5) Arabic, 41 n. 12; German, 35; (6) Arabic, 52 n. 24; German, 44; (7) Arabic, 74 n. 46; German, 64; (8) Arabic, 82 n. 9; German, 70; (9) Arabic, 83 n. 9; German, 70; (10) Arabic, 101 n. 34; German, 85; (11) Arabic, 101 n. 35; German, 85; (12) Arabic, 104 n. 39; German, 87; (13) Arabic, 127 n. 6; German, 108.

56. For al-Fārābī, see Arabic, 125 n. 4; German, 107. For al-Ghazālī, see Arabic, 4 n. 8; German, 4.

57. Arabic, 12 n. 8; German, 10; and Arabic, 56 n. 27; German, 48.

58. (1) Arabic, 127 n. 7; German, 109; (2) Arabic, 132 n. 18; German, 113; (3) Arabic, 163 n. 77; German, 145.

59. On Porphyry: Arabic, 73 n. 46; German, 63. On Galen: Arabic, 112 n. 49; German, 94. On the Stoics: Arabic, 73 n. 46; German, 63. On Ptolemy: Arabic, 131 n. 15; German, 112. On Themistius, Arabic, 51 n. 24; German, 44.

Averroes was fairly conversant with Avicenna's *Metaphysics* but not much with other commentators.

Can the revisions be attributed to a better knowledge of the Greek commentators? It does not seem to be the case. Averroes states that he is simply returning to what Aristotle himself said and that his previous positions were innovations of the modern commentators, i.e., al-Fārābī and Avicenna. In his first version he had not yet fully discovered how un-Aristotelian Avicenna is.

The first major change deals with the origin of sublunar forms.[60] In his first version, Averroes had maintained that from a metaphysical point of view all such forms come from the agent intellect. In the second version, he weighs the alternatives: either they come from the celestial bodies as they do in Aristotle's view, which is the correct one, or they come from the agent intellect as in the view of many later philosophers.[61] This is repeated a few lines further down.[62] Later on, Averroes states that "There is no need in natural things to introduce separate forms in connection with anything generated, except for the human intellect and this is what Aristotle really maintains and we have already shown this in our commentary (*sharḥ*) on this section of this science."[63] This seems to refer to the *Long Commentary*.

The second main shift in position concerns emanation and the validity of the principle that "From the One only the One can proceed."[64] In his early version Averroes had accepted many emanationist features including this principle. In the new version he rejects most of them, and this principle in particular, saying that such traits are not in Aristotle but are "the doctrine of the modern Islamic philosophers, such as al-Fārābī and maybe also of Themistius among the ancients." He ends by saying "We already talked about this in some other place,"[65] which could be construed as another reference to the *Long Commentary* or to the third discussion of the *Incoherence of the Incoherence* since in it Averroes agrees with most of al-Ghazālī's devastating criti-

---

60. This issue was carefully studied by Herbert A. Davidson in his "Averroes and the Active Intellect."

61. Arabic, 47 n. 19, *apparatus criticus*, n. 5; German, 289.

62. Arabic, 47 n. 19, *apparatus criticus*, n. 7; German, 290.

63. Arabic, 53 n. 25.

64. On Averroes' various positions on emanationism, see Barry Sherman Kogan, "Averroes and the Theory of Emanation," *Mediaeval Studies* 43 (1981): 384–404 (Kogan is rather puzzled by some features of Amīn's edition, but does not realize there are two versions of the *Epitome*; see pp. 387–90 and particularly n. 20); and a more compact version of it in his book, *Averroes and the Metaphysics of Causation* (Albany, N.Y.: 1985), 248–55.

65. Arabic, 153 n. 59, *apparatus criticus*, n. 8.

cism of emanationism. He even contends that some basic emanationist principle is an invention of the "later philosophers of Islam," and claims that on this issue al-Fārābī's and Avicenna's views are worse than those of the theologians.[66]

The second version of *The Epitome of the Metaphysics* shows Averroes further distancing himself from the Arab commentators. Averroes was always suspicious of some of Avicenna's views but with time he discovered that more of them had to be rejected as untrue and un-Aristotelian. This second version claims that the Islamic commentators are innovators and makes little reference to the Greek commentators.[67] This is not surprising since few commentaries on various parts of the *Metaphysics* had been translated.

Many scholars have claimed that in the *Epitomes* Averroes often takes liberties with Aristotle's text and does not hesitate to modify and at times to correct it. There is a clear attempt to integrate the concerns of the day into some kind of Aristotelian system. Aware of al-Ghazali's contention that most statements of the philosophers were not really demonstrative, Averroes deliberately elects to focus on what he deems to be scientific or demonstrative. This eliminates the "aporetic" character of Aristotle's philosophy.[68] The first versions show criticism of Avicenna's views but a clear reliance on the Islamic "Aristotelian" commentators and Avempace in particular when possible. These *Epitomes* are more compendia of the views of the Arabic Aristotelians than they are commentaries or even summaries of Aristotle's texts. One may even wonder whether they truly represent Averroes' personal and "original" philosophical views.

The revisions indicate that with time Averroes removed accretions inserted by the commentators in order to reach Aristotle's own view which often happens also to be the truth. Relying less on the Islamic commentators, he focuses much more on Aristotle's own words, and so is led to change his views on some issues. He does not hesitate to

66. Arabic ed. by Maurice Bouyges: Averroès, *Tahâfot at-Tahâfot* (Beirut: 1930), 173–262, see particularly pp. 245–46; English translation by S. Van den Bergh, *Averroes' Tahafut al-Tahafut (The Incoherence of the Incoherence)* (London: 1969), 104–55, particularly pp. 146–47.

67. Yet, according to Bouyges's index to his edition of the *Long Commentary* (Averroès, *Tafsīr mā baʿd aṭ-Ṭabīʿat* ("*Grand Commentaire*" *de la métaphysique*), vol. 3 (Beirut: 1938), there are numerous references to Alexander, a fair number to Themistius, several to Nicolaus of Damascus, three to Galen, two to Philoponus, a couple to the Peripatetics and the Commentators, two to al-Fārābī, one to Yaḥyā ibn ʿAdī, some twenty to Avicenna, and one to Avempace.

68. A feature already noticed by Gätje in his "Averroes als Aristoteleskommentator," 61.

name who misled him, but for the philosophical justifications of his moves he simply refers to other works.

Let us now follow Averroes' evolution from the first version of the *Epitome of On the Soul* to the *Middle Commentary* and then finally to the *Long Commentary*. The case of *On the Soul* is particularly interesting for our purpose since the *Epitome*'s preface indicated that the main source for Averroes' early work was the commentators and not Aristotle's own text. What role do the commentators play in the other types of commentaries on this same text?

IV. THE *MIDDLE COMMENTARY ON ON THE SOUL*[69]

The *Epitome* was provided with a long introduction, did not follow the traditional division into three books, and extracted from the commentators the universal statements most in agreement with physics and Aristotle's aim.

The *Paraphrase* or *Middle Commentary* presents a stark contrast.[70] There is no other introduction than the word "qāla," i.e., "he [meaning Aristotle] said." It reformulates nearly the whole of Aristotle's own text including the review of previous opinions and the dialectical passages. It is divided into the three traditional books, though there are further subdivisions according to the various powers of the soul.

On the other hand, commentators play very little role. Averroes names them only when dealing with two issues which preoccupied him for most of his career. The first is the importance of the sense of taste and its relation to touch. On this issue the *Epitome* was bristling with references to commentators. The *Paraphrase* names only one, Galen, and him only once.[71]

The second issue is of course the vexing question of the nature of the material intellect. Averroes is commenting on the beginning of book three, chapter four, in which Aristotle claims that the intellect, "since it thinks all things, [must] be unmixed as Anaxagoras says," and then concludes that "the intellect . . . is actually none of existing things before it thinks. Hence too, it is reasonable that it should not

---

69. Thanks to professor Alfred Ivry's kindness I have been able to use the manuscript of his forthcoming Arabic edition and English translation. There is an Arabic edition with German translation of the last chapter of this text as well as a series of useful studies by Helmut Gätje in his *Das Kapitel* (cited in n. 2 above).

70. Cruz Hernández dates it 1174 (*Abū-l-Walīd Ibn Rušd*, 56) whereas Gätje (*Das Kapitel*, 29 and 56) indicates that a Hebrew manuscript claims that Averroes completed this text in 1181.

71. The *Long Commentary* on this same passage, i.e., *On the Soul* 2.12.424b12–14, also refers to Galen (see Crawford's ed., p. 322).

be mixed with the body."[72] Averroes then concludes "this being the case with this intellect, its nature is nothing other than disposition only."[73]

This final declaration is followed by what Davidson calls an excursus of two pages which without further ado explains that the view just presented is Alexander's but that other commentators, at this point unnamed, think it is a disposition that exists in a separate substance, whereas for Alexander this disposition was in the soul. Averroes discusses then the problems arising from each of these positions and states that "the material intellect is something composed of a disposition found in us and of an intellect conjoined to this disposition. This intellect in so far as it is conjoined to the disposition is a disposed intellect rather than an intellect in act but it is an intellect in act in so far as it is not conjoined to this disposition. This intellect is the very same agent intellect whose existence will be shown later on."[74]

Averroes then concludes: "Both approaches to the material intellect have thus been explained to you, that of Alexander and others, and it will have become clear to you that the truth, which is the approach of Aristotle, is a combination of both views. . . ."[75]

Since the compromise position of the excursus contradicts what precedes it, one may wonder whether Averroes did not correct his previous view. A later passage reveals a further complication in returning to the position that the material intellect is located in the human being.[76] Yet, when he reached the notoriously difficult sentence, "But we do not remember because this is unaffected, whereas the passive intellect is perishable, and without this thinks nothing,"[77] Averroes now says: "You ought to know that Themistius and most commentators regard the intellect in us as composed of an intellect in potency and of an intellect in act, i.e., the agent intellect. As a composite intellect it does not think itself but thinks that which is here, when imaginative intentions are conjoined to it. Because these intentions perish, its intelligibles perish and forgetfulness and error occur in this intellect. Interpret in this way what Aristotle says according to what we have shown in our commentary (sharḥ, i.e. Long Commentary?) to Aristotle's statement."[78]

72. D. W. Hamlyn, trans., Aristotle's *De Anima*, Clarendon Aristotle Series (Oxford: 1968), 57.
73. *On the Soul* 429a18, Ivry's translation.
74. Further down, on *On the Soul* 429a18; my translation.
75. Ivry's translation with a modification.
76. Dealing with *On the Soul* 3.5.430a19–21 which is also repeated word for word at the beginning of chap. 7.
77. *On the Soul* 430a23–25, Hamlyn's translation, p. 60.
78. Ivry's translation with some modifications.

The *Long Commentary* on this passage[79] tells us that these lines can be understood in three ways: (1) according to Alexander; (2) according to Themistius; and (3) according to what Averroes has said. After presenting the views of Alexander and Themistius, Averroes concludes: "As for us, since we saw that the opinions of Alexander and Themistius are impossible and we found Aristotle's words clear according to our exposition, we believe that what we said is the view of Aristotle and that it is true in itself."[80]

The *Paraphrase* contains another allusion to the *Long Commentary*[81] while explaining the following sentence from *On the Soul* 1.4: "Thus thought and contemplation decay because something else within is destroyed, while thought is in itself unaffected."[82] Averroes spells it out thus: "By that which 'within the body perishes' Aristotle means the imaginative forms; and by 'that which recollects, loves and hates,' the practical intellect, which exists due to the imagination. This is indicated by his remark that in his view the intellect which abstracts intelligible forms from imaginative intentions neither comes to be nor perishes, though its activity does, perishing with the corruption of the subject in which it acts. We have, however, already shown this matter fully in the commentary (sharḥ) to what he says in this chapter."[83] At this point the *Long Commentary* simply refers to the interpretation which will be defended in book three.[84]

The two references to the *Long Commentary* and the excursus suggest—as Gätje has already hinted in his 1985 study—that Averroes revised his *Middle Commentary* after the completion of the *Long Commentary*.[85]

The *Paraphrase* does not use the commentators much and ignores Avempace who had been the main source for the *Epitome*, but it carefully discusses the Greek commentaries on the nature of the material intellect. For Averroes, it was the first opportunity to study carefully Aristotle's text. The revisions show greater knowledge of the Greek commentators.

79. Textus 20, Crawford's edition, pp. 443–55.
80. Crawford's edition, pp. 446–47: "Nos autem, cum vidimus opiniones Alexandri et Themistii esse impossibiles, et invenimus verba Aristotelis manifesta secundum nostram expositionem, credimus quod ista est opinio Aristotelis quam nos diximus, et est vera in se."
81. While commenting on *On the Soul* 1.4.408b24.
82. Hamlyn's translation, p. 7.
83. Ivry's translation with some modifications.
84. Crawford's edition, pp. 87–88.
85. Gätje, *Das Kapitel*, 29–31.

V. THE *LONG COMMENTARY ON ON THE SOUL*[86]

The *Long Commentary* must be studied in its Latin garb since only fragments of the Arabic have survived and the Hebrew translation derives from the Latin one.[87] It is a sophisticated line-by-line study of Aristotle's text. Averroes is using two translations, and examines their differences in at least ten cases. He notices three lacunae, suggests two emendations, and hints at four omissions. Five times he explains peculiarities of the Greek language to make the text clear, and on two of these occasions he compares Greek and Arabic usages.[88]

The text is divided into three books but the third book begins only at chapter four of our book three. The translator or scribe may be responsible for this division. Yet, if it reflects the Arabic original, then Averroes has highlighted the connection between sensation and imagination by grouping them in the same book, while emphasizing the uniqueness of the intellect which will be the single main topic of book three.[89]

As in the *Middle Commentary*, there is no introduction. The first words are those of the first lemma. Yet, in contrast with the *Middle Commentary*, it pays close attention to the whole text and refers much to commentators.

Among the Greek commentators, Alexander is the favorite (some fifty references and at least four quotations). Averroes refers specifically to his *De anima* and *De intellectu*.[90] He examines these texts so carefully that at one point, he even argues that there is a discrepancy between these two texts.[91]

As for Themistius, he is named some thirty times, mostly because of his *De anima*. Averroes names Galen eight times, but generally only in order to point to his errors.[92]

Other Greek commentators are treated as small fry. There are five references to Theophrastus, two to Nicolaus (of Damascus), one of

86. Critical Latin edition by F. Stuart Crawford, *Averrois Cordubensis Commentarium Magnum in Aristotelis de Anima Libros*, Corpus Commentariorum Averrois in Aristotelem, Versionum Latinarum Volumen VI, 1 (Cambridge, Mass.: 1953). An edition of the Arabic fragments is being prepared by Ben Chehida and Michael Blaustein. See: Abdelkader Ben Chehida, "Iktishāf al-nass al-'arabiyy lil-sharḥ al-kabīr li-Ibn Rushd," *Al-Ḥêyah al-Thaqāfīyah* 35 (1985): 14–48.

87. Gätje, *Das Kapitel*, 29, and Cruz Hernández, *Abū-l-Walīd Ibn Rušd*, 57, date it 1190.

88. Crawford's excellent index provides this information.

89. Gätje, *Das Kapitel*, pp. 36–38.

90. Crawford's index, pp. 575–76.

91. Crawford's edition, 483.

92. There are also some references to the physicians and one to Hippocrates.

them for his *Compendium of "De motu animalium,"* and five to the Peripatetics.

Whereas the *Middle Commentary* had ignored the Arabic commentators, this text refers twenty-five times to Avempace and to four of his works: *De anima, Conjunction with the Intellect, Farewell Letter,* and *On the Rational Power.* Obviously Avempace's work influenced Averroes the most since he refers only eight times to al-Fārābī and his *Commentary on the Nicomachean Ethics* (now lost), *On the Intellect, De generatione et corruptione,* and his *Elenchis.* Here again Averroes finds a contradiction between some statements in two of al-Fārābī's texts, i.e., *On the Intellect,* and the *Commentary on the Nicomachean Ethics.*[93] There is one reference to Abū'l Faraj Ibn al-Ṭayyib's *Commentary on "De sensu et Sensato."* As for Avicenna, he is nearly ignored, though his *De anima* was famous. His name crops up only twice, and the second reference is devastating: "Avicenna who does not imitate Aristotle, except for dialectics, but who in all other matters was mistaken and particularly so in metaphysics."[94] The Arab commentators *in toto* are referred to three times as "the moderns," and there are eleven references to the commentators, presumably both Greek and Arab.

Discussions of the commentators' views do not limit themselves to the two issues highlighted by the *Middle Commentary.* One finds them in every book. There is no doubt that Averroes has singularly improved his knowledge of Aristotle's text and of the commentators since writing the *Epitome.* The only constant feature is his contempt for Avicenna.

If we focus on the difficult problem of the material intellect, we can retrace some of his evaluation of the various commentators.

In book three, textus fourteen, Averroes contrasts the old Peripatetics, including Theophrastus, Themistius, and Nicolaus, to Alexander for their understanding of the material intellect. He contends that in construing the material intellect as a disposition in the human soul Alexander has left the Aristotelian fold and, therefore, the truth. Yet, the moderns, i.e., the Arab commentators, foolishly consider him as the only wise and perfect man because of his fame and because he is thought to be one of the good commentators. This is why al-Fārābī and Avempace followed him.[95] And let us recall that originally Averroes had adopted Avempace's position.

93. Crawford's edition, 433.
94. "Et hoc est propter Avicennam, qui non imitatus est Aristotelem nisi in Dialectica, sed in aliis erravit, et maxime in Metaphysica; et hoc quia incepit quasi a se" (ibid. 470).
95. Ibid., 428–33, particularly p. 433.

As we saw earlier, Averroes contrasts Themistius's and Alexander's positions on the nature of the material intellect and ends up presenting his own interpretation which he declares to be not only Aristotle's but also the truth.[96] The whole series of the textus discussing the material intellect explain Themistius's shortcomings with some restraint but attack Alexander with passionate vehemence.

Yet, probably the most telling passage is textus thirty which claims that Avempace was much mistaken. "What led him and for a long time me too in error is that the Moderns dismiss Aristotle's books to consider instead the books of the commentators and this particularly in what concerns the soul believing that this book is unintelligible."[97] This confirms our interpretation of the first sentence of the *Epitome*. And of course all these errors are Avicenna's fault.

So, what role do commentators play in Averroes? The answer is complex.

In the *Epitomes*, the modern or Arab commentators mold his thought to such an extent that he does not pay full attention to Aristotle's own text, and this most of all in the case of *On the Soul*.

In the *Paraphrase*, Averroes, at the request of Abū Ya'qūb, had to reformulate Aristotle's own text and to grapple with the difficult issue of the nature of the material intellect for which alone he makes real use of commentators.

The *Long Commentary* shows an intense and thorough examination of Aristotle's text in all its minutiae, and ample but critical use of all available commentaries.

The various revisions and the chronological succession of the three types of commentaries reveal that from the very beginning Averroes distrusted Avicenna as un-Aristotelian but followed rather meekly the views of the Arab Aristotelians and particularly of Avempace. In time and with better knowledge of Aristotle's text, he began to criticize the modern Arab commentators for their lack of true Aristotelianism and to make more sophisticated use of the Greek commentators. Yet, his final judgment seems to be that the only focus should be the truth, which often happens also to be Aristotle's own view, whose insight somehow had been obscured by the Modern Aristotelians and by the Greek commentators and among them Alexander in particular.

96. Book 3, textus 20.
97. "Sed illud quod fecit illum hominem errare, et nos etiam longo tempore, est quia Moderni dimittunt libros Aristotelis et considerant libros expositorum, et maxime in anima, credendo quod iste liber impossibile est ut intelligatur. Et hoc est propter Avicennam" (Crawford's edition, 470).

Contributors

John P. Anton is Distinguished Professor of Greek Philosophy and Culture as well as the director of the Center for Greek Studies at the University of South Florida. He has published on Aristotelian and Neoplatonic philosophy and is currently working on a volume concerning the history of categorial theory in antiquity.

Thérèse-Anne Druart is associate professor of philosophy at The Catholic University of America. She has published fifteen articles on Arabic philosophy and two on Plato. She has also edited *Arabic Philosophy and the West: Continuity and Interaction.* Her current research concerns the metaphysical foundations of ethics in Arabic philosophy.

Leo J. Elders, S.V.D., is professor of philosophy at the Groot Seminarie in Rolduc, Kerkrade, The Netherlands. He has published extensively on Thomas Aquinas, metaphysics, and the philosophy of knowledge. His most recent book is *Thomas Aquinas: His Life, Thought and Significance.*

Lloyd P. Gerson is professor of philosophy at the University of Toronto. He has a volume, *Plotinus,* in the Arguments of the Philosophers series. He has also published on Plato and Aristotle.

James Hankinson is professor of philosophy at The University of Texas at Austin. His research concerns Greek science, later Greek philosophy, and the philosophy of Aristotle. He has published *Galen on the Therapeutic Method* and has a forthcoming volume, *The Sceptics.*

Arthur Madigan, S.J., is associate professor of philosophy at Boston College. He has written on the Platonic and Aristotelian ethical tradition. He is also the translator of Alexander of Aphrodisias's commentary on *Metaphysics* 3 and is presently translating Alexander's commentary on *Metaphysics* 4.

Ian Mueller is professor of philosophy at The University of Chicago. His research concerns Greek science and philosophy, and he has published *Philosophy of Mathematics and Deductive Structure in Euclid's Elements*. He is currently translating Alexander of Aphrodisias's commentary on the modal logic in the *Prior Analytics*.

Lawrence P. Schrenk has published on late Greek and early medieval philosophy. His current research focuses on Aristotle's use of mathematics in scientific inquiry.

Steven K. Strange is assistant professor of philosophy at Emory University. His areas of research include Hellenistic and later Greek philosophy, especially Plotinus and Platonism. His translation of Porphyry's commentary on the *Categories* is forthcoming.

Index